STIMSON BULLITT

To Be
A
Politician

TO BE A POLITICIAN

STIMSON BULLITT

FOREWORD BY DAVID RIESMAN

Updated Edition

Willows Press 1994

Published by
Willows Press
1204 Minor Avenue
Seattle, Washington 98101

Distributed by
University of Washington Press
P.O. Box 50096
Seattle, WA 98145-5096

Library of Congress Catalog Card Number: 93-61492

ISBN: Case Bound 0-9631630-2-7
       Perfect Bound 0-9631630-3-5

The first edition of *To Be A Politician*
was published by Doubleday & Co., Inc., in 1959.

The second edition of *To Be A Politician*
was published by Anchor Books, in 1961.

The third edition of *To Be A Politician*
was published by the Yale University Press, in 1977.

Cover and text designed by Virginia Hand
Printed in the USA on 50% recycled, acid-free paper

To those who pursue the American Dream.

CONTENTS

FOREWORD

This is a book by a practicing lawyer, a Democrat of some political experience (mostly in his home state of Washington), little given to cant. Aspiring politicians who, like the author, are literate and either amateur or idealistic, or both, can learn much from it; professional students of political behavior, in and out of the universities, can also learn from it; and so can the great audience of citizens who might get better service from politicians if they understood the limits and opportunities of the profession, and for whom in any event the understanding of political life can make what happens in the world more meaningful if not less tragic.

Mr. Bullitt is not writing autobiography here; rather, he is writing essays which draw on his experience of what it is like to be a politician—about the company the politician keeps, the ethical dilemmas he faces, the encounters that wound, that educate, and that inspire. He is a salty man, without false heartiness; a brave man, without false heroics; a thoughtful man, without pretensions. What distinguishes him is the capacity to confront the experiences of turmoil the politician has, especially during campaigns, while saving something of himself for reflection and perspective: to be at once insider and outsider.

In introducing the first edition I commented particularly on the importance of what Stimson

Bullitt had to say in a country that holds a dangerous disdain for politicians. Having read Lincoln
Steffens early, I grew up without this disdain, but
found when I began teaching law forty years ago
that my students, and markedly so the better they
were, held politicians in complete contempt. I looked
around then for books which would reveal both the
essential humanity and decency of many politicians
and the inescapable functions they performed, and
did not find many. Mr. Bullitt's would have been an
enormous help. Today, after Watergate and the
general loss of legitimacy of virtually all established
authority, I believe it more than ever essential to
restore the legitimacy of party politics and politicians. However, I do not believe that cynicism in
general and contempt for politicians in particular
are brought about by television. Children's cynicism
is not so much nurtured by the discovery that
Wheaties do not make champions as by hearing
their parents' acerbic remarks about presidents and
other political leaders. These usually unintended
lessons from parents seem to me more important
than the risks of conditioning through television to
which Stimson Bullitt addresses himself in his final
chapter. There is certainly now an even greater
danger than in 1958 of the public's being taken in by
politicians who pretend not to be politicians, but
instead pretend to be ordinary men and women of
the people who are not going to get tangled up in all
the vast complexities of government.

The view held by my students and by many
college students the country over, then and now,

deprives public life both of needed actors and a critical audience—for how can an audience be critical if it assumes that all stagecraft is mere illusion put on by charlatans? I share Mr. Bullitt's opinion that on the whole our representatives, especially if they draw on a district of some heterogeneity of interests, give more disinterested and less parochial service than we ask or expect of them; and there are many congressmen of broad horizons who represent voters who neither know of their best work nor would care about it if they did.*

It is to the essential task of separating the problems of politics as a generic calling (in Max Weber's sense) from those peculiar to the American scene that Mr. Bullitt addresses himself with wit, learning, and casuistical sensibility. Politics in the

---

*In my judgment—this is not an issue Mr. Bullitt discusses—congressmen and senators may have broad horizons intellectually but since so many of them are lawyers or, in quite a few cases, former academics, they have rarely had the opportunity to run large enterprises. They have managed a staff of several dozen people, to be sure swollen by volunteers and others during campaigns. I believe one needs in the presidency individuals who have had to manage the complexities of large organizations: these might be governors, mayors, university presidents, or executives of large high-technology corporations or nonprofit enterprises. To be sure, this is no salvation: Woodrow Wilson had been president of Princeton and governor of New Jersey, which did not save him from self-righteousness and intransigence as president. Conversely, it is possible to learn on the job, and many presidents coming from the Congress have done so. (Lyndon Johnson is something of an exception here, for he actually managed the Senate, but, as Doris Kearns observes in her compassionate biography *Lyndon Johnson and the American Dream*, this was not an ideal preparation for the presidency.)

My friends might think it inconsistent with the foregoing that I did support Eugene McCarthy's candidacy. I believed that if nominated, which was unlikely, he could be elected (for he held appeal for conservatives), and that he would end the war in Vietnam; he was not impressed by generals, and he had a certain indolence which attracted me, for I have feared activist presidents, at least in the foreign sphere. Eugene McCarthy was not likely to lead a crusade of the bored, whose implicit and explicit dangers Mr. Bullitt penetratingly anatomizes in chapter 14.

age of nuclear fission has become even more urgent than hitherto, and its very seriousness is a drawback in competition with commercial or do-it-yourself entertainment, particularly among an electorate that expects to be amused but also, having become more literate and sophisticated, is not so readily amused as in the days of long sermons and courthouse antics. I very much agree with Mr. Bullitt that television sets a model of entertainment alongside of which politicians, like preachers and professors, must seem either flat and pedantic or seek for hyperbole and dramaturgy which undermines their very function. Mr. Bullitt's experience as a campaigner was that of accosting prospective voters at factory gates, taverns, street corners, and shopping centers; he was hardly ever questioned about a stand he had taken. Many whom he approached were indifferent; some feared that the approach was from a bum or a drunk—and some that it was from someone who wanted to warn them that they live in a dangerous world where some choices are more difficult than deciding which horse to bet on or which jar of peaches to buy. What politicians fall back on is their personal flavor, or charisma. Nevertheless, Mr. Bullitt asks *cui bono?* and he skirts as close to an answer as many social scientists and novelists have done. He notices that ambition, if not overpowering, can be a kind of substitute for character: it can force people to do unpleasant things and, if the rules of the game are clear and well enforced, keep the contest within bounds. And he realizes how hard it is for Western man, put on a racecourse, not to run—even while capable of simultaneous awareness that it is absurd.

It is not only ambition that forces people to work hard; people who assume positions of leadership, whether as university presidents or political executives or in large corporate business, have enormous pressures on them which they cannot readily delegate, especially in the chronic emergencies in which many people in such positions now live. Not enough talented people enter large organizations to provide a cadre of leaders. I know that among the students I see in selective colleges, many of the ablest are seeking—perhaps in vain in many cases—the seeming independence of medical or legal practice, occasionally academic life, or work in the arts. In the field I know best, that of higher education, high pay does not attract the ablest people to the presidency, for it is well known that presidents become the targets of hatred and suspicion when they are in the position of having to manage, not growth, but decline, while facing the envy of the faculties who, though really in charge, blame the executive for not getting more money for them or other amenities to which academics became accustomed in the boom years of the last several decades. Mr. Bullitt suggests a sabbatical for politicians every dozen years, perhaps with the person in question moving to another state, institution, or country, and thus finding a change of pace—a good idea if one could work it out.

The advantage of a position of leadership and of the education that sometimes but not in-

variably helps pave the way, whether fairly or unfairly, toward such a position is that it increases the
range of one's ability to enjoy interesting company,
both as part of one's work and during what remains
for leisure time. In no previous period of history,
Mr. Bullitt observes, have people of talent had the
opportunity to associate on a worldwide basis with
other people of talent, thus increasing their own
range of cultivation and interest. To be sure, one
can be acquainted vicariously with greatness through
reading, wherever one lives. But Mr. Bullitt is aware
that at its highest reaches American society stretches
people: it almost compels them to work hard; it
brings them into company which is intellectually if
not morally superior; it allows them to choose their
friends on the basis of interest rather than of ethnic
or geographical parish.

But Mr. Bullitt also points out that this
possibility of self-selection is likewise a kind of self-
sealing which cuts the talented off from the less
talented. This is the theme of a new chapter con-
cerning ability grouping (chapter 15). People want
for their children in school, as the sociologist Everett
Hughes has observed, "equality plus," that is, at
least as much as the next person's children and a
little bit more. This is segregation, not by class or
race, but by culture and talent, and it runs counter
to the leveling and populist tendencies in our society,
which gain support from those, themselves often
among the most talented, who attack such voluntary
grouping as "elitist" and seek, for example, to get
rid of such selective public schools as the Bronx

High School of Science in New York City, or the old black Dunbar High in Washington, D. C., from whose severe classical training came many of the black leaders of the previous generation, who went on to major selective colleges and to distinguished careers.

In the original edition of his book, Mr. Bullitt concluded with a fascinating chapter, "Leadership among the Leisured," in which he suggested some of the basic changes in social structure and stratification underlying the then current political tides. He has developed further in this new edition his concept of society as torn between the tensions of meritocracy and those of egalitarian leveling. He sees talent as distributed in the shape of a Gaussian bell curve in which there are a number of extremely talented people and an equally small minority of wholly inept or marginal ones at the bottom; the vast bulk of society are of middling ambition, middling talent, middling levels of grievance, envy, generosity, and affluence. Some of those who at the top of the bell-shaped curve benefit from inequality of esteem and reward will side with those at the very bottom, while the large bulk of those who benefit from inequality or who, while moderately affluent, fear to fall back into poverty in a world of seemingly diminishing resources will be more afraid of the social inefficiencies of extreme polarization, a theme Mr. Bullitt takes up in chapter 15, than they are ashamed of privilege. Much of part IV of the book is taken up with the issues with which the politicians of today and tomorrow will have to cope, for Mr.

Bullitt sees issues as a way of avoiding the boredom that turns many away from politics.*

While I find it difficult to envisage how politicians can defend meritocracy or ability grouping in the face of populist attack, Mr. Bullitt in his new chapter 15 argues that the flattening or leveling of society is unlikely for reasons already proposed: while no theoretical defense of inequality will convince the passionate levelers, as long as most people believe themselves middle-class, it is unlikely that they will side wholly with the levelers. I wish I could see a way to raise the issue above the current levels of cliché and polemic, but perhaps such a remark neglects the power of imagination Mr. Bullitt would like to see politicians develop, allowing them to seize the initiative and create issues rather than react to those created for them by events or massed minority constituents.

Had Stimson Bullitt not been washed out of the race for Congress in 1952, he might well have become a leader in the House and shown himself to be a practical and reflective idealist, energetic enough to serve both his constituents and his country

---

*Whether survey data bear out this notion is open to question. In a new introduction to his book *Rebellion in the University* (Chicago: University of Chicago Press, Phoenix Books, 1976), S. M. Lipset shows that the more highly educated college students of the present time as well of the late 1960s are issue-oriented but not attracted to the political process; they are better, as Mr. Bullitt himself recognizes, at acting as veto groups through litigation or environmental action, etc., than as traditional party partisans. In spite of all the pressure to gain votes for eighteen-year-olds, and then to urge or shame them into voting in 1972, there were many nonvoters both among the disenchanted elite and the generally bored nonelite. In the 1976 presidential election the proportion of voters among youth and among the general population fell to even lower levels, less than the already low American norm.

and, beyond these, that voteless and all too voice-less constituency: the planet and the unborn. But it is time for me to end my own speculations and let the reader enjoy the flavor of Monsieur Montaigne of Seattle: his wisdom, his wit, his detachment, and, what is so seldom combined with these qualities, his underlying compassion.

DAVID RIESMAN

PREFACE

As a former politician, blessed with leisure and obscurity, I reflect upon the calling that has absorbed me. This book examines the life led by politicians, their conditions of labor and habits of mind, the qualities that their work demands, and some of their trade secrets. Comparing their vocation as a way of life with private pursuits, it looks at the changing relationship between citizen and politician and the effects on the governmental process. It considers the quality of truth in politics. It considers what it is to be a politician.

May the boundary between the roles of citizen and politician be made low but sharp? May it be put low enough to be more easily crossed on the way back to private life, so that politics as a temporary profession may not deter the entry of men and women good enough to have something to lose? Yet, can the politician's role be clearly differentiated from those other vocations also engaged in the management of affairs?

What effect does personality have on communication between citizen and politician? How do certain aspects of personality bear on a politician's value and success? What kind of personality in a politician can enable him best to reconcile his duties of democratic leadership—to give direction and to be responsive? How are the qualities of independent character and inner purpose in a politician related to the need for him to serve, survive, and lead?

Some politicians and some citizens deem that the politician's duty to the public's current wishes forbids the exercise of conscience or judgment; this belief merges the roles of governing and governed and is reinforced by the supposition that since no man is an island, one might as well become part of the sea. Can we obtain definiteness rather than isolation in a politician's personality, diversity among politicians instead of diffusion within? How do these conditions affect the politician's performance? How does the flavor that he gives to his constituents shape the way his constituents relate to him?

Refusing to assume that man is born to trouble or to nothing more than cultivated comfort, a politician can aspire to a better scheme of things, a scheme that might be brought to pass with politicians' help. Although most utopias cannot be reached, and of the rest most are found wanting when attained at last, they should be sought. Yet pursuit is arduous for a politician because these golden lands recede before him, as the sparks fly upward from a campfire, disappearing in the dark. A politician's service as a part-time pilgrim depends at least on public acceptance of him in this part. A central question of a politician's conduct is how he can fulfill today's needs and wishes of those to whom he owes a duty, while he keeps his singularity and tries to lead his constituents toward his vision of an exalted polity; how he can be a man after their own hearts, yet listen for a drum beyond their earshot and "step to the music which he hears, however measured or far away."

My intention is not to encourage those who consider entering politics either to go in or to stay out. It is to offer them comprehension with which to make their choice. The purpose of this book is not to persuade anyone to respect politicians or even to give them pity or affection so as more easily to suffer them. My aim is to give the reader better understanding of this vocation so that when he measures a politician's character and record of performance he may apply standards that not only fit what is and what can be done, but also are a guide for what a politician ought to do and be.

NOVEMBER 1958

The original book was written during the country's Eisenhower years and my late thirties. This revised and expanded edition has been written mainly during the country's Nixon years and my early fifties. In the intervening period changes of method have left many conditions and questions facing politicians much as they have been for a long time. A lot of people have come so to detest politicians that they do not even consider rehabilitation for them, only damnation. Such people think that to examine this occupation would be unrewarding at best and that any attention to its members should be left to others, as we leave to social workers, therapists, and guards the requirement of going among some of those we choose to shun. But without arguing the merits of politicians compared with the rest of us, it should suffice to justify this study that so long as we retain a representative government, politicians will matter more to our lives than do those who follow other ill-regarded lines of work.

In this book's new version, some parts of the old have been removed: items that time has proved, or reflection has discovered, to be untrue; remarks that had lost their appearance of wit; and items that, though true, did not seem important enough to justify their dullness or smell of the lamp.

Added has been discussion of the ways a politician's life and work have been affected by changes in the political process since the earlier edition was written. These include the further decline of parties, though not issues, and the concurrent rise in the importance of personality and money in the campaign process. Television, with a force of its own and in part both cause and result of the latter two factors, affects politicians profoundly. The impact of the politician's personality projected on the screen at home shapes citizen attitudes toward him or her; and the cost of broadcast time influences the conduct of all who must pay the price.

Our new power to make drastic and irreversible changes in our surroundings has sharpened a politician's dilemma between his constituents' wishes and rights to enjoy the fruits of exploiting natural resources and their wishes and duties to provide for posterity. Issues likely to perplex all who perform any civic function—with politicians the central performers—are determining how each others' personalities shall be shaped by the powerful methods that we have learned, and when segregating each other according to apparent personal gifts makes opportunity for self-fulfillment less equal and the society less just.

It may be fitting to offer a glimpse of what has taken place in my life during this period, so that the reader may judge whether to read and, if so, where to add weight, where to subtract, and what adjustments for bias to make. Although engaged in politics for ten years before the original book came out, after that I did little in politics and was not in public office. Much of ten years I spent in charge of a mass-communications company (television stations, movie making, publishing a magazine). I did considerable work as a lawyer and citizen on measures to improve the campaign process: defending the constitutionality of money disclosure laws and trying to shape campaign broadcast reform legislation. Late in 1966, I put some effort into opposing our war policy. Much of my time has been employed in the parochial but varied experiences of a lawyer and citizen engaged in the community.

In recent years, many of my best hours and days have been devoted to skiing and to climbing wilderness peaks. These isolated pursuits may have helped a bit with perspective, but at the expense of touch with the world of affairs and how one stands with others. I tried to influence events, mainly acting through business enterprises. I laid things on the line for several social and economic policies I believed in, and in the course of committing money and reputation lost considerable of both (some of the reputation loss coming from the fact that some of the money lost was other people's money), but kept some, remaining rich and not wholly ignored. I continued to observe and reflect on the politician's calling, and to read for enjoyment and to seek the education I did not achieve in school.

DECEMBER 1975

This is not a how-to-do-it manual; rather, it is in part a what-it's-like picture of the politician's profession, an occupation peculiar to the democratic process. Much of the content addresses an underlying theme: the question of free choice as a member of society.

JULY 1993, SEATTLE

I | The Profession

Chapter | 1

POLITICS AS A CALLING

To enjoy politics one must enjoy people; it helps if one likes them as well. A politician wants and tries to like people. He must be with them, and a friendly relationship makes it easier for him to satisfy and please. He meets and works with every kind. He is enabled to associate with the best, and compelled by duty and circumstance to spend time with some of the worst. Near the centers of government, which has come to reach us all, he is invited to open almost any door; and the universal franchise makes him practice unrestricted social intercourse. His uncommon relationship to people requires him to develop a singular attitude toward them. He must be sensitive to all aspects of their personalities, including their changing opinions of him, yet be numb to the pain of their rebukes.

A politician should feel at home in both the abstract and the concrete. He needs to think along the boundary between the general propositions of the schoolroom or the cloister and the specific problems of the business office or the shop. To get along in politics one's inclinations should be balanced between people and ideas. One too concerned with people may lack judgment in his decisions of public policy and campaign for office as though he were in a popularity contest. One who puts too much emphasis on issues forgets his fellow citizens, each of them, whose welfare is the object of his work. Free from the facts of human needs, here and now, he risks becoming dogmatic. His grand designs may so enchant him that he forces others to accommodate themselves to the symmetrical perfection of his program. China, France, and Russia in their periods of dynamic absolutism have been afflicted by those hard men who impose a platform as an iron frame, while America suffers from men who would rather be liked.

It is impossible to master or even to learn a great deal about all the subjects to be tackled—war, peace, education, money, jobs, prices, energy, diplomacy, ecology, justice. . . . A universal genius could not be expert in all. An able politician is neither an amateur nor a specialist. He is a general practitioner.

A politician's work has come to differ less from the work of those who manage society in other fields. In antiquity, the skills and functions of the military, business and government were united in one man, as in some Roman leaders who in one career would manage farms, administer a province, negotiate a treaty, judge disputes, collect rent, debate laws, and march on Antioch at a legion's head. Then for a long time these skills and functions were apart. The Confederacy's performance was impaired by combining in Jefferson Davis both military and political strategies. Conversely, their separation benefited the Union, whose generals either admitted or demonstrated their unfitness for politics. Now these functions are merging again. The change tends to be more drastic for the officer and executive than for the politician, who has long been attending to a little of everything. This extension of his range has made a politician's knowledge even broader and more shallow. Having children and trying to answer their questions is a good preparation for a politician, who must deal with many things he does not understand.

In the political world the grasp of abstract ideas is better than it is in business, but not so good as in the university. Among politicians the comprehension of specific problems is also intermediate, not so good as it is among businessmen but better than it is among academics. Writing of politicians, Macaulay declared, "The perfect lawgiver is a just temper between the mere man of theory, who can see nothing but general principles, and the mere man of business, who can see nothing but particular circumstances." Although the average politician's intellect falls short of that in some other professions, in politics one can acquire a better comprehension of the forest, together with its trees, than in any other field.

An American politician does a job and plays a part. He serves as both a craftsman and a symbol. The higher public offices used to bear more moral and emotional color in the public eye than other occupations, except perhaps that of the clergy. The standing for all has dropped, but politicians remain symbolic, even though many people are disappointed.

A superior politician combines two contrasting qualities: In the details of his work he is flexible, yet the outlines of his personality are definite. The flexibility is necessary to do justice under the democratic process, and also to permit him to survive in politics. His nature must be well enough defined for him to know who he is, so that his policies may cohere. Few great public men have differed from this pattern, and in none of them was it reversed— none was without direction or identity yet stiff in execution of detail. But the proportion of those in politics who have a well-defined character is exaggerated in the public mind, because an outward sign is often mistaken for proof of an inward grace. Both the old identifying features (a forelock, a brown derby, red suspenders, or an underslung pipe) and the new (mannerisms or total appearance— visibility of face and figure in cartoons and on the screen having relieved the need to identify by costume props) are evidence only, and often overrated.

A constituent's patriotic idealism or self-esteem is shown by his disappointment at a politician's failure to meet the standards of merit that the constituent thinks deserved by his country, his community or himself. But from this falling short of an ideal standard, for the citizen to presume his representative's inferiority to politicians of another time or place (whose merits he has heard of or imagined) confuses an expectation with a wish. If his clay-footed senator is one of the Senate's best, he should recognize the depressing fact. To appreciate comparative worth among politicians is to face reality and to give them their due, as did André Gide when the foreigner asked, "Who is France's greatest poet?" and he replied, "Victor Hugo, alas."

Because politicians are regarded as necessary evils, both their conduct and existence are condoned. It is thought that by the necessities of his profession a soldier must kill and a politician lie. Most American citizens are given better government than they realize, and most politicians are better public servants than many people think. The more complete and accurate information that citizens now receive about candidates and their records tends to eliminate the worst knaves and fools from among elected officials. In general, as in other fields, the quality has improved as the profession has grown more competitive, although the magnitude of the problems has increased faster than the average quality of the membership has risen.

One cause of the disparity between popular belief and fact is ignorance of how much a politician is affected by his instinct of workmanship and his desire to be liked, respected and reelected. People are confused by their own contradictory attitudes toward public leadership: On the one hand is the notion that most politicians are rascals, based partly on evidence of it in the period following the Civil War and the example a century later of one misplaced lawless opportunist and his accomplices; on the other hand is the admiration for institutions of government, compounded of reverence for tradition and pride in the merits of the city, state or nation as symbolized in its government. It is not generally realized that politicians are steeped in the same patriotic myth that is common to other citizens who grew up in this country. With some truth, critics charge that public office corrupts. But where it embodies high tradition from the past or a society's hopes for the future, public office often elevates its holder's conduct. Madame de Stael wrote, "Men collected in a public assembly generally end in electrifying themselves with the sparks of mental dignity." The mansions and temples of government in state capitals and in Washington encourage not only vanity but upright conduct.

To enter politics at the bottom is easy and good sense. Competition is mild, and one may practice in an arena where mistaken judgment is not fatal. Among professionals, however, the game is played for keeps. Survival depends on quick resourcefulness and judgment which comes partly from experience. A few people in public life but not in politics can make up for lack of cunning by common sense and purity of heart. The danger line is crossed when one starts to appear in the papers. From then on he will be saddled with his record and penalized for his unpopular companions or unfortunate remarks. On the congressional level the players are skilled, most of them seasoned by years in minor leagues. The only way to learn the system well is to see its whole range. Those who enter politics late in life, and start in high office, are led by ignorance into errors that are avoided by those who realize the nature and significance of the work done by people down the line.

Going in quite young has its drawbacks too. If success comes soon, perspective first is lacking and then is distorted, like that of high school athletic stars in later life. If success comes late, one may stay in too long, and such service may become rigid or shapeless. The profession should be populated at all ages between adolescence and senility. Since the early bird does not necessarily have an advantage, it is better to prepare and to observe while waiting as the outward eye looks for an opportunity and the inward eye is open for a call.

The most important reason for starting as a part-time apprentice is that one may at the same time learn politics and another trade. The risk is slight that one will stay an amateur so long that he becomes a dabbler. The choice does not matter much, but a private calling is essential to the politician who is brave and wishes to be free. Like Cincinnatus, he should have a plow standing ready for him in a field at home. This goes for everyone, despite the independence of his means. Even a strong-willed politician's flesh is too weak not to be chilled by the prospect of a long drop. Without a happy alternative, an acrobat's net, he cannot afford the independent judgment which he must have to do his duty. Through the window he sees the old men sitting on the courthouse lawn; unless he can afford to lose he may think, "There . . . go I," and keep a wetted finger in the air. Such timidly submissive service to constituents is less than they deserve, although they may be given what some of them demand. And on those terms politics is not worth its price. The Book of Common Prayer addresses God, "whose service is perfect freedom." But base obedience to others' whims dissolves a man's identity by his immersion in the mass.

To succeed in American politics, one must win the acceptance of many people and the approval of some, but compared to what other fields require, the approval needs to be more widespread and need not be as strong. As always, success depends on both circumstances of background and situation, and on personal qualities. But the balance has shifted weight toward personal qualities. Accidents of prejudice or birth are smaller factors now. Being a nonwhite, a Roosevelt, or a Kennedy has diminished as an exception. Whether your parents helped you—or perhaps pressed you—to get an education counts more. A distinguished origin, such as a Mayflower ancestor or a log cabin, is worth less now than it was before, while qualities of ability and personality and of experience common to the voters are worth more. Scandal among one's kin is not much of a handicap except to a candidate for local office in a small town.

Some people have advantages available to them in the form of status, connections or inherited wealth, factors not a part of their own personality or the result of their own efforts. In many situations, if one's gifts of privilege are used to further personal aims, his talents atrophy because they are not whetted on other people's skills. On the other hand, if one's outward gifts are used either not at all or only toward ends unconnected with his career, he misses the chance to put himself closer to a spot where his inner gifts will be most effective. In fact, the time spent in diversions to collateral ends handicaps one who competes with those who focus on a single goal. A person who uses money for play, status for security, and connections for social pleasure loses out to one who has none of these but puts all his time into his career's advance.

And where is the line to be drawn? One who stays within the shelter of his family business is not likely to develop unless he runs the firm, rather than working for it, and unless it must compete, instead of being just a collection of investments. But in politics, as for one who enters a profession in which his parent has been distinguished, it is wise to make full use of those advantages that are outside one's self and that mankind has chosen to applaud so much less than those gifts that happen, equally by chance, to be located within us. Politics is so competitive that there is no risk that a person's powers will decay if he employs his outward gifts to help him toward success.

Among politicians one finds cowardice, dishonesty and pride, but little sloth, lust, cruelty or greed. Contrary to popular fiction, Americans eminent in the management of affairs make poor symbols of evil. We do not elevate Caligulas and Borgias, who "drink iniquity like water." Although some politicians have colorful personalities, few successful ones have lurid faults.

In politics, voluptuaries are even more uncommon than ascetics. Ambition makes most successful politicians impose on themselves disciplined habits of restraint from vicious pleasures. They have little time for self-indulgence. Even when they have a moment with nothing to do but degrade themselves, they generally can resist temptation because they prefer success to pleasure. To obtain the secrecy necessary for vice is often more inconvenient for them than for obscure men. However, some high-ranking politicians are promiscuous with women. After long neglect, their wives cool toward them. They are away from home much of the time and often drink enough to forget some of their duties when an opportunity comes to hand. Because they are celebrated figures, the flattery shown by their favor substitutes for time-consuming preliminary pursuit. Some female staff members blend appetite with hero worship. But the main cause, these men's driving egos, overshadows the supplemental causes. They take women less for pleasure than as signs of success, like exclusive club memberships and addressing notables by their first names. Their practice proves the narrowness rather than the breadth of their interests. Denied the ancient privilege of pushing underlings around and the chance to take revenge on peers, these men would feel they were missing out if they did not indulge in the surviving prerogatives of rank that remind them of their success.

Some people mistakenly think politics endurable only for a puritan who likes to show off. They see the politician as a person exposed to the sight of all and held to the level of rectitude of a schoolteacher in a small town or a man of the cloth, while subject to derisive criticism that may be even harder to take than the insulting condescension accorded teachers and parsons. But in fact the public insistence on observance of domestic moral rules is not strict. Divorce and infidelity do not win votes, but neither one is any longer a crippling handicap, even for the highest positions, unless the circumstances are an open scandal. In such matters, most voters condemn a politician not for private immorality but for demeaning his office.

The speech of politicians tends to be as drab as their sins. They find it harder to be amusing than they once did. Having to tell people about serious problems which the people have to decide, politicians are not even as entertaining as they were in the days when rhetoric and elocution were taught and learned. Few people now can hold an audience with talk unless they are professional comedians, actors in a dramatic performance, reporters of news, or public figures telling important decisions. Growing up over a hundred years ago in Kentucky, where few diversions were offered, my father learned to speak in a way more amusing and charming than anyone I have known in my own generation. In Dublin, during the years near the turn of the century, in an atmosphere in some ways like the Reconstruction South, the gift of gab flourished. It was said that Oscar Wilde's wit, at which London marvelled, in Dublin would have gone unnoticed.

Educated for utility instead of pleasure, contemporary politicians are unskilled in the art of amusing by their speech. They fail to attain even the level of declamatory rhetoric. Part of their failure to amuse owes to their lack of training to write and speak. Some people have come to regard inarticulateness as an adornment of personal style. Schools have shifted emphasis from the art of communication to other things. The language has been debased and to meet new conditions it has been rapidly altered and stretched. Politicians are unable to use the tools of language to communicate well because of the decline in both the fitness of the tools and politicians' skill in their use.

At one time a candidate could develop and improve an important speech by practice, repeating it before many small audiences. For three years before he carried away the 1896 convention with his "Cross of Gold" speech, Bryan had been giving it in the Mississippi Valley. Now a political speech is heard by most interested listeners the first time it is delivered. This difference resembles that between plays performed live in a theater and those performed over television as a one-shot performance. When a candidate does not broadcast, the groups he addresses are small, and what he says is so informal, open-ended, limited to parochial concerns, and varied by answers to questions that not much language becomes constructed into a design.

Other causes also contribute to this dullness of speech and address. As in politics, few men successful in managing affairs in private life have clear-cut individuality, and in each field their character type tends to be uniform. A major reason that does not apply to politicians is the increase in specialization. One bent on success would fall behind in his race if he were to spend time learning things in many fields. He could not acquire more than a superficial knowledge of each. Of course, it is a drawback if one's knowledge and skill are narrower than the limits of the job, and the limits do widen at each higher level. If in competition in a narrow field one can achieve enough superiority to rise to the broader levels, then he can effectively employ what broader outlook and knowledge he may have but did not use. Yet even up there most of the world's knowledge is still outside.

Many of these able Americans in private life are dull in speech because their attention is kept within the immediate limits of their work. Politics makes dull men, but for a different cause. Burke said that the law sharpened a man's mind by making it narrow. Politicians' minds are rarely narrow but often flat. Most are full of fascinating experience. But a politician is inhibited by the hazards of his profession. Seldom are his comments on the world amusing or clear-cut. Distrustful even of an audience of friends because he knows that every sentence from his mouth may be taken someday by itself and used to harm him, he is bound to the formula for dullness: accuracy and completeness about details and vagueness about general ideas. His talk of facts is constricted to banality by his need to be correct. For the sale of stocks and bonds it is almost impossible to draft a prospectus in language that will be eloquent yet satisfy the SEC. Ogden Nash's poem contrasting accuracy and wit contains the line "If it's right, it's trite." Yet when a politician gives his own opinions he shuns exactitude. His words have rounded edges for he knows he may be understood. Clarity is perilous unless transfigured by enchantment, a blend given only to those who speak with the melodic line of a Mozart. And even they dare not sing out for fear some unresolved chord will be plucked from the score and used against them. An ex-politician no longer fears to fascinate but often is too old to learn.

For those who manage affairs, the daily life of incessant work toward a single goal results from an egocentric nature and causes a dull one. On their way upward in a hurry, they lack time for reflection or idle curiosity. Although some of their faculties are highly developed, they tend to be indistinct in personality. An important cause is the intensity of competition, partly brought about in turn by the horizontal and vertical extensions of opportunity— to choose one's vocation and to rise in it. Christopher Fry has Moses say, "The golden bear Success hugs a man close to its heart, and breaks his bones." Except for a few whose remarkable qualities enable them to retain their identities, politicians lose their sharp edges on the way toward the summit, a table top covered with ivory billiard balls—and some impressive exceptions. Thomas Mann wrote: "In an age that affords no satisfying answer to the eternal question of 'Why?' 'To what end?' a man who is capable of achievement over and above the average and expected modicum must be equipped either with a moral remoteness and single-mindedness which is rare indeed and of heroic mould, or else with an exceptionally robust vitality."

One who wishes to excel as a lawyer should foreswear politics. John Marshall wrote to his youngest brother, Louis, my father's great grandfather:

> However seductive may be the splendor of political life to a distinguished politician and statesman, it can afford no compensation to a gentleman not possessing an independent fortune, for the solid advantages to be derived from close attention to his profession.

As in any other competitive field, an almost exclusive attention is essential both to preeminence and to first-rate performance. But for one to be competent in his practice, political activity is compatible, even congenial, with law. To look at this another way, if politics is one's main interest, law is a good home base. Although this factor is overrated, a legal background is a help in the performance of a politician's job, because the work experience of a lawyer, even a specialist, covers such a wide variety of knowledge in his community.

One may seem better prepared for politics by a background in business than by a background in law because business and political decisions both deal with possible future events, while arguments before a court look mainly to the past. Also, in appeal to voters, a background in small business probably ranks above one in law, which is a less popular profession in this century than it was in the last. However, experience has shown that business life does not produce superior politicians. The deficiency of business as a training ground may be its concreteness and lack of necessity to consider abstractions, even though it deals with intangibles such as money and price.

Law practice is a castle that one can leave for a venture in politics. When the fortunes of war or his own taste require, he can return to it more easily than to most other lines of work. "During my various excursions into public life," Henry Stimson once recalled, "I always felt that I remained a lawyer with a law firm waiting as a home behind me, to which I could return on the completion of my public task and where I could always find awaiting me congenial friends and collaborators in the law." As for any sustained personal associations of my own, except for a few family blessings, my law partners have constituted my greatest pleasure and honor.

And law is a worthy and satisfying alternative to politics. A person in public life can afford to take a more upright course if he is aware that his constituents lack the power to banish him to anything worse than the conditions of a lawyer's life.

For one who does not hold public office, to use politics as a means to increase one's law practice is not very effective, although fairly innocent. It makes one well known but not in his capacity as a lawyer. If his political activity makes his practice flourish, he finds that he has ceased to practice law; he is retained not for his skill with the lawyer's tools of analysis, debate and scholarship, but either for his "connections," whom he tries to persuade in matters where the official decision is to be made by standards that are mainly subjective, or for his knowledge of the maze through which he guides his clients. He is a salesman or a seeing eye. The only resemblance that his work bears to that of a lawyer is the title under his name on the office door.

A businessman rarely gets his money's worth from "influence" peddlers, who foster his delusion that they know the passwords. Most people have as much success if they approach an official without an intercessor's help. To get an audience with a politician, no matter how august, you need not be his friend. High public officials are easier to approach than other busy men. It is no handicap that your closest contact with important politicians may be no more than a handshake with Hubert Humphrey or a signed picture from Ike.

Some lobbyists are paid a lot because they know high officials and are thought to have their ear, but a lobbyist's power is less in those he knows than in those he represents. Few are like the Pope in having power without any armored divisions. The effective ones are those who marshal the things that influence politicians: vocal constituents, campaign contributors and persuasive information about the matter to be decided. Without this leverage behind him, a lobbyist coaxes and appeals to old acquaintanceship in vain. He is known to be an agent for pay. A politician may yield to evidence, logic, temptation or threats, but he will not do much wrong to help the money-making of a friend.

The devices used to influence political decisions are spread across a moral spectrum. At one end are bribes and blackmail; dispassionate argument and information are at the other. The persons range from criminals to upright citizens who exercise their right of petition to improve their government or to protect another right. The steps between are neither high-principled effort nor statutory crime. They include promises, eloquence, entertainment, telegram avalanches, desk-pounding delegations and investment tips. Whether using them is a breach of civic duty or whether yielding to them is abuse of public trust depends on: the methods' irrationality and force; their use by other contending parties so as to compel their adoption by all in order for each to hold his own; and the existence of an objective standard by which the choice can be made in the public interest so that reasonable people can agree on a single course.

A government official who is hired by another person has been bribed to use his power against the public interest. If his power is real even though his position is private in form, a different law applies, but the morals are the same. If, like Senator Bricker, his excuse for his retainers from a railroad is his sincere belief in railroads' right to preference in public policy, even if he is telling the truth he still foregoes the right to change his mind. On the other hand, he cheats his customers if, like Lord Chancellor Francis Bacon, he takes money and then does the right thing or, if the matter is one of opinion, follows his own best judgment.

To enter politics costs a person little in his vocational progress. The return is the rub. The likelihood that they cannot recover their former private stations deters many good men and women from a whirl at politics. On returning, a person often is set back further in his private career than if his time away from it had been spent in some neutral occupation such as the armed forces.

The politician may have to enter some new line of work. Doors are slammed shut behind one who undertakes elective public service. It is feared that a teacher might corrupt the youth with evil mysteries that have been revealed to him. One employed in business loses caste but usually is allowed to return so long as he has not opposed his employer's interests or contradicted his beliefs. A lawyer always can resume his practice, but he, too, is set back. Some people assume that he lacks judgment, or that his practice was so poor he ran for office in order to better himself. Others fear to entrust their substantial affairs to a man who may be orating on a platform instead of tending to business. In the time spent away from practice he falls behind his colleagues in attainment of learning and skill. Perhaps lawyers suffer less blame than others for entering politics because some people do not expect more of them.

The prospect of the stony ground on which a politician tends to fall when he returns to private life keeps some inferior people in politics at the same time that it keeps good ones out. Although it is well for the roles of citizen and politician to differ in texture and color so that each person may better know who he is, the transition between should not be hard. Except by change in public attitude there does not seem to be a way to lower the wall that impedes the healthy tidal flow between politics and private life. A smaller sacrifice should be exacted from a person who comes back from politics. Politicians more easily can be righteous if the cost of defeat is lower; they more easily can be wise if they are sometimes out of politics; and good people are encouraged to enter politics if the price to them on departure from it is not so high. (A politician should be able to say to himself what Burke wrote to his constituents, declining their offer to renominate him to Parliament in 1780: "By being returned into the mass of private citizens, my burthens are lessened; my satisfactions are not destroyed. There are duties to be performed, and there are comforts to be enjoyed in obscurity, for which I am not without disposition and relish.")

A permanent career service in elective office, implied in the proposals for special training of prospective politicians, is impossible under our electoral system. The examples of England, France, and Japan give it little appeal. Not all the arguments for a permanent career apply as well to politics as to other work. After a time the public tires of a person who no longer has anything new to tell or give them. Perhaps this is right and not to be regretted. Since a person's effectiveness as a teacher and guide depends partly on his personality and approach to life, his power to contribute may be reduced after he has performed before the same audience for long. The present extensive media exposure, by making people bored soon by a personality, perhaps will shorten political careers, while it may enable a more prompt recognition of merit. A politician's assets include outlook and character, as well as training and experience. Few retain enough perspective without recurrent periods in private life. During the height of his career as chief of Israel, Ben Gurion left office to this end for a year on a farm. Theodosius did the same, to save skin rather than soul, until he was called to lead and rule the Roman Empire. Tiberius, more from calculation and taste, secluded himself for seven years before he reached the top.

A politician may try to make a free society as either a liberal or a conservative. Without liberty, an orderly society can be stagnant and unanimous but not stable or harmonious. As ends in themselves, order is futile and security ignoble, although both are indispensable conditions to political liberty which, in turn, is an essential means to a free society. Although this, too, is not a final end, politicians do well to treat it as one.

Liberals and conservatives occupy opposite sides of the same coin, which represents not all political attitudes but only those that contribute to constitutional liberty. One half prefers to pursue this aim with emphasis on boldness, experiment and direct liberty. The other half puts more weight on prudence, preservation of the best that already is and maintaining that degree of order that is essential to liberty.

In their thinking, liberals put more emphasis on principles, form and structure. Conservatives look at society as a continuing organism, shun formulae, revere tradition and fix their attention on the concrete. This generalization is complicated by

attitudes toward previously accepted principles—
the conservative mind's attachment to them and the
liberal mind's willingness to reject them. Liberals
err by chasing rainbows, conservatives by forbearing to chase.

The two complement each other, and society
needs the stimulation of adversaries and the choice
of alternatives. Differing in emphasis only, they
stand together against those who prefer the swerv-
ing road between tyranny and chaos.

Those who are neither liberal nor conservative may be found on another coin. Its occupants
may be classified as "fanatics" and "agnostics."
Fanatics advocate change because their minds are
closed to any deviation from the absolute pattern to
which they are committed, while a liberal may advocate a change because his mind is receptive to
new ideas and their application. Fanatics oppose
change from an undiscriminating attachment to
things as they are, while a conservative may oppose
a particular change that he thinks would cause the
loss of some presently desirable elements of a free
society.

While fanatics lock themselves to notions
that contradict the principles of an open society,
agnostics are indifferent to political ideas. Of those
agnostics, some stay out of any part in public life,
while others engage. But whether such a person's
activity lies within or without the political process,
whether he is a hermit or a dictator, his purposes are
wholly personal, without reference to political ideas.
Although he may use or even enjoy ideas, he is

indifferent to their significance or truth. The better-known men of action in history have tended to be agnostics (like Bismark) or fanatics (like Lenin). Almost all the more productive creative thinkers in politics have been liberals. Hospitality to new ideas and willingness to dare unblazed trails are a condition of pioneering thought, or of action recognizing such thought's merit and shaping it into policy.

Here we are concerned with political attitudes that affect action, not with thought aimed at changing others' thought. Some radical, illiberal thinkers, "sedentary fanatics," may contribute social value. Where their endeavors are confined to thought not aimed at inciting immediate action, their intolerance of others' rights and interests may be harmless, while their expressed thought goes forth at its peril, subject to rebuttal, and their fundamental thinking may illuminate parts of life for us all and suggest innovations that we want to make.

Except for agnostics, most politicians have genuine beliefs, despite the widespread genuine belief that members of the opposition express only a pose. Some leftists believe that they hold their convictions solely because they see the truth, that to pursue ideals one must be poor, yet that the conservative rich act as they do only to reduce their taxes, that they follow their policies only as policies, not as beliefs, that they do not believe in the nonsense they spout, that it is all cold-blooded self-interest on their part. This so exaggerates the rationality of the rich and the unselfish idealism of the poor that one is tempted to retort that the ideal to which society should aspire must be poverty, as the only condition that produces merit.

The occupants of the two coins differ not in their intensity of action or momentary state of mind but in approach to social problems. Members of the bad coin cannot be distinguished from members of the good one on the ground that the former favor drastic action or rigid inaction. A conservative may resort to violence in order to preserve constitutional liberty from subversion. A liberal may resort to violence in order to overthrow a despot and obtain or restore constitutional liberty. The one may be primarily attracted by the element of liberty, the other by the element of order.

One may choose a faction, a party or a set of colleagues to match his beliefs. But he does not choose to be a liberal or a conservative, because that characteristic is so much a part of one's personality type, as illustrated by Herr Settembrini and Herr Naphta in *The Magic Mountain*, that one has no choice.

However, the expression of one's outlook may vary with one's situation. The independence of liberal and conservative attitudes from particular policies when unconnected with circumstances cannot be better illustrated than by the career of Halifax, the English statesman of the Restoration and the Revolution. Moving to meet the needs of the time, he shifted to the right when events were moving too fast, and to the left when they were going too slowly. (For this admirable consistency he was attacked as a turncoat.) To shift one's position in this way is more difficult where party boundaries are mainly ideological, so that a shift means a change of party, than it is in the United States, where at any given moment each major party contains among its members almost every currently held political belief.

Neither a liberal nor a conservative should be blamed for allies, enemies or policies from the distant past. There is no more reason to think that the liberal mind forever favors free coinage of silver, a stronger central government and a curb on the railroads than to think that the conservative mind continues to oppose women's suffrage or to favor monarchy, primogeniture and hanging for stealing a sheep.

To relate gradations in the liberal and conservative ranks let us consider a clock face. Conservatives are located in the upper righthand quarter (1–3) and liberals in the upper lefthand quarter (9–12). Fanatics and agnostics are mingled throughout the lower half (3–9).

At 12, the liberal and conservative outlooks merge. There sits Halifax. Beside him are the conservative Tocqueville and his liberal friend, Mill. Another balanced pair who stand a few minutes apart near the top of the clock are Churchill and Franklin Roosevelt. (Isaiah Berlin referred to them in their relationship as "royal cousins.") The former, though belonging on the right of 12, had a boldness of imagination and a devotion to liberty which are consonant with a liberal mind. The latter, though properly classified as a liberal, had an attachment to his country's traditions and resources that fit the conservative pattern. Going down the clock, those on the left embody progressively less of the conservative outlook, and vice versa. As they drop below 3 and 9 they pass the pale bounding the company of politically civilized men and women. At 6 are those who are often noticed but never missed.

While the liberals' impact on events has been more dazzling, and their names are found in greater numbers in the history books, the conservatives' impact has been of equal weight. They have administered and executed the policies formulated by liberals, and interpreted and applied the laws that liberals have devised. Few have made substantial changes in the direction of human society except in the negative, and important, respect that if they had not acted as they did, the course would have been different. Rather than innovate, a function essential only by the decade, they have kept the world spinning in its grooves, day by day. At a distance, the significance of such a conservator is obscured by his lack of glitter. His role, like that of rearing children, is not the conspicuous kind that gains notice from succeeding generations. But on its performance depends the maintenance and endurance of the human race. Conservatives may perform a major part in preventing mankind from destroying itself, whether the earth is depleted, poisoned or scorched.

✧ ✧ ✧

What are the rewards of this calling? It gives the pleasure of dealing with people, the fascination of work with ideas, the challenge of problems important to all the world, the excitement of sharing in the "action and passion of the times," and the satisfaction of helping to operate one of the great inventions of human kind. At a time and place more harsh than here today, Achad Ha'am declared:

> I live for the perpetuation and happiness of the community of which I am a member; I die to make room for new individuals who will mold the community afresh and not allow it to stagnate and remain forever in one position. When the individual thus values the community as his own life and strives after its happiness as though it were his individual well-being, he finds satisfaction and no longer feels so keenly the bitterness of his individual existence, because he sees the end for which he lives and suffers.

Often a politician of many years finds private life unsatisfying. Even after circumstances isolate him, his ties to politics remain intact. Few can retire and, like Diocletian or Garner, find their gardens more diverting. Politics holds the attention of most veterans to the end. Not until six months before Andrew Jackson died at seventy-eight did he feel that he could write a friend, "I can now say in truth like Simeon of old, 'Now let thy servant depart in peace'"—and even then he was rejoicing at the election of Polk.

Chapter | 2

MOTIVES AND INCENTIVES

Men and women are drawn into politics for a combination of motives; these include power, glory, zeal for contention or success, duty, hate, oblivion, hero worship, curiosity and enjoyment of the work. According to motive, they are drawn by the incentive of some corresponding aspect or condition. In most cases, the incentive is the mere general opportunity to satisfy the motive. For one who seeks a self-testing device, the structures of politics may be like peaks to a climber. But in some cases a specific thing is an incentive. A person in whom the motive of the public good first was implanted by family tradition or by reading lives of great men may be inspired to action by some current issue that stirs him. Another, like James Fenimore Cooper, whose reading of a worthless novel provoked him to quit his work and write a good one, may decide that he can, and therefore should, give a better performance than that of some officeholder who appalls him.

Each change in social relationships has been followed by a resulting change in moral obligations. The feudal relationship imposed the duty of loyalty up and down. A century ago, Sir Henry Maine wrote, "The society of our day is mainly distinguished from that of preceding generations by the largeness of the sphere which is occupied in it by Contract." The contractual relationship exacted the duty to keep one's word. Now, the individual's relation to others, and his moral duty as well, are being shifted toward larger groups, primarily the community or state, and away from other individuals. Good citizenship in its broad meaning has become a primary moral duty, and politics its largest means of fulfillment. Politicians are assigned a major share of turning to the better the strong social forces that are at large.

The questions placed before American politicians today challenge the intellect and inspire patriotic effort: how to control the weapons of mass destruction; how to protect individual freedom in an urban society as organized groups that shape our living conditions grow ever larger, more impersonal and more interdependent; how to keep a continental economy steady yet allow experiment, how to plan for coherent measures yet respond to the democracy of cash, how to make the system give us plenty of goods and services, justly distributed, at least cost in human and natural resources; and how to treat the worldwide revolution, calling for effort to enable the poor abroad to improve their lives without impairing ours too much.

The shift of population to the cities leaves many of us lonely. *Magna civitas, magna solitudo.* But often what the migrants left behind was worse. Sam Rayburn recalled his boyhood on a Texas farm: "We were consumed by loneliness." Where government covers large numbers, so people apply public policies to others unknown to them, political skill is challenged less by how to alleviate the loneliness of urban life than by how to mitigate the harshness of rules made uniform for justice but unvaried by individual particularities. In *War and Peace*, Pierre Bezukhov stands captive before one of Napoleon's marshals:

> At first glance, when Davout had only raised his head from the papers where human affairs and lives were indicated by numbers, Pierre was merely a circumstance, and Davout could have shot him without burdening his conscience with an evil deed, but now he saw in him a human being.

The whirlpool of politics offers oblivion to some. As part of changing crowds, one is absorbed in varied and incessant activity, never compelled, and seldom allowed, to sit still and expose one's mind to fundamental thoughts. Physicists think matter to be an insubstantial swarm of related events, and so to knowing eyes the universe looks like air over the railroad tracks on a hot day. (Justice Holmes said that science "has shaken established religion in the minds of the very many. It has pursued analysis until at last this thrilling world of colors and sounds and passions has seemed fatally to resolve itself into one vast network of vibrations endlessly weaving an aimless web, and the rainbow flush of cathedral windows, which once to enraptured eyes appeared the very smile of God, fades slowly out into the pale irony of the void.") To those with little comprehension and perspective, who are not bound by an explanatory dogma, politics resembles this phenomenon. One also can reach oblivion in other ways, and unaccompanied, through stimulants, depressants or a meditative trance. Granted the longing to escape one's self, the choice of means is a matter of taste, and politics appeals to those who prefer flight in company of a sort. The profession is filled with gregarious "workaholics." Politics does not attract those people who wish to hold on to themselves yet find that politics jostles them off balance. The unrelenting scramble to reach and hold office gives to some a longing for the refuge of the bench.

Others enter the profession because it provides them with a medium through which to pursue a philosophy of conduct. One often starts with youthful reflections about what he should make the purpose of his life. He who chooses politics may have a firstrate mind but rarely is a deep thinker about ultimates and almost never is trained in philosophy. He may have heard of Rawls or Wittgenstein, but the construction of his cosmos is likely to be an amateur job, helped by models from the ancients. He may suppose that his object is to do God's will, but his ignorance of this leaves him where he started.

Is the world a moral gymnasium in which everyone should spend his life in exercise of high principle so that mankind one day may constitute a sort of moral Olympic team? If he decides that mankind is perfectible, he begs the question again, because what do we do when all of us have become angelic toward God and each other? Does the earth become a monastery? How does a band of angels fill each day? Where pain and evil are abolished there is no work for the good. What if he decides that evil is here to stay, limiting our powers but leaving us with a choice of ends? If he expects eternal struggle and failure, for what should he work and fight? If he decides our proper goal to be an unattainable City of God, he still does not know what such a commonwealth is like or even how to use his powers to establish morality, as distinguished from socially well-adjusted people's conduct, which tends to be what we regard as right.

Should he try to bring to pass a static world of cultivated materialists? Is the graceful use of leisure our proper end? If exclusive, is it even a satisfying end? Now that many of us are becoming free to consume much of our lives in pursuit of our pleasures we discover that they pall sooner than Andrew Marvell expected when he told his coy mistress that if only they had infinite time he would enjoy spending a century in praise of her eyes and forehead before he went on to other things. Is a life of elevated play redeemed by conduct that is temperate and correct? Man's aspiring nature enables him to fly upward, but where and for what? Even on pragmatic grounds alone, discovering new ends is called for now because without them few people can be content.

When I was a boy, Sunday was the single day
of leisure, and for most it was a day of rest. Many
people spent it sitting in a chair, because earth was
moved by pick, shovel and wheelbarrow; forests
were logged by ax and cross-cut saw; and bricks
were carried up ladders on hod-carriers' backs.
Now we must consider, if not yet decide, what to do
with the time and energy bestowed on us by our
technology and social organization which have
substituted their services for the sweat of our brows.
Our efforts might not be productively spent if all of
them were devoted to the continuing problems of
distributive justice as to material comfort and
pleasure beyond austerity. What do we do with the
rest of our energetic time? We can have aimless
flight from boredom or we can pursue our favorite
utopia. What are we free to do in our pursuit of
happiness? Create beauty and search for the truth.
If he has no gift for either, one may enter politics to
make a society that permits others to do both.

Politics offers more incentive when goals of
policy can be seen and are approached. The periods
of consolidation are less tempting than the periods
of advance. In the middle 1930s, although the means
were in dispute and were matters of experiment, the
general aims, such as protecting investors from
deceit and ending mass unemployment, were stars
to follow. These no longer show the way. The
problems of that time have in part been solved, have

diminished, or have passed away. For a long time thereafter they were talked about as though they still existed; to end our troubles we were urged merely to redouble the force with which we applied old tools such as deficit spending, easy credit and giving organized labor a helping hand. The new problems have taken a long time even to be recognized as the first step toward their mastery.

Especially during slack times, some people prefer to discern problems and shape long-range goals. For this they must sit on the bank of the stream. They cannot be politicians too. A politician is not only without honor in his own land, he is not a prophet anywhere. He learns his lessons from the prophets, whose sights are farther ahead. He is too busy with current emergencies to chart the stars, although he can follow them. He is a pilot, not a navigator. As Long John Silver told his fellow pirates in *Treasure Island*, he can better steer a course than set one.

There is a stronger incentive to jump into the fray when the major parties are sharply divided by issues. The parties' paths diverge, converge and sometimes even cross. When they are almost Tweedledum and Tweedledee, about the only persons to enlist are those more interested in organization than in issues, or those who enjoy combat for its own sake. A prospective politician may look at the parties as Buridan's ass looked at the two bales of hay.

A clear-cut division recruits not only more politicians but better ones. The public interest is served by having able people in both parties, but it is harmed by those who enter politics without caring which party they join. An inconspicuous danger is those men of common sense whose policies are neither guided nor distorted by philosophies of government. Unless a politician believes in some of the stands he takes he is almost sure to follow a wavering line of expedience. A politician with direction of his own, by attracting others of his kind, keeps the parties apart. The outs look for, and in this case easily find, reasons to disagree with the ins. But where the ins are led by men and women who stand for everything and nothing there is little with which the outs can join issue, and so the parties converge.

Some young people choose to join a party that has many members in office. They like to be identified with a winning team and enjoy the warmth radiating from those in power. When they go to meetings, instead of adopting peevish resolutions criticizing the current leadership they hear firsthand reports of meals at the White House and almost-classified matters of great import.

Others have an investor's approach. Like Caesar, who joined the broken faction of Marius, they prefer to enter a party at a low point so they can ride up with it. Where a party is weak and small a new arrival may be welcomed with hospitality. His recognition will be quicker and his apprenticeship shorter than where the ranks are crowded and places of responsibility are more sought after and more tightly held.

To some people politics offers a better opportunity for success than they have in other vocations that may attract them. This incentive applies to many women and also, in a declining degree, to men, such as Truman, whose formal education is unequal to their abilities. Some are late bloomers, who did not acquire self-discipline and directness of purpose until after they had compiled poor school records, providing weak credentials for a job. Graduates of obscure professional schools have been more likely to enter politics than those from the leading schools because in politics their undistinguished formal training is not held against them. The fact that their kind of school experience is common to more voters may give these persons more appeal, although that advantage has lessened

In politics are so many men and women of low ability in relation to the work to be done that the scene sometimes looks like a struggle between the one-eyed and the blind. This condition deters those with discriminating taste, while it attracts the ambitious who hope to take advantage of soft competition. On the other hand, the presence in politics of men able to climb high but likely to do harm repels the squeamish, while it inspires idealists to battle. In the past a common dangerous type has been the fanatic with a mind like a locomotive, who is willing to stamp on whomever might stand in his way. A menace now is not a dark, unrelenting oppressor but a decisive weather vane, who measures the wind's direction, then bolts headlong that way to run interference for his constituents; he is a warm and shiny salesman who rehearses his sincerity before a mirror every morning and burns a candle to opinion polls each night.

The quality and congeniality of the company in politics are a stronger incentive or deterrent than when there were more self-willed men who knew where they wanted to go and did not pay much attention to the scenery on the way. A rise in average levels of quality and ability among politicians invites more people than it repels.

Prosperity works both ways. Easy living makes one less inclined to submit to the hard grind of politics. Yet easier fulfillment both of obligations for family support and of the need for self-support enables people to enter politics who otherwise would feel they could not afford it. Prosperity's effects on prospective politicians and young athletes are alike, deterring some from turning professional and enabling others to take part as amateurs.

When ready to retire, some persons run for office to obtain a final adornment to a successful career or to pay a debt to the community in which they have flourished. But regardless of such a person's motives, whether generous or immature, unless he enjoys the daily work itself his performance will disappoint his constituents, and his experience will disappoint him.

A candidate for county commissioner told me that his motive was "prestige" in the community of which he was the leading disk jockey. By the change in employment he stood to become less widely known and far less popular. Yet he wanted the job so much that he shaved his beard.

A voter's motive is thought to be negative more often than positive. Yet many people are lured into political activity for the first time by enthusiasm for a politician whom they admire, while a comparative few start with a purpose of inflicting a defeat. On the other hand, this may be the sole motive of a person who files once again for office after having been rejected by the people and licked by an opponent. Those in a similar position who are less consumed by a thirst for revenge or a need to prove or justify themselves are able to stay in private life because they know that for one who returns to politics with no other purpose than this, "The pleasure is momentary, the position ridiculous, and the expense damnable."

Often public life suggests to onlookers the splendor and simplicity of grand opera. But a politician feels more like one member of an orchestra that is improvising with intricate subtlety. He is absorbed in details that in sum encompass most of life but that, unlike opera, seldom are larger than life, just as the common speech of Britain's kings was not in fact as eloquent or deep as the language given them by Shakespeare.

For centuries young men have bounded into

politics, fired by Plutarch to play some heroic part in their country's history. Euripides wrote:

> Thou hast heard men scorn thy city, call her wild
> Of counsel, mad; thou hast seen the fire of morn
> Flash from her eyes in answer to their scorn,
> Come toil on toil, 'tis this that makes her grand,
> Peril on peril! And common states that stand
> In caution, twilight cities, dimly wise—
> Ye know them, for no light is in their eyes
> Go forth, my son, and help!

However, as the opportunities to rise in other ways have expanded, the chances for glory have contracted. As objects of worship, God and man together have gone down. Heroes are less to be adored or even recognized as such. With a general equality of comforts, the need for vicarious living is lessened, and with the diminishing attribution of personal responsibility, sainthood is abolished along with sin. Especially in politics and war, glory's value has become hardly worth its price.

War's increasing destructiveness has narrowed its utility as a policy. War's increasing specialization and collective organization have made the soldier's profession less glorious. For other reasons, the utility of politics has been enlarged, while the glory of political leadership has suffered a corresponding decline. Power has been scattered so that there is less of it to go with the glory. It has become harder to hold a conspicuous place in the direction of affairs, both public and private, but more so in government because the leaders are more vulnerable. (In big business, where men on top enjoy a hidden eminence, taxes on income and estate transfers have caused some shift in incentive from wealth to renown within the ranks.) Some persons deny that any superiority exists in order that their own may not arouse envy. The crowd's resentment of the heads that show above it makes ambitious men try for concealed power and let the glory go. He who would serve his community must take short and patient steps to bring about slow change. No longer can he stand before his city like Hector or Horatius and strike decisive blows. One has a better chance to play the hero in the fields of entertainment and sport.

One who would be a politician must attend political meetings to gain acceptance from people who can advance or impede his progress, and he should attend them to learn a civics lesson. The equalizing effect of the right to vote extends beyond the polling booth to political gatherings. On such occasions, people who elsewhere would be graded in a hierarchy treat each others as equals. This educates by humbling one and reassuring another, according to need.

Some enter politics to become the center of attention. Self-preoccupied, they may not always boast, but in conversation refer everything to them-selves. Such a man often thinks of himself as an institution. In the past some of these have been successful demagogues, but their kind is becoming extinct along with the backwardness of the regions in which they prospered. Not many of them now go far. Some never win an election. Others drop out after a short time. A few are bright enough to discover their shortcoming and have enough ambition and capacity for growth to subdue it.

Many successful politicians have an equally narrow but more sophisticated selfishness. Subordinating present gratification of their pride to long-run fulfillment of their self-serving aims, sacrificing vanity to ambition, they forego praise for the sake of self-advancement. Instead of talking about himself such a politician flatters others to get his way, never letting his ego impede his own eventual success.

In pride, politicians range between two extremes: at one end are the haughty who are concerned with government for, but not by, the people and whose paternalistic attitude is often a mask for class prejudice; at the other extreme are those who imitate and grovel. As times have grown more democratic, the midpoint has moved toward the sedulous apes. No living politicians resemble Coriolanus, who generated resentment even in his day by a proud and stubborn temper that put the public interest below his ego, and who insulted people in the effort to avoid debasing himself by flattering them. Woodrow Wilson, who stood about as far on that side as any successful American politician in this century, wrote in 1884, "I have a sense of power in dealing with men collectively which I do not feel always in dealing with them singly. In the former case the pride of reserve does not stand so much in my way as it does in the latter. One feels no sacrifice of pride necessary in courting the favour of an assembly of men such as he would have to make in seeking to please one man." One wonders how he would succeed today.

Politics is an all-or-nothing venture that does not easily fit into the scheme of a person who enters it to fulfill part of an aim that is wide rather than high. For example, to give his profession skilled service, to do his duties as a parent and citizen, to play a musical instrument, and to have some good times. A friend of mine who fits such a pattern became an able physician and leader in his profession, as his father was before him, and an effective poker player, kept his good health, and has six sons and a sailboat. One ambitious to attain a large number of achievement units but along a broad front rather than up a long ladder, one who would rather excel in the decathlon than in a single event, may find himself handicapped in politics by his rivals' preference to excel in politics alone.

Directed at unbounded ends, diffused but strong ambition is to be distinguished from making one's life a comprehension of several human interests, with the placid intent of acquiring attainable moderation and the preference for harmonious shape to one's life rather than a high score. Rounded balance can be attained without making enemies or sacrifices. But willingness to make them is a condition of ambition to travel the longest distance that one's capacities allow toward moral, social or vocational goals. Even for an opportunist, ambition, aimed at the conquest of circumstances, not adjustment to them, can be exercised only by sometimes standing for principle or asserting interest and thus risking offense to others. This applies no matter what measures are taken to fulfill ambition, whether they be stands on public policies, efforts to get rich, attempts to enable one's child to become a superior person, or struggles to win a zero-sum game and thus make others lose.

Although this diffused ambition, growing more common, gives some security by spreading the risks of failure, it is more difficult to practice than a single-goal ambition. One aiming for multiple goals must compete with single-track persons, each on his own track. He rarely rises far in politics, not only because he gives it part time in competition with others who give it all their time, but also because he may not be competing as hard in the total of his pursuits. He may put out less effort because he is not surrounded by persons competing on his own terms for the same goals and because he does not have models of his own kind of success to emulate. He may be perplexed with continual decisions about allocating his time and effort among his concerns. Wondering when to leave his office to do some civic or domestic function, he may envy the singlemindedness of a van Gogh, absorbed in direct pursuit of one object.

Diffused ambition may become less difficult and more competitive. As it becomes more widely held, it may handicap one less in competition for supremacy in a single field because there will be a smaller proportion of single-field competitors and a larger proportion of competitors for whom the goal in question is only one of several aims. Yet, if this outlook is held for long by many, then for each set of goals a heroic model of achievement may be established by those persons who have advanced the farthest in their concurrent journeys, measured in series on the several tracks. As the Greeks did for their ideal of *areté*, we may define the models further by charting these constellations of aims. Such models can help a person with multiple goals to keep up with the single-goal person for whom there always have been dramatic examples of his kind of success, like Alexander's monument, before which Caesar wept in Spain. Both the presence of these models and the new subscribers whom they tended to attract would stiffen competition for a cluster of aims. The result may be to shift some intensity of competition from single to multiple goals.

Some stay in politics because they like the work. Gregarious, energetic, internally secure, they enjoy the attention and acclaim and do not mind the knocks. Children, debts and other hostages to fortune do not trouble those to whom the stony road of politics is like the brier patch to Br'er Rabbit.

Chapter 3

LIABILITIES

One who enters politics must realize that he is to live dangerously. In business, the line between the red and the black divides anxiety and comfort, but a businessman can survive a bad year; in politics .01 percent of one's biennial gross vote can mean the difference between prosperity and ruin. Some politicians would call it the difference between anxiety and ruin.

Between politics and other professions runs a deep crack. At the bottom are a lot of nice fellows. A defeated candidate, conscious of this hazard, often resumes his former work with desperation rather than enthusiasm as he hustles to make up for lost time.

For an active intellect the most severe condition of politics is to abstain from the full and constant use of one's powers. One must be willing to submit to boredom and make the effort to conceal it. Insofar as a politician works with organizations his patience is taxed by tedium such as service on committees engaged in administration (e.g., organizing a dinner meeting or picnic), a function suited to a single person. Most political meetings are dull enough to spur the ambition of impatient people. By custom, a private has to sit through them in silence, an officer is allowed to speak, and a general may arrive at the end to make the main oration, during which he may while away the time by listening to his own voice.

To converse on public affairs is often stimulating. To compose a speech on some important issue is satisfying. To deliver it sometimes is exhilarating. Those occasions on which one is able to entertain or amuse a responsive audience are great fun. But much of the public relations work, in and out of campaigns, is sitting through long meetings where the business transacted and the ceremonies performed are almost identical with what took place at the meeting the evening before, which was dull the first time; then at the end, one must circulate within the group as it breaks up and greet strangers or acquaintances with a cordial handshake. Politics, like parenthood, is less paternal than it used to be, but it resembles parenthood in the drudgery that is a part of both.

In politics, the rate of pay is modest, although not as low as one might think from the complaints of some. Expense is high, and much is not tax deductible. Because, unlike happiness, money-making can be best achieved by direct approach, politics is no place for anyone who wants to make big money, or, unless he has it already, to live on a scale of comfort that requires it. The main loss of income caused by politics is not the drop, if any, in actual net income on entering public office. It is rather that following a period of political activity the long-run level of private income falls below what it would have been if the person had stayed where he was and polished the handle of the big front door. Although having done time in politics is likely to reduce a person's total lifetime income, this loss, because evenly spread and deferred to future years, is a weaker deterrent than the conditions, say, of becoming a physician, where austerity comes at the start.

Some other lines of work take as much effort, but except for some kinds of medical practice, none allows less time free from the cares of the job. The hours are too irregular and long to permit a satisfactory family life, although extensive political activity can be postponed until the children are of such an age that no one suffers much from your absence except your spouse. After sundown far from home a politician may remind himself, "I have promises to keep, and miles to go before I sleep."

Cirrhosis of the liver has been called a journalists' occupational disease; to say the same of politicians would exaggerate only a little. Drinking often becomes a problem, deriving from long meetings and conferences under conditions that encourage it in hotels, lodge halls, restaurants, airports and homes. Social conventions permit it, and exacting thought is not required. Artificial aid may seem almost imperative to men who feel they must be as genial as a ski instructor playing Santa Claus in conversation with the fiftieth stranger they have met that day. It is hard not to tire of playing the cheery friend to all the world and the devoted slave of one's constituents. But in this profession are some teetotalers and few drunkards, because ambition is to politics what hope of profit is to business,

and it is strong enough in most politicians to protect them from the allurements of drink.

It would be less perplexing to be a politician
if one did not have to learn to make, and practice
making, a living in two ways, as a politician and in
some private work. In order to live, and also to
acquire the respected status that will help him to be
elected, he must apply much of his time to acquiring
knowledge and practicing skills not directly connected with public affairs, and which may not be
easy for him or of special interest to him. For
success in most lines of work, a person's choices of
activity in other, unconnected fields and his failures
or successes in them are irrelevant. A physician's
practice is not impaired by the fact that stocks
always drop as soon as he buys them, nor is it
assisted by the fact that he is a noted poet. But one
trying to establish himself as a politician is measured
to some extent by the nature and quality of his work
performance outside politics.

A politician is helped or hurt in politics by
both the choice of his private work activity and the
level of his private success, which have less effect on
his political success than does the nature of the
private work itself. He may be shunned as unsound
if he is known as an artist, good or bad, and some
voters may doubt his interest in the public welfare
if he has shown himself to be a gifted speculator, no
matter how legitimate. For him to excel in certain

fields may handicap him more than if he failed. Having gone broke as a storekeeper did not cost Lincoln or Truman many votes, but either man might have found it hard to reach the White House through the needle's eye of the summit of the country's biggest bank.

In many constituencies, the public respect and confidence necessary for election are harder to acquire if one does not wear the mantle of the man of affairs. Some people suspect the ideas and proposals of one who does not accept tradesmen's values. Having "met a payroll" has lost its appeal, but long-sustained effort in the management of affairs continues to be an important asset in earning the respect of one's fellow men. Some teachers who enter politics surmount this handicap by superior knowledge of the subject matter in politics and by skill in presenting it to their audience. However, some experience acquired in the management of affairs is not merely relevant to questions of public policy but is an essential condition to political competence.

All in all, because a person's political ideas or abilities to apply them may be worthless, the practice of his private profession can serve as a useful end and a safe hedge to the bets on which part of his life is committed.

Because life is too short for him to master two trades, a politician sometimes learns little more about public office than how to attain it, like a student who fails to get an education because he concentrates on grades to keep his scholarship. Few are frustrated for long by this thinly spread application of their time. Most either do not mind it, become resigned to it, or quit. Even if a politician's main interest is politics, so long as he enjoys people and the busy life of affairs, in or out of government, he is not much discontented by the differences in subject matter between his public and private callings. Also, if he prefers politically unacceptable work, this fact may prove to him and others his lack of fitness for politics.

Mendès-France said, "To govern is to choose," but a politician's choices give offense. He does not coldly call them as he sees them. No one thinks him a mechanism that makes automatic choices as an agent of the Law, which he applies as though it were a T-square or a spirit level hanging from his workshop wall. Everyone knows he cares about his decisions. As both referee and advocate, he plays in a game for which he helps to make the rules, and the rules are the object of the game. He is less protected than unknown umpires, temporary jurors or majestic, impersonal judges. Seldom does a trial court ruling hurt more than a few, but a strong, revengeful group is ready to be kindled by a governor's appointment or a legislator's vote. No politician can have as few critics or ill-wishers as a Hank Aaron, a Jack Benny or a Lotte Lehmann. Because a politician estranges many people by what he does or fails to do, popularity, in contrast to notoriety or fame, is harder to attain or to keep in politics than in some other fields, although many politicians have a craving to be liked.

When public opinion about a policy issue is widely held and in sharp contradiction to what a politician thinks is wise or just, he has to yield in principle or power. He must choose between conforming to the public wish and disregarding the sentiment, thereby inviting defeat at the next election. Like an actress asking a casting director for a part, his response to these distasteful conditions depends on the comparative pulls on him of his principles, his ambition and his taste. The most public-spirited citizen has the right, sometimes the duty, to say for himself, "The public opinion be damned." But even if at times a politician does not follow public opinion he always must give it respect.

Another hazard, less real than apparent, is the restraint on free speech. The argument goes like this: "On most jobs your speech must be circumspect in the presence of employer, clients and customers, but after work you may say what you please; a servant of the public, however, whether actual or aspirant, never can escape the agents of his employer; such continual discretion is an inconvenience requiring severe discipline until it becomes a habit." This overstates the difference between the speaking conditions of public and private life. The practical limits on unpopular speech are similar for a politician and any private person whose position is a responsible one in the conduct of affairs. A man's associations often compel him to be silent so as not to hurt others close to him in his business or his firm. The silence of business life is more absolute than the cautious reticence (or windy ambiguity) of politics. In general, compared with that of private life, speech in politics is less free for casual conversation, yet more free for issues. A politician may feel he should refrain from grumbling to a friend at lunch about the cost of haircuts because this remark might start a rumor that he is "against the barbers"; yet without disloyalty to his associates he can lead a street march for one side of a disputed issue, while if he were not in public life he might feel embarrassed to appear at his place of work the morning after such a performance.

To be a brave and useful politician you need not speak out boldly whenever you differ from your associates or party. Political ties have their loyalties, and there are occasions when one must keep silent, or else blunt the thrusting edge of his convictions. Here comes the time for anxious study and balancing what is to be gained by speaking out as against waiting one's turn. Without sacrifice of the public interest, a compromise can be struck between saying nothing about anything and letting the chips fly.

A politician's duty demands candor, while his survival demands discretion. As much as possible, he must refrain from criticism of individuals and groups, except by inference; such talk is the main source of antagonisms. The public interest does not obligate him to make truthful statements about the truthfulness of used car dealers or gun lobbyists. Referring to a distinguished Roman reputed to have been the son of a gladiator, Tacitus wrote, "I would not publish a falsehood, while I shrink from telling the truth." Asked to evaluate a colleague of little merit but to whom loyalty is owed, politicians give blurred and evasive answers insofar as they value the truth. Such lack of candor should neither surprise nor offend one whose question has unfairly presented a choice between betrayal and falsehood.

When asked about a pending issue, a politician ought to speak out clear and straight. But one may mitigate the enmity of those who feel the other way by phrasing one's declaration in terms that accommodate the audience. General answers of opinion are more likely to inflame than specific answers of fact. Arguing the merits of a specific solution to a problem is safer than asserting controversial principles, which may antagonize whether understood or misunderstood, and more useful than asserting principles on which everyone agrees.

On the whole, speech is as free in politics as in at least some important walks of private life, and thought is more free. Private citizens often become so molded by their work that after five o'clock they think and speak the way they do while on the job. In 1940, an advertisement in the *Chicago Tribune* declared that, "In a last stand for democracy, every director and officer of this bank will vote for Wendell Willkie." Those labor union spokesmen who used to claim that the Taft-Hartley Act had repealed the Thirteenth Amendment did not exemplify such frozen thought only because most of them either did not believe what they said or erred from lack of knowledge; they were irresponsible or ignorant, but not true believers.

A businessman, conformed by his eagerness for money, recognition or power becomes as empty as his counterpart in public life. Even more so, because in many walks of private life thought is numbed by the pursuit of money, while in politics the strife, in part, is over ideas. The habit of expressing ideas, even if not one's own, is a help. Most conversations in which politicians take part are the same as those of other people, confined to small talk, big talk and shop talk. But despite the prudential bounds to politicians' speech, the subjects of their conversations cover a wide range.

To stand up for principle is no harder for a politician than for a private person. The latter may have more chance to explain his position to those whom it offends. But in politics the action of standing up tends to be taken before a crowd, which lets a speaker's feelings remain more protected within himself than when he confronts another individual, the more common situation in private life. Political communication's current shift from public meetings to the media makes even more impersonal the atmosphere in which a politician declares a position that may please or offend. His thinking can be more independent of the audience, more concentrated on the subject matter, when he is looking at a camera lens or speaking to a mike. Face to face with another person, you are exposed to his reaction to you as a person. A crowd, visible or invisible, may do you harm or give you help, but it will not scowl or smile.

The actual choice of a side on an issue is as perplexing for a politician as for a private person, and when the side is publicly taken the exposure is the same whether one is in or out of public life. But the decision to take a stand at all, preliminary to the decision of what stand to take, is easier for a politician than for a private person because by doing nothing a politician cannot escape criticism. Like a driver approaching a fork in the road, he knows that if he falters cars behind will honk. For him to get moving takes less effort because outside pressures overcome his inertia, jarring him loose from his resting place. By denying him the choice of doing nothing, they both narrow the alternatives that face him and impel him to take one, although the choice itself still falls on him. For an indecisive person, politics often is less difficult than it looks.

When a private person sees a hot public issue he can stay in the shadows without disapproval. Even when asked, the private man can safely say, "I pass," while politicians must explain their indecision. If they fail to fulfill their publicly recognized duty to take a position on important issues they suffer the consequences of showing themselves evasive or weak. Ignorance, either admitted or claimed, cannot excuse them. If they do not meet an issue they must pretend illness or claim that the issue does not exist. Visits to the hospital are impractical, and it is uncomfortable to be scorned by both sides of a controversy for dodging it. Therefore, the decision to take a public stand on an issue requires less effort of a politician than of private persons, who are not goaded into action and who have little to lose by standing pat.

A politician is exposed to abuse by opponents, critics and constituents. Anyone is free to attack him and his family with falsehood or with painful truth, and many do. The low risk of either legal liability or public disapproval makes the half-truth a common device. Some news reports of a campaign resemble the ship's log in which, after the mate had written, "Today the captain was drunk," the captain wrote, "Today the mate was sober."

A politician may expect two forms of assault: on his principles or policies, and on his character. One who calls for a tariff cut on certain goods is damned by their local producers as a traitor and a cad. It is not hard to get used to such invective, just as a surgeon becomes inured to the flow of blood. A politician is consoled by the belief that he is right and that some others agree with him. Abuse based on the things he stands for is faced without concern by any sensible politician as a hazard of his job. After a local convention, I saw a leading member of the U.S. Senate pushed backward across a hotel lobby by a drunk who prodded him with one thumb and dropped cigar ashes on his tie while scolding him for his vote on a measure that had affected a commercial interest. The Senator kept repeating gently that he certainly respected the man's opinion. At last he backed into an elevator, which lifted him to a room filled with adherents and smoke, where he could expect to be put upon again.

In the other form of attack, no matter how preposterous the charges may be, lies about a politician's character upset and embitter if their nature so combines with the climate of the time as to make some of his fellow citizens accept them as true. Even for a veteran the hurt remains acute. He cannot prove his innocence and has no fair way to hit back except perhaps by ridicule, such as Franklin Roosevelt's taunts at "Martin, Barton and Fish" and his defense of his "little dog Fala." But ridicule works only when the audience is not too distrustful and it is available only to politicians with enough wit and commanding presence to put across their gay contempt. Striking from the ambush of a pseudonym, a Nixon agent falsely charged Senator Muskie, himself two generations from Poland, with having made an ethnic slur. When Muskie showed his pain, he was removed as Nixon's strongest opponent by voters who took his response as proof that he was weak.

An impersonal attitude toward personal attacks reduces the shock and helps a politician to react with more calm than a layman would, just as an athlete is not depressed or offended by bumps he takes from other players in the course of a game. At a Senate committee hearing a certain McCarthy told a cruel lie about the young colleague of a lawyer named Welch, whom he thereby drove to tears, although Welch had a cool head and long experience in courts. Not even such a thing as this would make many politicians cry. However, players in a body-contact sport need only keep in mind that their opponents feel no spite, while a politician must try not to remember, but to ignore, that his assailants often mean their blows to hurt; and therefore his defenses can be pierced.

Those attacks not proclaimed to the world but delivered to you alone do not impair pursuit of your ends, but their severity tends to make them the most deeply offensive. Worst are the cowards who strike from ambush: with anonymous malevolent letters, postcards, phone calls, an occasional telegram. Neither plausibility nor accountability blunts their knife.

To a politician whose policies have followed the middle of the political road, abuse is like a wind blowing across it. He may drift over to the lee side for refuge and a kind word, or else lower his head and butt it at his critic in anger, like the man who took the pitcher to the cellar for his wife. After he tripped on the top step and tumbled to the floor below, his wife called down, "Did you break the pitcher?" "No," he replied with an oath, "but I'm going to break it now!" On the other hand, a politician with a keener sense of survival though no more courage may try to refute his accusers by moving to join them on the windward side of the road.

As for physical attacks, the violence common to American life largely leaves politicians alone except for those who hold or seek the office that provides the only human symbol of the nation, an emotionally concentrated bulls-eye. Most politicians sustain less risk of violence—whether a bloody nose or a hole in the head—than does a door-to-door salesman or someone engaged in a boundary dispute or a custody fight. The principal form of physical invasion to which a politician is exposed is not an injury but an offensive intrusion on his person—a plucked sleeve, jostled hip, grabbed lapel, dug rib, slapped back, poked chest or breathed-on face.

Men shrink from politics because they can be ruined by enemies. Friends are trouble, too. The truth is hidden from a politician to keep him cheerful, or twisted to make him a more fiercely aggressive campaigner. A license to cheat the public by deceiving its servants often is assumed by persons who are otherwise upright.

Friendship is difficult. A politician sees many people but few of them often and over a long period. He loses friends when he acts or speaks against their wishes or beliefs. His profession is small, and the turnover is high. Few among those of his companions who remain follow the pattern of his location as it shifts between hometown, county seat, state capital, and Washington. Long-lasting friendship is difficult because "in the frequent jumble of political atoms, the hostile and the amicable ones often change places." A politician has few friends, and among them he is sure of few but those he knew when he was still unknown.

However, do the rest of us have it much better? Family ties can provide a cushion. Shared experiences may forge a comforting bond. Conrad recalled "as good a crowd as ever fisted with wild cries the beating canvas of a heavy foresail; or tossing aloft, invisible in the night, gave back yell for yell to a westerly gale." Many lawyers enjoy splendid comradeship together, but fellowship is less than friendship. In a hierarchical business organization friendship is restricted by inequality of power over each others' careers. If you seek friendship with your boss you may both fail and impair your standing as well. If you allow yourself to become friends with a subordinate you may hinder your efforts to do right by your employer and by other subordinates. A middle-aged man, parting after dinner with a set of well-behaved couples at a friend's home, wonders, "Is that all there is to friendship?" The orderly grooves that they have come to follow keep relations tepid. Those present may be quality folk, not chattering the evening away on kindergartens, mortgages and golf, or even Michelangelo, but they do not come to grips with each other or with fundamentals. Always at a distance from best friends who never drop their guard, one may feel wistful yearnings for intimacy, ardor, human dealings with some bite, for the society of characters in Russian novels, whose first words on being introduced are a question such as "Do you believe in God?"

Is not loneliness the fate of the well-differentiated person wherever he finds himself? In public life he may receive inspiring loyalty that goes far to justify his personal isolation. But along with hero worship, now less common and less strong, such loyalty is in decline. Skill at expression with language helps but leaves one on a largely solitary journey. Even Flaubert, himself no mean hand at reaching others with his words, acknowledged that "human speech is like a cracked tin kettle, on which we hammer out tunes to make bears dance when we long to move the stars. . . . Speech is a rolling mill that always thins out the sentiment." One fortunate enough to enjoy the companionship of himself still tires of it often. Anyone with a clear-cut personality is fairly sure to feel lonely, whenever he stops to think of it. Joyce wrote, "We cannot give ourselves, it is said: we are our own."

A politician may be lonely but he cannot be alone. About public leadership Montaigne wrote, "Ambition is of all others the most contrary humor to solitude; glory and repose are things that cannot possibly inhabit in one and the same place." Some kinds of ambition do permit solitude, but ambition for power and glory during life does not.

Because politics is urban, a politician may frequently praise, but seldom enjoy, nature's beauties. The only exception is a part-time politician like the farmer who goes to the legislature in winter. On a summer afternoon a politician may attend a union picnic at a lakeside park but he cannot stroll alone among the green and rolling furrowed hills of cultivated land, nor can he climb up cloud-capped towers above the snow and heather slopes and beneath the splendid, silent sun and then stride down the granite ridges feeling like a winged steed.

One's dark and cozy zone of secrecy or of intimacy with a few is smaller for a politician than for a private person. A larger proportion of a politician's family and business matters—his "private" affairs—and details of his daily life is exposed to the knowledge of those who are not in his confidence than is the case with private persons. He is less free to draw the curtains, relax, and be "himself." Of course, to have less privacy than is allowed to private persons is no hardship insofar as it does not deny a person comfort. Some thrive on it. This exposure makes them feel not naked, but clothed in protective company; not invaded by the eyes upon them. but sustained.

Immersion among those with whom his connection is thin or cool denies a politician both solitude and intimacy. His exposure to everyone bars him from the steady company of those whose values, tastes and experience fit his own. A private citizen can find or gather a congenial circle and stay within it; he can avoid the rest. But a politician consorts with all. Perforce, a few of them are sure to strike discord with each other or with him. Even if this appetite for people is indiscriminate, he must suffer some whom no one could enjoy and others to whom he tastes bad.

Recognition for accomplishment is passing and uncertain. "It's not what you've done, it's what you've done lately" (or probably will do). This political proverb describes a fact that is in the public interest though often disappointing to an individual, as it was to Churchill in 1945. Nor is merit given full credit. Acts of generosity, conviction or even courtesy are discounted as done for political gain. The practice of virtue is as it is in private life; for some external rewards, waiting for heaven is one's only resort.

A politician may receive gratitude for his acts of public service and he may be pitied for his misfortunes. In politics both gratitude and pity vanish as quickly as do these fleeting sentiments when directed at someone in private life. In a politician the transience of gratitude is the same as it is for others who feel it toward him, as any president or governor knows when he appoints a judge.

Pity toward politicians is more common than gratitude. Even the most gallant election loss inspires little pity, but it often is felt for personal misfortunes unconnected with failure, such as a death in the family. This pity is genuine and, because the politician is well known, widespread. President Truman's approval ratings in the public opinion polls rose when his mother was dying. President Eisenhower's partially disabling illnesses increased his support from some voters as much as it reduced it from others. Pity, creating public support, flowed toward Senator Ted Kennedy for the loss of his three brothers and of his young son's leg, and toward George Wallace on the loss first of his wife and then of the use of his lower body. Because pity can motivate votes, a politician's misfortune may be · offset by befalling him at campaign time.

The risks of becoming a megalomaniac or a cynic are not like Scylla and Charybdis because one can succumb to both at once. The altitude of some offices encourages delusions of grandeur which are latent in many of the men attracted to politics. A politician who plays the big shot in order to meet the expectations of some constituents runs the danger of coming to believe his own pretense. The pronoun he uses for himself shifts from first person singular to first person plural (combining the imperial "we" with the mock modesty of team spokesman), then is replaced by his name, to which he refers as though he were an institution. Some dream that destiny has chosen them to legislate in marble halls. Others give less thought to whether their country's money is going to bear a graven image of their heads. A state senator told me, "How I hate to see my name in the papers. It's always something bad. I could be reelected forever if I could only stay out."

If a politician reveals a touch of cynicism, humbugs in a swarm embrace him. Like everyone, he sees the world through his experience, and these companions confirm his cynicism. The pressure to be cynical is strong, and the withering effect of cynicism is hard to resist. He can be lonely, discreet and thick-skinned, yet remain himself. But if he becomes a cynic he is an altered man, and a hollow one. He can escape this penalty, however, if he takes care not to expect an improbable rate of progress or level of goodness, and if he does not lose his nerve.

Under the temptation and pressure to respond to popular wishes and beliefs a politician may become nothing but a suggestion box for pressure groups, like the Emperor Claudius, "who had neither partialities nor dislikes, but such as were suggested and dictated to him." This hazard has increased, despite the reduced emotional impact of the public will since the crowd's roar, compelling music to his mind, was largely replaced by messages filtered through the media from an invisible crowd. The public will is stronger, and a politician need no longer fear that by obedience to it he may forfeit his colleagues' respect. A dreadful private evil of public life is this corruption of personality, which produces men who have lost their savor and are "neither fit for the land, nor yet for the dunghill."

In conversation, most people combine two approaches to what they hear: Consider the statement's content and try to discern the speaker's mind and determine what response would be most effective to achieve one's wishes in respect to him. But, like those theorists of teaching method who advise, "Teach the child, not the subject," such a faceless politician ignores the content of others' speech to him except as related to the others' feelings. He listens to one addressing him as though he were administering a Rorschach test, not curious to know what the ink blot is trying to say but only what the person tested thinks about it. The crowd plays Hamlet to such a man's Polonius, prodding him to shift his interpretations to please them. An echo board with nothing of himself to give, he may be addressed in the scornful words of Conrad's captain to the outcast, "What is there in you to provoke?"

One can lose his soul anywhere, of course. Politics allows two protections from this risk: one is a moderate ambition, enough to maintain one's effort and purpose; the other is an alternative trade as a hole card to remind the politician of a further chance for service in another worthy calling after his defeat.

A politician has to keep his place. He will be found at fault if he is either undignified or arrogant. The former sin is venial, the latter cardinal. As Tacitus pointed out, men "scrutinize with keen eyes the recent elevation of their fellows, and demand a temperate use of prosperity from none more rigorously than from those whom they have seen on a level with themselves." The quality of a politician's bearing is measured against the background of his rank. Arrogance in a coroner is dignity in a governor.

Egotism is increased by the sweet music of applause, but humility is also induced by the conditions of a politician's life: to be told off and have to beg his daily bread from face to face. A successful politician has a strong ego, but he lacks that kind of pride that inhibits him from asking for help.

Sometimes politicians are driven back to private life by exasperation with their constituents. People often resent a politician for his failure to be both delicately responsive to public wishes and a self-sustaining leader who leads. He disappoints them if he is not at once a thistledown on the breeze and a game fish that swims upstream. Politicians are directed to be both responsible and responsive, to be guided by the inner voice of personal principle, judgment and foresight—and by all the voter's wishes. Yet a politician is excoriated for failing to do both.

These contradictory demands resemble the layman's expectation that the law provide both certainty and the determination of each case by fireside equity. Hiram Gill, a former waiter, was elected mayor of Seattle on a closed-town platform. He kept his promise and was dismissed from office at the next election. He ran again on an open-town platform, was elected, kept this promise, and was again defeated. This puzzled Gill, who just wanted to be mayor.

Macaulay wrote, "In all ages and nations, the politician whose practice was always to be on the side which was uppermost had been despised." Yet if he fails to skate into membership of each new majority as it forms, he is blamed for being out of tune with the times. Because to follow the shifting center of power is now constitutional and often approved, the meaning of the label "opportunist" is less definite and reproachful. Political opportunists now are not courtiers in a usurper's train but men who rise to high station by legitimate means: obedience to public wishes by policies to the merit of which they are indifferent.

Another attitude that makes for disappointed citizens and exasperated politicians is people's dislike of a cocksure manner and their concurrent wish that a politician be sure he knows the answers. Since they did not elect him to doubt and ponder, they do not want his trumpet to give forth an uncertain sound. They want a humble messiah. In their attitude toward politicians, some people oscillate between cynicism and intolerant perfectionism, between regarding politicians as knaves and fools and expecting them to be impossibly wise and brave. Such a citizen expects the worst, yet is furious if he gets it. More than that, he expects politicians always to follow that course of policy that he, the citizen, thinks right, yet keep majority support so as to win reelection and thereby continue to serve.

A politician also knows that many of his constituents wish him to perform the functions of his profession yet be "above politics," where Eisenhower tried to be and where they think Lincoln was. For a politician's personality, still another aggravating contradiction is the common wish that he be both subservient and dignified, that he run petty errands, and run them as though he were descending Sinai with tablets of stone.

Imperious negative demands by constituents, often opposed to each other, may discourage one who thinks of going into politics. They intimidate politicians and stifle their enterprise. Subdued by threats, politicians often, in order to survive, resort to "the usual substitute for wisdom in waiting for the folly of others." In dealing with one's supporters, and with other pressure groups, one could learn from the football coach who hoped his team would lose no more games than just enough to "keep the alumni sullen but not mutinous." Indifferent to anything beyond their single purpose, these bitter citizens are less offended by sins of omission than by one act that they regard as wrong, even though combined with a record of good deeds. The same people who denounce politicians as pliant lackeys will call for dismissal of those whose position does not fully fit their own on some single issue, such as abortion, the Middle East or possession of pistols.

Politicians well may say to one another,

"Constituents do make cowards of us all," and tell their fellow citizens, "He that depends upon your favors swims with fins of lead."

In several walks of life, the deference given to what the crowd prefers has been increased by its newly accurate measurement. Cost accounting teaches restaurant operators to speed up the turnover and concentrate on the most popular items of food and drink. This enables customers to be served at lower cost but at reduced pleasure for those who put high value on wider choices and more time to talk. Sales and profits records have taught book publishers to concentrate on a few titles that many will buy, at the expense of many titles that would give pleasure and benefit to separate audiences of a few each. The precise accuracy by which audience preferences are measured for periodicals and broadcasting stations has induced their managers to choose material to be dispensed more on the basis of magnifying audience than of presenting (some would say imposing) some of their own tastes and values. Entertainment supplants information; the sensational wins out over the elevated, the instructive or the wise.

A closely similar process has been operating on politicians. Long ago, leaders (insofar as they cared) could measure the public's reaction to their performance no better than by observing more sullen than usual tugging of forelocks or, less often, dancing in the streets. When votes began to be taken and counted, it was possible to determine citizens' appraisals of candidates' past overall performance and comparative characters.

Now politicians can act not on comments about the past but on today's requests. They can learn, as never before, what their constituents prefer on each public issue, what will provoke them, what they may tolerate, what is the priority of their wants. The reports' narrow margin of error has caused politicians to defer more than before to voters' preferences. Knowing public opinion on every question, knowing that the constituents and the lobbyists know that the politician knows, the politician feels pressed to gratify them.

The shift from vague notions to precise knowledge, from the stale to the immediate, induces politicians, from democratic duty and survival urge, to shift the emphasis on what they seek from the public's welfare to its wish. Substituting opinion polls for their own judgment of the general good, they respond to momentary public whims. If the constituents would rather eat the seed corn than go hungry, the politician will show them the granary key.

Foucault argued that to discover closely measured probable consequences enables public policies that bring to pass more detailed and far-reaching consequences—a government that can see the sparrow fall may decide whether and where it shall fall. Such an increase in governmental efficiency does not always increase human freedom or happiness. Concern has been expressed that this condition may do harm by leaders manipulating citizens, but a like harm is done where the process is reversed.

In a bygone day, public leaders treated all others as children who did not know their best interests and must have their rules and policies chosen for them. Now politicians earn the citizens' hostile contempt for giving the term "public servant" the connotation of messenger boys and scullery maids. Their masters despise them as such, reacting with anger at being given that for which they asked.

Lawyers are widely disliked, but capable people nonetheless are drawn to the law by the money, the fun and the cocoon of colleagues and clients. Politicians do not make lots of money and they must associate with one and all. Quality folk, whose merits earn them open doors to more than one vocation, pass up a trade the public scorns.

We can do without high quality politicians less readily than we can survive second rate lawyers, televangelists and headwaiters. Democracy and politicians go together. Without politicians we can have government— perhaps, for a while, government better than we deserve—but it would not be democratic government. Democracy is impossible without politicians, and without democracy politicians have no place in government. Would those "curdled indignants" (Riesman's phrase) who revile politicians, whom they identify with their troubles, prefer the critical decisions of their government to be made by any one *but* politicians? By admirals, aristocrats, bishops, bureaucrats, commissars, courtiers, dictators, dukes, emirs, emperors, owners of major league franchises? Would they prefer their armed forces to be headed by the officers' choice, their police chief to be named by the cops?

Chapter | 4

DILEMMAS

A politician must draw delicate moral lines, and with little guidance. He can but dimly descry the never-ending shoals among which he must navigate. When he performs his function of shaping public policy by striking compromises between conflicting interests and opinions, or by resolving his equally conflicting loyalties, it is wrongly claimed that he is compromising principle (his own and others), and therefore lacks it. Recognized canons of professional ethics might reduce this disapproval and help to show him where his duty lies. If he knew his adherence to a set rule would not put him at a disadvantage with his rivals who had accepted the same duty, he would be encouraged to raise his standards of practice. Such a code, like a minimum wage law for competing employers or a racial non-discrimination ordinance for apartment house operators, might as much enable as compel. But the moral perplexity of political decisions results not so much from the lack of norms as from the inherent moral ambiguity of the decisions, making it impossible to develop standards that could help much.

What should be the rule for evasive answers, or the one for unspoken lies? How far should a candidate be held accountable for defamatory rumors that his supporters start? What should be his attitude toward a low-caliber running mate for whose selection he has had no responsibility except the remote one of membership in the same party? May he protect himself by displaying disapproval of the other, or does duty to his party constrain him to pretend respect?

Should a politician accept help from contributors with dishonest motives? If he does, what does he owe them? They expect a payoff and deserve a double cross. He can choose the latter only once. Few have the chance to handle this problem with dispatch and satisfaction as did Scoop Jackson who, after his election to the Senate in 1952, received predated checks from men who despised what he stood for and had supported his opponent, but wished to do business with Uncle Sam. Gracious letters of thanks were sent to the donors explaining that he could not use the money, since his bills were paid, but that, knowing how devoted they were to his principles, he had endorsed their checks to his party's state committee.

In deciding whether to accept a contribution, should a candidate distinguish between a frank sort who states his conditions when he offers money and a discreet one who does not? That is, are express contracts worse than implied ones? In the latter class, does it make a difference whether the candidate knows of the offeror's business interest in governmental favor, and whether it is present or prospective? Is it all right if there is no meeting of the minds? How long before a campaign or after it may money be accepted?

How should he respond to offers of institutional support from unions, chiropractic societies, trade associations and other special-interest groups? In most elections a substantial measure of such help must be obtained to win. Yet most such groups give assistance as their end of an assumed bargain. Some help without asking, then come around with a request.

How specific must a candidate's answers be, and how sincere? Voters share the blame for politicians being vague. May he declare as his opinion what reflects his own record and what he thinks to be the view of most of his constituents, yet in truth is not his own? May he give a truthful answer as to his intended course but a false explanation of the motives that determine it? On a certain issue, if he sees a conflict between the public's wish and welfare, and he decides to heed the wish, may he give the public welfare as the reason for the attitude he takes?

What must the officeholder do when he finds himself imprisoned by his own supporters who favor him on principle because of his policies? If, on principle, he changes his policies to conform them to his change of mind, will he lose his supporters, who will believe that he has lost his principles?

How narrow must a special interest be, how far in contradiction to the general good, how strong the pressure from the group that represents it, to make submission to the group's request not obedience to the people's will, but acceptance of a bribe or flight from a threat?

How far may a politician deviate from the

truth in unimportant things? Dishonesty about trifles is a dangerous habit because it is hard to keep within limits, but there it does no harm. A witness may not be impeached by proof that his testimony contradicts what he has said about collateral matters. Like other artists, a politician may be allowed a license to improve a tale. On the Chicago plane with the Massachusetts delegation to the 1956 Democratic convention, James M. Curley told me that FDR had betrayed him and that after he had uncovered the depths of the President's baseness he addressed him in the words that Cardinal Wolsey spoke "to Cromwell who had condemned him to death and then had come to visit him: 'If I had served my God as well as I had served my King [substitute Roosevelt], He would not have left me naked and helpless before mine enemies.'" Imagine Mayor Curley's Boston crowds when he would put himself in the place of a cardinal defying Cromwell. Shakespeare gave the dying and ruined Wolsey similar language, in a speech addressed to Wolsey's former servant, one Thomas Cromwell, a ruthless agent of a ruthless king, and a remote collateral ancestor of Oliver, who was born sixty-nine years after Wolsey's death.

In the day of rule by kings, a courtier had the duty to impart painful facts "without wounding the delicacy of a royal ear." In addressing his masters, a politician is called on to learn and exercise this art. How does he locate the range between the limits that duty and survival set? The duty is to tell the citizens the truth to enable them in turn to do their

duty of forming public policy or considering suggested alternative policies. For survival, he must
avoid giving too much offense. Twenty-four hundred years ago Isocrates wrote that citizens "like
those who cultivate their favor better than those
who seek their good".

Duty often calls for sincerity, while survival
often calls for good manners, of which insincerity is
the essence. Unlike a courtier, except in urging the
defeat of his incumbent opponent he does not have
to advise his constituents to correct their mistakes
or faults. He need tell them nothing irrelevant to
the problems that confront them both. He would
not have to inform a group of Irish that Saint
Patrick was English. Nor must he express invidious
comparisons in personal taste, such as to say what
he thinks of beehives, naturals, corn rows, and
crewcuts. The hard choices come where the politician must decide whether to tell citizens the fact,
as it appears to him, that a certain policy that they
may authorize will hurt them later more than help
them at once. Most kinds of fiscal responsibility
illustrate this kind of bad-tasting truth.

In action, a politician has the duty to carry
out the wishes of his constituents as modified by his
conscience and judgment. But in speech he has the
duty to tell people the truth about public affairs.
Except in a crisis, plain medicine will not be swal-
lowed by more than a few, because so many people
prefer happy-ending fairy tales. Even with Hitler
across the Channel, the harsh dose of "blood, sweat,
toil and tears" could be presented only in a setting

of invigorating rhetoric. The most socially valuable politicians master the art of dispensing sugarcoated pills. But a large proportion of the less adroit political pharmacists yield to the temptation to hand out candy as safer than trying to express truth in a palatable form. In choosing what to say, many politicians find it hard to resist the urge to follow Marshal Field's motto for his store: "Give the lady what she wants."

How much of the truth should a politician withhold from his constituents when public knowledge would not make people angry with him but in some way might do them harm? When should a politician let his constituents know facts that would help the constituents make their basic decisions of national policy, yet would give another nation's hostile government advantage against our own? Should an economist's report predicting a business depression be released if the politician reasonably expects that public knowledge of this report would depress business conditions even more than the report predicted? When does this kind of statement resemble screaming "Fire!" in a crowded theater, in which there is in fact a fire? And when is withholding it an unjustified treatment of citizens as children who are to be sheltered from facts that would confuse or hurt them? How should a politician balance the harm that disclosure might cause the commonwealth against the advantage to the commonwealth of the citizens' right, and free government's necessity, to have the whole truth for citizens to govern well?

And how far should a politician go in presenting to his constituents information that they need but that provokes some of them to resent him because they think national security is impaired, because it embarrasses leaders with whom they identify, or because it makes them uncomfortable by facing them with moral complexity? By pretending that their duty to provide the whole truth is absolute, some politicians pass on to their constituents all the facts they learn in order to escape responsibility for these hard choices. In the name of national security other politicians have gone the other way, withholding facts that could do the citizens no harm but that would reveal the politicians' own mistakes, or the mistakes of a bureaucrat whom they wish to protect

Another problem, in Gibbon's words, is "the deep and dangerous question, how far the public faith should be observed, when it becomes incompatible with the public safety." When may a treaty be broken or a defense contract canceled? When may persons who have not been proved insane or charged with any crime be confined on the apparent probability that they will do harm?

How to present an issue to the public is a puzzle. The antiquity of the age-old problems proves their insolubility, added to the complexity that marks most political problems. A simple problem soon is solved or disappears as such. To oversimplify is to

mislead, yet a politician has to simplify, not because the average voter cannot understand a clear and thorough explanation, but because he will not listen long enough. It is difficult to explain an issue in terms that are accurate, simple and brief. Those politicians who produced the Federalist Papers and the Gettysburg Address grasped the problem's root, understood their audience's minds and expressed themselves with clarity and art. Men and women on that level have passed through the smoky tunnel of polysyllabic gobbledygook and come out in the pure air on the far side. But except for those lofty few, a politician is left with the dilemma: to speak at length and not be heard, or to speak briefly and either mislead or be misunderstood.

A speaker is tempted to make promises when he is unable to hold his audience by entertaining it as an Alben Barkley or a Stevenson could do. For example, a local candidate for prosecutor promised to throw all sex offenders in jail, "even the innocent ones."

Ambition to achieve may be a productive force. Ambition for power and glory often corrodes and makes a person good for little. Yet to achieve much in politics requires one to climb to dizzy heights. So to do good one must tread the brink of hell. Men and women forget to treat high office as a tool and not a prize. To measure achievements in politics is difficult because they are obscured by the power and eminence that often accompany, but do not prove, achievements, and because instead of being solved, each problem always seems to be replaced by the next.

❖ ❖ ❖

A politician may be tempted to be vulgar. If he is a sucker for pomp, he may think vulgarity a way to resist the temptation; or if he has succumbed he may try to conceal his condition by a coarse mask. Like Congressman Boykin with his repeated motto, "Everything is made for Love," he may think vulgarity a shield against the hostility of those constituents who equate refinement with that extinct snobbish ruling class whose manners and education were an ornament. He may agree with those people. Vulgarity is often ineffective, and its wide acceptance lowers the aesthetic tone of public life. A few men only pretend to be vulgar, and make the most of both sides of the street, like Connecticut Governor Wilbur Cross (former Yale English professor) with his cultivated diatribe against baths. Some confuse vulgarity with the politically priceless common touch. When they aim at the latter they hit the former. Some, like Lincoln, embody both. Others have the common touch uncheapened, like the Emperor Augustus, who did not need a prompter when he called each senator by name and who was liked and trusted by the people because he knew the names and numbers of the gladiators at the games, or like Senator Robert Kennedy who, when Dr. King had been shot down, stood on an Indianapolis ghetto streetcorner—and quoted Aeschylus.

✧ ✧ ✧

What company should a politician keep? Unless he spends time with those who suffer from injustice or misfortune of a kind that public policy can relieve or correct, he is likely to lack the sympathy necessary to do right by them. This rule applies to him for every group that has its own special problems. As to those groups of which he sees little, he is an absentee politician and tends to neglect or mishandle their concerns. Without continued contact with a group, he cannot do a proper job for it. He lacks the knowledge needed for sound judgment and the indignation or pity to inspire him to act with force. Without association face-to-face, the inspiration still may be found in either of two types: one with a sensitive imagination or a self-propelled lover of mankind. But in most cases only personal contact can give understanding of each singular group.

If a politician acts in ignorance of his constituents, he will make policy in one of two ways. If he fits his policy to the only class or group that he knows, he harms other groups that differ from it. If he conforms his policy to the whole constituency's common denominators, the policy, though less harsh, still is wrong because any policy that fails to provide specific variations to meet the differences of each group imposes rules of a more strict uniformity than is suitable for a society that tries to grant diversity not only to individuals but to groups as well.

If he fails to consort with the wise and able, he may not develop his wisdom and abilities to their highest point. Without the regular company of his peers, his effort is likely to slacken and his perspective to blur. One who reaches high estate may be like the priest who was appointed bishop; his friend told him that never again would he hear a candid word or eat an ill-cooked meal. When one is among peers, his jokes must be funny to get a laugh.

Because of these conflicting needs—to improve his powers and to know the situation of those he represents—a politician is blessed if he has a receiving apparatus sensitive enough to detect the people's thoughts in a short time and if he has the gift of letting people know that he respects and understands them despite the fact that he does not often come among them.

A politician has to stay close enough to an organization, whether party or personal, to employ its force and depend on its support, yet far enough apart from it to show his independence and keep from being identified with its excesses. Truman went to one extreme, and Eisenhower the other.

In office, a politician, like a journalist, has one of the moral problems of a ruling class, close association with other community leaders, which makes him reluctant to treat them with justice when punishment or criticism is deserved. He weakens his impartiality, as well as his perspective, if he confines his associations to fellow big shots. Even if he does not tolerate their misdeeds, he feels inhibited by fellowship. To give his government its due, he need not go far toward the classic examples of stern adherence to the state in preference to personal ties. When the first Roman consul, Junius Brutus, learned that his sons had conspired to restore the tyranny of Tarquin kings, he told the lictors to do their duty with an ax. (The royal family had put to death his father and elder brother, so perhaps concern with treason to his family rather than to state dictated his choice and he was not a model patriot after all.) Xicotenga the elder ordered his son killed for plotting to betray the Conquistadores. James Lynch convicted his son of murder, condemned him to death, and then, finding no one willing to do the deed, executed him with his own hand in the Galway City Square, dismaying the locals at the impersonality of the Saxon approach to law. And Stephen Boileau had his godson hanged for theft.

Like most of us, a politician feels a strong pull to treat with scrupulous consideration those people with whom he deals in person and is on good terms, and to overlook the rest. At worst this narrow loyalty becomes honor among thieves; at best it earns the compliment that "if he's bought he stays bought." At seventy-six, John Quincy Adams wrote, "Throughout the course of a long and diversified public life I have considered it among the most impressive of my duties to render liberal justice to every individual with whom I have ever been associated in the public service, whatever my personal relations with him may have been, public or private." Even for Adams, cold to men and hot for principle, the ideal of justice for all was hard to attain.

A politician's intentions may be good, and he may give to the corrupt only the appearance of corruptibility, but if he acts in a way to suggest the thought, or encourage the hope, that those who cultivate him can have their way with him, he makes himself bait for the wrong appetites. His plight resembles that of Red Cross women on a jungle island wartime base because the congestion of petitioners keeps all but the most ruthless and aggressive from reaching his presence. Attracting unattractive attention from unattractive persons tends to make him a misanthrope or a pushover, to turn him too far away from people and too close to principle, or to corrupt him.

One tactical problem for a politician is how he can show the world all the rectitude he has, and maybe more to boot, without offending the gentlemen of easy virtue with whom he sometimes has to deal. A person does not deserve, and cannot long enjoy, the title of politician unless he conceals, or fails to feel, disgust for knaves or impatience with fools. In this his work differs from some occupations in which one is shielded from both.

It is more difficult for a politician to be severely just with those he knows and understands than tolerantly merciful to those whom he does not. How should he cultivate intimate knowledge while avoiding ties of interest and affection? The more knowledge he has of something (or someone—the more delicate problem for him), the better he can comprehend it and explain it to others, but the greater difficulty he may have in detaching himself in order to be fair. Too close association with the people involved may make him partial to them (if not cynical from disgust with them) and inhibit his criticism of them.

Also, he fails when he makes allowances for all human actions by his understanding of the actor's motives and the causes which have shaped him. Such a passive course contributes nothing to truth or freedom. Life may be meaningless, but politics is not. Albert Camus, with his concern for the ambiguities of moral responsibility and the difficulties of passing judgment, may give insights that inform our personal outlook on life, but a politician must bear the burden of playing god, or at least he must play judge. He does not sentence anyone for eternity but he has the duty to hold up standards and not only to act according to them but also to measure others' actions against them.

Until recent years there was a greater willingness to pass judgment on both issues and persons. Despite the ardor of personal relationships, less effort was made to understand people, who were measured more by their conduct alone, without adjustment for their nature and condition. This new concern for explanation of conduct is accompanied by a more flexible standard of responsibility, an increased toleration of misconduct. Although his duty says he must, a politician finds it hard at once to judge and understand. Most politicians are dis-

posed to lean toward judging issues and understanding men.

A member of Congress has the ethical and
practical problem of balancing duties that conflict
often in purpose and always in allotment of time. An
important one is to help and represent his constituents with their personal problems with Uncle
Sam, that is, to serve as a mediating agent between
citizens and government. The administrative branch
has become huge, impersonal and complicated.
Sometimes a citizen's legitimate efforts are frustrated by the inertia or indifference of a government
office. Often his congressman is the only person to
whom he can turn who can intercede to expedite the
matter or in some other way to correct an impending
injustice. Another duty of a congressman is to see to
it that his district is not deprived of its fair share of
federal funds.

Both of these functions, errands for constituents and money for the district, are subordinate to
the process of shaping national policy. Many
members of Congress and their constituents forget
that times have changed and think that what is good
for their district is good for the country, or do not
care whether it is or not. They think, or assume
without thinking, that exclusive attention to the
district at the expense of the region or nation will
improve the fortune of the district in the long run,
that the primary aim is to win a multilateral tug of

war for pork barrel funds with 434 other congressmen who still feel themselves Kentuckians or Vir-
ginians first and Americans second. The truth of
the trickle-down theory as applied to the central
government and those who inhabit each of the areas
that it governs is not yet widely understood. And so
long as the tug of war is practiced, even a sophisticated congressman must do his share of tugging to
protect his district's share, and thus perpetuate the
game.

The dilemma between a politician's judgment
of what is right and his constituents' wishes is more
easy to resolve in favor of the former to the extent
that his constituency is diversified. A group demanding one thing will have no special rights to it
from the politician who represents its members if
another equally deserving group asks for the opposite. In such a case to disregard the wishes of
some of his constituents is not a breach of trust
because it is a necessity, and obedience to the will of
all his constituents is not a duty because it is impossible. This is a great asset of the presidency,
which is subject to less pressure to be parochial than
any other elective office. But a diversified constituency does not always leave a politician without
hard choices. His constituents may disregard their
conflicting interests and unite in contradiction to
something else: foreigners, humankind, the unborn,
his conscience, his principles, his judgment.

A politician must serve several masters and serve them well. He tries to reconcile the never-ending conflicts between the things he is supposed to do, the elements of which cannot be codified: the duty to obey the wishes of his constituents and to follow his conscience or judgment or both; the duty to do the right thing and the necessity to stay in office to get the right things done. He must get along with constituents who think all economies should be made at the expense of Somewhere Else, and also with the elected representatives of Somewhere Else whose constituents feel the same way. He has to choose between a direct and immediate benefit to his district and a long-run, indirect one through the welfare of a wider unit, the state or nation. There may be the choice between success and fame (for a governor or senator) or the choice between fame and greatness (for a presidential nominee), and the fear of missing both.

How can a politician give direction, yet be the public's agent; how can he both lead and obey his principals, how embody his constituents' aspirations without becoming their lowest common denominator? Because it is no solution, it does not console a politician inclined to lean toward independence of his constituents' wishes to remind himself (or try to justify himself to others, by reminding them), as educated politicians have often tried to do, of Burke's remarks to the voters of Bristol, declaring that a legislative representative's duty is to exercise his judgment for the whole commonwealth rather than to be his constituency's pliant hireling. In Edmund Morgan's words:

> If the representative loses his ties to his constituents, the government ceases to be representative; if he and his colleagues lose their responsibility to the whole state, the government itself ceases.

Self-deception makes these contradictions harder to resolve. Politicians can fool themselves all of the time. With fervent earnestness, dairy area legislators contend that margarine is unhealthy, un-American, and against the laws of supply and demand. A feeble invalid (Glass, Mundt, Wagner, Vandenberg) convinces himself that he can serve the public interest better by keeping his seat (although unable to rise from it unaided) than by resigning to permit his replacement. A politician is tempted to tell himself that his ambition or fear of failure is obedience to the public will, so that he pretends the people are the sun whose beams it is his duty to reflect as a sort of governmental moon. Those distributors of popular entertainment who refuse to take responsibility for taste assert the same defense. In either case the opinions of mankind are given abject homage instead of a decent respect.

A politician's most fundamental dilemma confronts him when he disagrees with his constituents. When should he lead and when should he obey? What rule can tell him when he ought to disregard their wish so that he can serve their welfare? Sometimes the question is confined to disputed judgment, such as proposed vaccination, fluoridation, or birth control clinics, which the majority fears or hates but the politician thinks will make almost everyone happier. Often, if he cannot reconcile conflicting loyalties, he must choose—as between a majority of constituents and a minority. A variant conflict—often in appropriations and appointments—pits the general good against his personal loyalties to colleagues, friends and supporters, sometimes an indirect help to the general good.

How does a politician decide when to shift his loyalty to a group other than the majority of his constituents? How are his loyalties to be measured and weighed? At what point does one's loyalty become misguided, and at what point does it end? How does he decide how hard he should fight for the comparative advantage of his constituency over others? The factors are too complex and variable for criteria to be laid out, much less settled, for drawing these lines. Without guideposts a leader is subject to being swayed one way or another unless he has a rigid personality which itself denies him perspective and realistic judgment. The lack of any catechism makes a superior politician much to be admired.

The most uncharted territory of all through which a politician must sometimes make his way is where he must decide whether to substitute not only his judgment but also his morals for those of his constituents. When should he discard expedience—the wishes of a majority of his constituents—

in favor of a course he considers morally right toward others? When does his duty direct him to practice moral leadership by asserting his own moral principles? If citizens wish to indulge their passions, pride or prejudice, ought he enable them to do so? He is supposed to appraise the moral quality of his own impulses. Does it follow that he has the prerogative to judge when his constituents' wishes are evil appetites? When both he and most of his constituents are of two minds on a subject, does a politician in a constitutional democracy have a duty to impose his superego, prevailing over their ids? Directed only by his pity, should he donate public funds to starving foreigners abroad when a majority of his constituents would prefer a tax cut?

And when should he call on others to exercise *their* courage? Anyone can have peace by knuckling under, but to win or save the freedom of one's community may both require and justify the use of military force. In *Utopia*, the people waged war for three purposes: to defend their own territory when invaded, to deliver the territory of an ally from invaders and to free an oppressed nation from tyranny.

The weapons of mass destruction perplex as well as threaten us. If we refuse to fight we may have to submit to others, yet if we give up peace to preserve freedom, we may lose both by destroying established society, if not humankind as well. Here we cannot hope to muddle through by a continuous balancing act—preparing to win a war, avoiding the last step into it, and yet being evidently willing to take the last step so that others will not call our bluff—because the tightrope is too long and our own due care alone is not enough. The Pearl Harbor attack reminds us that leaders of even an industrially advanced nation can be utterly reckless. Safety is not assured by the consoling fact that this dilemma faces everyone, nor by the balance of terror which makes bullet-headed generals of powers hostile to us hesitate to do more than thunder at each other, "Delenda est Chicago." Our strongest potential enemies are unwilling to be Samson pushing at the pillars, and no one wants chaos, even though some do not care about freedom and some are indifferent to death. But although no strong group on earth is led by beasts who wish mankind had but a single neck, the structure of opposing forces is so unstable that a chance incident may set in motion events that will bring on doomsday. To solve this problem will take more than courage and a steady nerve because no answer lies in policies that have yet been tried.

As the moral question of calling on others to take up arms has diminished, another has arisen. In Bertrand Russell's words, "It is difficult to refuse a certain sympathy with the Irishman who said: 'Posterity never did anything for me, why should I do anything for posterity?'" Yet a politician often must consider whether to make a permanent change in the surface of the earth or to commit economic resources that in part will be paid for by the children of those who make the commitment. What is he doing to or for the unborn? Does his action build or preserve for their benefit while he lays a charge on them that is a fair bargain, or does he dissipate his generation's inheritance rather than pass it on? He must not only compare the merits of alternative undertakings but also balance the present interests of his constituents against the interests of people who did not elect him and whom he will never know.

In the past, we were too busy scrambling, taking care of the living, to have time to consider mouths that did not yet need to be fed. We lacked our present technology which gives us both power to alter the future and leisure to decide how to do so. In ancient Rome, the word *gloria* connotated a concern for posterity. Men strove for fame so that their names and splendid deeds would be known and admired by later generations. Now we can touch those who come after us by setting the conditions of their lives in most respects. We no longer are limited to tree planting, to the building or destruction of cities and to the setting of good or bad examples of individual conduct. By spendthrift ways we can leave a patrimony of poisoned ocean and eroded land.

It may become easier for us to sacrifice for posterity now that we recognize that the only sense in which we are immortal is through our actions, whose consequences ripple on until Judgment Day, long after a gravestone or a thought preserved on paper is gone. We know that our identity soon is lost. We have ceased to believe in an afterlife and we know we soon will be forgotten on earth because we have become aware of ravaging time, that "bomb that splits the most august temple open, if indeed the wanton savagery of men does not anticipate death's weapon," in Lewis Mumford's words. Since most people promptly drop from memory after death, records of individual achievement—the ghostly pattern of all remembered persons—cover only some of those whose ability and luck gave their performance an identity that endured for a while before the signature wore off.

> The Vanity of Fame, which at best is but the Shadow of great Actions, and must necessarily vanish, when destructive Time has eat away the Substance which it follow'd.
>
> CERVANTES

Both the good and evil that we do live after us; only our name is interred soon after our bones. One's capacities and years lived relate to the depth and length of the furrow dug and left behind, not to its existence. Marx wrote that all "history is nothing but the actions of men in pursuit of their ends." Our immortality in this sense is limited only by the causal chain descending from our actions, coming to an end when the chain is broken, when the laws we know cease to operate in that part of the universe where the consequences of our actions have been felt.

How far should a politician push for the interests of the unborn, with whom many of his constituents do not yet identify? To serve the unborn, should he try to diminish their numbers? A baby has enforceable rights, and some claim rights for an inchoate baby in a woman. If the future babies inside a baby were acknowledged as having political interests that a politician is justified in protecting, such recognition would not abate the politician's dilemma, though it might advance the interests of the human race.

When constituents insist, *carpe diem*, I want to get mine now, should the politician gainsay them? This is a new, public version of an old, private problem: whether to take the cash and let the credit go, as Omar advised (winning an all-time acceptance record for serious advice) or to take psychological promissory notes in the form of satisfaction at thinking that your actions may gain your ends long after. Dying at thirty-two when he took an Austrian bullet as he marched before his troops at Marengo, General Desaix is said to have murmured his regret that he had not done enough for posterity. But to consider posterity may be—and perhaps ought to be—harder for a politician than for an officer in a fighting army, one of whose biggest commitments of life is his risk of death.

In resource consumption and use of sewage and chemicals, a politician's dilemma may be blunted by price rises and pollution, which give enough people a present interest that accords with the interest of the unborn. But the issue of preserving that part of the natural wilderness that is beautiful makes him face a choice as easy to see as it is hard to resolve. Should he let the wilderness be transformed to something else—whether it is plundered as a mine or cultivated as a garden—that concurrently increases his constituents' material comforts and denies their descendants their chance for aesthetic and spiritual satisfaction from what, in Justice Douglas's words, is "the very core of America's beauty"?

Only recently has wilderness beauty been recognized, although green trees have long possessed charm in their beholders' eyes. Valerius Asiaticus "opened his veins, but not till he had inspected the funeral pyre, and directed its removal to another spot, lest the smoke should hurt the thick foliage of the trees." The chance to enjoy wilderness beauty comes from leisure. The taste grows from personal cultivation, discontent with other things, familiarity with the subject and reassurance that danger and discomfort are slight. Macaulay wrote:

> A traveler must be freed from all apprehension of being murdered or starved before he can be charmed by the bold outlines and rich tints of the hills. He is not likely to be thrown into ecstasies by the abruptness of a precipice from which he is in imminent danger of falling two thousand feet perpendicular; by the boiling waves of a torrent which suddenly whirls away his baggage and forces him to run for his life; by the gloomy grandeur of a pass where he finds a corpse

which marauders have just stripped and mangled; or by the screams of those eagles whose next meal may probably be on his own eyes.

Burt wrote of the Scotch Highland scenery:

> It is a part of the creation left undressed; rubbish thrown aside when the magnificent fabric of the world was created; as void of form as the natives are indigent of morals and good manners.

The poet Gray wrote of a celebrated grand and lovely outlook over Italy:

> Mount Cenis, I confess, carries the permission mountains have of being frightful rather too far; and its horrors were accompanied with too much danger to give one time to reflect upon their beauties.

And Goethe passed through the Alps with his carriage curtains drawn.

Just as those phrases that become clichés are ruined from overuse because they are the most vivid and eloquent in a language, so the most beautiful wilderness places need the most rigorous protection from becoming loved to death. Compare Lake Tahoe, as described by Mark Twain in *Roughing It*, and as it has become. At Yosemite one must stand in line for a place on the trail or the cliff to climb, and at Mount Rainier's Paradise Valley the trails are paved.

In the city, "vest pocket" parks can work well, but each wilderness tract must be large. When put next to our dynamic activities, the ingredients of wilderness cannot be kept in a stable and unchanged relationship with their surroundings, like peacocks on a shaven lawn.

The total wilderness territory must be both large and well-protected. It is preservable but can be neither expanded nor restored, while that proportion of the world's increasing human race that has the taste and time to enter and enjoy the wilderness is rising, thus multiplying the pressures, which are incompatible with the requirements of wilderness. Unless the number of persons allowed to enter is rationed, the wilderness will be lost.

Like saving for future consumption, providing for the unborn compels present sacrifice. Although those who value the wilderness multiply, their total still is small in proportion to those who seek to exploit it, whether by use for pleasure or by development for profit. Since the biggest threat to the mountain wilderness comes not from loggers and miners but from recreational users, the main measure is to restrain ourselves from converting wilderness to other forms of outdoor pleasures. Part of our timber needs may be supplied from tree farms in unappealing places, and the rest may be satisfied by use of substitutes. The consumption rates of metals made from ore may be reduced by conversion, recycling, conservation and other measures. But natural beauty, unlike energy and artifacts, cannot be replaced. *Solitudinem faciunt, pacem appellant.* We have the power to make a desert and, perhaps, to make peace but we cannot make the kind of wilderness we want. All we can do, and only through political leadership, is to keep what is.

We will lose a lot forever unless our remaining wilderness be kept as "true" wilderness. For us as members of humankind, it constitutes a singular and complex museum piece of what has been our long-time home. For us as Americans, it leaves us a link with our start in this hemisphere, "an Errand into the Wilderness."

Among the particular groups that benefit, one is commercial. A wilderness provides economic as well as social benefits to the surrounding area, serving as functional backstop and visual backdrop for businesses that depend on outdoor recreation in or by the woods and mountains. This branch of enterprise has grown until its potential dollar worth (and on a perpetual basis) to most regions exceeds that of the extractive industries in the same places. Advances in technology reduce the importance of raw materials' existence, and advances in transport and communication reduce the importance of raw materials' location. To leave the wilderness exposed to steady erosion by us, by our machines, and by the forces of nature acting on land that has been torn open by men and machines prevents much money from being made.

Other wilderness beneficiaries are noncommercial. A few make frequent, direct use. Members of a larger group, but still a small one, make occasional direct use. A large group, the size of which is hard to measure, never enters yet receives satisfaction from awareness of the simple presence and availability of the wilderness, the knowledge of one place not treated as wet clay, perpetually remodeled. The Psalmist sang, "I will lift up mine eyes unto the hills, from whence cometh my strength." To know some hills that will still be there the next time one looks up may give security through a fixed reference point in a perplexingly mobile world.

In a society governed by the popular will, the difference between statesman and demagogue seems to be mainly in length of view in action. Whether he guides or follows depends on whether a politician urges people to pursue an end for which they have no taste but which, in his foresight, he knows they would like if they attained it or approached it for long; or whether he endeavors to lead the people to attain what they already want. The demagogue who gives the people what they want has fewer dilemmas, and they are mainly tactical. He may enjoy an immediate ascendancy over the statesman who does not. But if the statesman manages to stay in action long enough, people may discover that his proposals better fit their long-run needs which one day become their wish.

The demagogue may be more useful than the wholly nonpolitical person who does not look beyond himself in that the demagogue to some extent identifies the happiness of his constituents with his own happiness. He resembles an overly permissive parent who puts all family decisions to a vote in which the children are controlling. When the demagogue helps his constituents to attain their longed-for diet of whiskey and sugar he at least is seeing farther than the person who is satisfied merely to attain this for himself. Even Satan was applauded by his adherent fiends when "for the general safety he despised his own." Of course, where a politician offers a policy for the sole purpose of using it as currency with which to buy advancement, his view is no more expanded beyond himself than is that of a promoter who sells stock to the public without concern for its worth. His view is longer, however, if he aims for satisfaction through satisfying others and because the conditions for his life are more likely to fit his wishes if his fellow men are attaining their ends, which attainment makes membership in the society more comfortable, satisfying and safe.

A statesman's efforts are based on conceptions of greater magnitude in time and personal relationships. He undertakes to restrain his constituents' immediate self-defeating aims, to discern the attainable good by looking beyond their horizons, and to lead those who will follow him toward this envisioned good. He realizes that the best thing for himself is for the human race to be proceeding in the direction of what in twenty years it will realize it wants the most.

Where leaders are exposed to strong public pressures, the difference between demagogue and statesman is small. How far can a politician let the duty of responsiveness push him toward indulging his constituents before his efforts are transformed from public service to demagoguery? Adlai Stevenson said that the hardest thing about a campaign is "how to win without proving that you are unworthy of winning." To extend the line of a politician's own prerogatives is up to the politician, just as an oligarch bears the burden to withdraw it. The citizen can help by setting his own balance: vigilant to thwart autocracy (a threat no longer from elected men but from bureaucratic practices that they permit), yet tolerating initiative by those whom he elects.

A thoughtful politician may be inclined to extend his prerogative far, to keep the bit in his teeth when he reflects that despite his limitations his wisdom is likely to exceed that of the average among those constituents who compose the majority forming an opinion on any issue. A constituency would have low standards or bad luck to elect a politician whose wisdom and knowledge were not above the average of the whole. Also, the citizenry cannot deliberate as a group to get the best of each other's thought; that is one of the reasons why his office was created. He knows that even if he does not play on people's fears and hates, he sins by doing the devil's work to please his constituents. (We hanged German and Japanese officers, who had let prisoners be killed, for failing to adhere to proper limits on the interests and wishes of their home folks.) He is aware that majority public opinion is not always wise or good. It may be either consciously or unconsciously wrong, erring in one direction:

immediate and parochial satisfactions. It favors the moment and the community, the here and now. It gives excessive consideration to me and to today, and not enough to thee and to tomorrow. Majority wishes often represent the community's needs for today, but they sometimes conflict with the group's welfare which is often the world's future needs.

But then the thoughtful politician pulls back on asserting his prerogative when he remembers other things. Like most people active in the civic affairs of a society that has a strong democratic tradition, he feels the force of the principle that the people are paramount, and that he should discern majority public opinion on any issue and humbly say, "Thy will be done." He knows that his particular function creates a duty that contrasts with that of the press, which ought to report but not reflect the mood of its constituency. (The press may display the mood but not express it, not report that the home team won just because the rooters wanted them to win. Its role is to communicate to the audience, each organ obedient to its own minds and consciences, not the public mood. One may be tempted to be characterized in the words of Isaiah: "How beautiful upon the mountains are the feet of him that bringeth good tidings, that publisheth peace." But the temptation must be resisted if publishing war is closer to the truth.)

Then a politician's wish for survival— meaning short-run survival—bids him to indulge the people in their mistakes. He knows they sometimes do not find out whether they have a good servant until after they have fired him. "Having many times opposed [the Athenians'] inclinations, forcing them against their feelings to do what was their interest, [Nicias] had got himself disliked."

Last, a politician knows he may be mistaken because of the limitations on his knowledge and comprehension. He cannot be sure of his own judgment. He remembers that in measuring present value, future pleasures and pains, like money, must be discounted. He may be reminded that the worth of granting leaders unfettered discretion is belied by the Vietnam experience and many others. Unlike a scientist who refuses to accept a hypothesis until he has verified it by examining all available evidence that may prove or disprove it, a politician often lacks time for study and always lacks controlled conditions for tests. He must act on his hypotheses, which are often hastily formulated, and which are measured, if at all, only by looking backward on his acts.

Not only may he be mistaken. His constituents may be right. The story was recorded of the ancient Roman whose friends reproached him for divorcing his wife: "Was she not not beautiful? Fruitful? Chaste?" He took off his shoe and held it out, saying: "Is this not new? Is it not well-made? Yet not one of you can tell me where it pinches me." Awareness that his constituents may be more right than he may inhibit a politician from imposing his own singular judgments on them. This knowledge not only operates on him through conscious thought but it accentuates its strength by encouraging him to deceive himself.

In an exercise of judgment, only time will tell who was right, and the time tends to be long. When I moved from law practice for a stint in charge of a business, I thought the function would resemble piloting a plane—as you pushed and pulled levers the dials would register changes in direction, altitude and speed. This illusion was dispelled by the discovery that managing a large organization resembles piloting an under-powered tanker: When you turn the wheel or push the engine room telegraph the ship does not soon respond. My days were spent alternately frustrated at the seeming futility of my current efforts and startled at current results of things done years before and since forgotten. To the time lag is added the uncertainty that your ship will ever turn as you direct. Compared with business, the results in government sometimes are even more incalculable and long delayed. Business responds to direction with more promptness and precision because its functions are narrower and more subject to measurement and because business management calls for a degree of presumption, tunnel vision and impatience that among politicians is less common (as well as less desirable) than among able business executives.

In politics, not only is the wait for results often longer than in business, but even after the results appear, their merit may not yet be shown. The telling time tends to come later than the next election day. If events ultimately vindicate him, the politician thereby may be enabled to win an election many years after his act. But to survive until then he may have to yield to what the public wants. In *The Statesman*, Henry Taylor observed that a politician "should steer by the compass, but he must lie by the wind." How far may he do things which, in his judgment, are against the public welfare in order to satisfy the public wish so that he may stay in office where he can serve the public welfare?

When a politician thinks of changing his position, one factor that he considers is how citizens may react. What is the citizen to think?—The politician is insincere? Conditions have changed, justifying or appearing to justify the shift? He is capricious, even though sincere? His previous position was careless and imprudent, based on ignorance and lack of concern with the matter? He has changed his values on where to draw the line between his opinions and his constituents', although all opinions and conditions have remained unchanged? For his notable flexibility and adroit affiliation shifts as he gracefully picked his way through times of rapid change, keeping his feet on top of the turbulent heap, Talleyrand was scorned as a cynical disloyalist. His biographer commented: "In politics, innovation is always betrayal."

A constituent less readily may forgive a politician when events show him to have been mistaken and applaud him when he turns out right, if they have differed on a moral issue than on a matter of judgment. In the latter case, no one knows for sure what is right, while in the former case each knows what is right, and the constituent may feel ashamed of himself and resent someone whom he may think to be self-righteous. When a politician makes people sacrifice for their own good, they may never forgive him the price he made them pay. Their virtue may have been for them an inadequate reward. If time proves that he acted for their long-run welfare, the facts they may acknowledge, but the demonstration of moral superiority they may be unwilling to gulp.

II | Methods

Chapter | 5

COMMUNICATION BROKERS

The mass media have done to the campaign system what the invention of accurate artillery did to the feudal kingdom: destroyed the barons and shifted their power to the masses and the prince. While the Reformation removed the intermediary between deity and communicant, the media substitute themselves for the party in an intermediary role, enabling more nearly direct contact between politician and citizen because they transmit more and translate less. Without the media, candidates are as lost as once they would have been without the Party apparatus through which to operate. Candidates now pay less attention to district leaders than to opinion polls, and citizens no longer need party workers to advise them how to vote. For most of our nation's first century, most voters did not know what their Presidential candidates looked like; to many, not even a blurred likeness was available. But now that a citizen can see and hear candidates on a screen at home and read and hear news written by the best journalists from a variety of points of view, about candidates' public and private lives, he does not heed the precinct captain on his block.

Television broadcasting of political speeches has changed their style, especially in statewide and national campaigns. The universality of coverage—augmented by the press—keeps a speaker from taking extreme contradictory positions—saying he favors something when in the country and opposes it when he is in town. Language is more internally consistent (though not otherwise more logical).

The comprehensiveness of the audience inhibits the use of words and manners offensive to some ears and eyes that would not have been found at a political rally in the past. Speaking to a cross-section of opinion, rather than to a group comprising a single viewpoint, moderates the tone. Also, despite our lifted interdict on words and subjects, we have become restrained in accusatory speech, having shifted our euphemisms from sex and toilet functions to personal attacks. Even guttersnipers' charges now are mild. Instead of hammer blows, they employ circumlocutions, code words and language more snide than either sharp or blunt.

Although a politician constantly seeks to have his word spread abroad by the media, he is often disappointed when they do. Sometimes he is exasperated when his statement is twisted, muddled or even reversed, and sometimes he is sorry when his words are transmitted precisely, letting everybody know his indiscretion or mistake. No matter what justified and bitter indignation the media's treatment provokes in him, he neither screams nor bites unless he is a fool or loses self-control, because he knows that they will have him to kick around if they choose. When next he sees the reporter he pastes on a grin as does a salesman when he meets a big customer who has told him off.

Seldom is a written statement misquoted, because falsehoods are easy to prove against the perpetrator and hard to excuse as a mistake. Spoken statements are often falsely quoted, a result of the hasty process and the reporter's limitations (of capacity rather than character). Electronic transcriptions mislead less than do printed reports. Audio and video editing may distort a statement, of course, but in common practice news media do not. For half a century periodicals have quoted things I have said—as athlete, wartime serviceman, lawyer, political candidate, business executive, civic activist, author and parent. Every quote was inaccurate. I could not always remember just what I had said but always could remember that I had not said what the paper or magazine printed as mine. Some errors were insubstantial, but many made me squirm. By contrast, among the few times I have been interviewed on the air, some broadcasts made my toes curl, but the blunders were my own.

In their pursuit of free communication, citizens need the media as much as politicians do, and the media make them equally frustrated. People always have risked deception by the untruth of an expression's contents. In the means of transmission itself one could be deceived only by the speaker's plausible manner and the symbolic sanctity of some writings that induced reverence without rational support. Now new forms of deception inhere in the communications' procedure. They include teleprompters, lighting and multiple-system editing that relates sight and sound, cunningly joining Esau's hands and Jacob's voice. For a journalist's elaborate tools to present a fair picture, he must make delicate judgments. Plutarch wrote that "we would wish that a painter who is to draw a beautiful face, in which there is yet some imperfection, should neither wholly leave out, nor yet too pointedly express what is defective, because this would deform it, and that spoil the resemblance." Equipment that can quickly record face and voice encourages the media to use actual human expression thus reproduced rather than relying on simulation by actors' imitation and sound effects. However, it also enables deception, and the temptation and probability accompany the opportunity.

Although in the law of commercial fraud, half-truths are recognized as falsehoods, in politics and journalism they often are treated as the most venial of sins. The device is not new. More the scholar than the propagandist, Saint Jerome remarked that Saint Paul, who wrote of a Greek temple dedicated "To the Unknown God," had lifted this out of the full inscription that the altar in Athens bore: "To the Gods of Asia, Europe, and Africa; To the unknown and strange Gods." However, the media have made the half-truth more effective because clarifying questions cannot be asked by the receiver of a message. On the other hand, journalists' reports can encourage politicians to cleave to the truth.

For politician and citizen to perform their functions for a free society, they need to send and receive thoughts through the media with freedom. To consider how to enable this, we may examine the nature of communication liberty and the policies resulting from traditional doctrines. One who practices free communication enjoys three elements of choice: diversity, definiteness, and desirability. Diversity here means the product of the number of available choices and their difference from each other. Except insofar as choices differ, multiplicity does not make them diverse—like the choices offered by a sideboard bearing thirty plates of ham.

> In fact, it is possible to interpret the information carried by a message as essentially the negative of its entropy, and the negative logarithm of its probability. That is, the more probable the message, the less information it gives. Clichés, for example, are less illuminating than great poems.
>
> NORBERT WIENER

Definiteness here means the completeness, accuracy, and precision of knowledge of each alternative: the fidelity of the photographs that one's mind is given about his choices. They cannot constitute diversity unless one can tell them apart. Definiteness depends on the clarity of both the choice itself in its appearance to any person (how clearly does the map define the routes) and the person's capacity to discern his choices (how well he can read the map).

Desirability here means how much one wants to take part in a given thought in relation to his other wants. He has no free choice—because this factor is missing—if he wants only things unavailable to him or if he wants nothing.

The absence of any one element wholly denies free choice, regardless of the size of the other two. Each depends partly on the person. Diversity is limited by one's powers of action, definiteness by one's powers of observation and judgment, and desirability by one's intensity of desire for any of the available choices.

If a person's relationship to the communication system were thought of as a telephone switchboard, then diversity is the number and variety of plugs, definiteness is the precision by which they are differentiated, and desirability is the degree to which the person wants to take part in conversations enabled by the board. Each person's switchboard is built in part by the causes that have shaped him, in part by the technology that has made the communication system, and in part by the society's practices and rules.

Our doctrines for free speech and press largely derive from the principle stated in the *Areopagitica:* "Let [truth] and falsehood grapple; who ever knew truth put to the worse, in a free and open encounter?" It is as true as ever but does need to be carefully read to remember the qualification. Aristotle recognized that a free and open encounter was essential when he observed that one utility of rhetoric was to equalize competing advocates because the right should be expected to prevail by its own weight, so that when judges decided wrongly the defeat of truth and justice was caused by their advocates' fault in giving an unskilled argument. Failure to remember that grappling is not enough without the free encounter gives the false assumption that if we merely watch the tossing waves of communication, or even waves of controversy, we can expect to see the truth come soaring up from them, like Venus or Polaris.

A laissez-faire policy toward the commerce of thought enables some of the wrong kinds of the fittest to survive. Like economic liberty, communication liberty depends on competition, which often does not stay open unless organized society keeps it so. This requires not the rules of the alley or jungle, which describe what is, but the rules of the playing field, which prescribe what ought.

Although a free and open encounter is an essential tool for approaching the truth, its presence does not assure success— either truth or more freedom. Thomas Erskine confidently declared to a jury, "The changes produced by such reciprocations of lights and intelligences are certain in their progressions, and make their way imperceptibly, as conviction comes upon the world, by final and irresistible power of truth"—but he addressed these words for the prosecution in criminal proceedings against a man for having published Paine's *Age of Reason*. Livy wrote that the Romans "never were worsted in an open fight or upon equal terms." Well, hardly ever. And the same goes for encounters of truth and falsehood. We depend on probabilities only, but the method offers the best odds.

Freedom to give and receive thought used to be narrowed in two ways: choice of fellow participants and choice of what to write or speak. Technical and economic limits on the communication system's capacity allowed a person to reach only a few others, and the patterns of practice did not stimulate those who took part.

To criticize the authorities or suggest a different outlook on life threatened the society's frail structure, subverting the underlying order on which social freedom of all kinds depends. This risk itself restrained some people, and most were restrained by governmental sanctions, imposed by reason of the risk and extended by the authorities' self-protective wish to prevent even such critical words that would not threaten society's fabric.

Those in charge more freely could indulge in reacting as affronted, and public opinion was less fastidious about punishment. The law came down hard on those at society's bottom who spoke ill of those at the top. When John Adams stopped in Newark on his way from Philadelphia to Quincy, he was greeted by a crowd and by a committee that saluted him by firing a cannon. A bystander said, "There goes the President and they are firing at his ass." Luther Baldwin replied that he did not care "if they fired through his ass." Under the Alien and Sedition laws he was convicted of speaking "seditious words tending to defame the President and Government of the United States," and sent to jail until he should pay his fine and court costs. Now, even in a society such as ours, where private physical violence is common, fiercely disparaging words by the small about the great are not punished because they are not regarded as doing criminal harm.

For long, communication liberty has been sought, and with success, although less than one might expect nineteen centuries after Arrian referred to "liberty" and "free speech" as "those grand old words." Expression is substantially exempt from threat that it will be suppressed. Governmental inclinations are curbed. Private suppression continues to be a real problem but not a severe one because the main practices are indirect and they inhibit more than they gag.

In some ways, freedom to deal in thought—produce, deliver, obtain, consume, exchange and record—has been increased most by the expanded scope of the media. We have come far from the condition in which what we call a chapter was called a "book" because a volume would be cumbersome to handle if it contained any more words. The new technology brings sender and receiver closer by letting them reach each other faster and at greater distances, by more complete and accurate transmission of expressed elements, and by handling a greater volume of traffic than was permitted by pigeons, pony express, parchment scrolls and fences over which to chat. A microphone enables a sender to reach a multitude of receivers, and a library enables a receiver to reach many senders. The communication system has grown more efficient and integrated until it approaches the pattern of a seamless web. Many communities have distribution systems with a capacity not far short of the limits of their inhabitants' personal capacity to take part.

The risk of reduced capacity is slight. This was not so in 1637, when, as a measure to control the press, a Star Chamber Decree limited England to four type-foundries. But those who want to restrict communication freedom aim to confine some particular notion or kind of thought, and it seems no longer feasible to restrict all transmitted thought as a means of restricting that which a censor thinks would do harm.

However, despite the expanded scale of communication available to everyone, the communication system threatens freedom through its own size, complexity, imbalance and operating rules. The old problems of suppression and capacity have been succeeded by new ones. The simplest form of thought delivery—person to person—calls for little concern. But where thought goes between an individual and either an organization or a distribution system in which one voice reaches many ears, or the other way around, both the policies and the moral consciousness have lagged.

When our doctrines were developed, during the period between the British civil war and the ratification of our Constitution, senders varied, as always, in their appeal and persuasiveness, but, provided they were allowed the right to try, they were roughly equal in the size of audience they could reach.

Since then, a disparity of means has opened among senders. Some can reach myriads, while others leave their sheets under a few windshield wipers. The range has widened not only in numbers reached but in impact as well. Long ago, a person had only two ways to reach many people: shouting to a crowd or carving on a rock. The new means to reach a multitude have great extent and force. Those who direct the mass media may be many things, good or bad, but they are not fugitive pamphleteers. One of the chief problems pertains not to being allowed to speak, but to reaching a large audience. William Lloyd Garrison, the Abolitionist editor, wrote, "I will be heard!" Except for those like him who sit at the keyboard of a mass communication organ, how many of us could say the same?

The right to howl in the wilderness, pass out handbills, address passers-by on the sidewalk, and run off copies of one's own work on a copy machine gives unequal freedom where others can reach vast numbers through the big distribution systems. The low cost processes of turning language from one's mind to print and then reproducing it have given print, without a distribution system, no more impact than unbroadcast speech. Putting a thought into print used to be enough to win a chance for acceptance, as publication implied a substantial readership among literate people. Now for one to reach many minds, a distribution system must augment the print.

Speech for some is more tolerated than free, having become freedom of whisper or freedom to shout into an unconnected mike. The soap box or parade or picket line that the media do not pick up—as an exercise of free speech plays little more part in the passage of ideas through society than did the old practice of letting a condemned man harangue the crowd before he reached Tyburn gallows. The notion that free communication, as a practical matter, means permission to release your thoughts has lost its truth, resting on the no longer sound premise that you can count on being heard as well as anyone else whenever you get something off your chest.

For a politician to perform his function well, he and his constituents must have access to each other. He can make himself accessible by heeding his mail and people who talk to him alone and in small groups. But those who wish to reach him are few, while sometimes he needs to reach most of them, and, in the large numbers that compose modern constituencies, only through aggressive media does he do this well.

Those organs that enable one sender to reach many receivers with an impact greater than a circular letter are oversubscribed. Prospective senders seek time or space that exceeds the supply from an organ that obtains attention by putting its product into the presence of many people—on the screen at home, on a speaker in the car, rolled up on the door mat—and holds the attention by using appealing material. For advertisers, the demand is economic;

for the rest, personal desires or institutional purposes impel the seekers. Lacking guidance of past experience, we have not yet developed theoretical standards of fairness for those access opportunities that cannot be made equal for all.

A politician's most effective means of access to most people is television, and his main barrier is cost. Its impact makes TV almost essential for a campaign, while its cost makes it prohibitive for many, yet not only is there a high overall cost—getting into the game—but the unit cost is often high compared to that paid by others who use the medium.

In most mass-medium solicitations prospective takers of what the speaker offers compose a substantial proportion of the audience. But in a nonpresidential campaign, the proportion of the TV audience that the solicitor seeks is small. Many of the audience are not registered voters in his constituency. In primary races, many of the remainder are excluded by their registration with another party or attachment to it in other ways. Since advertising rates are based mainly on the total audience size, the candidate is subjected to a unit cost for reaching members of his target group higher than that sustained by most commercial sponsors. In general, the larger the constituency, the smaller the spread.

Yet where used with skill, television is a method so efficient that a small amount of broadcast time could provide an informative campaign. Faster and at a lower unit cost than any other way, television can acquaint hundreds of thousands with a candidate's personality, enabling a campaign to be short and cheap.

This cost factor's most harmful consequence is its tendency to exclude candidates of merit—as well as candidates who lack both merit and money. Not much access to this powerful instrument is available to those who neither are rich nor show enough probability of winning to attract campaign contributions. Except for incumbents, the latter status can be attained by few.

When our doctrines were formed, attention was confined to the right to declare a statement or pass it on. Because those who sought to speak or print stood in the bullseye, the policies for liberating commerce in thought concentrated on speech and the press, the two items on this subject that we put in our Bill of Rights. Those who needed the protection of legally defensible rights were street corner orators and embattled pamphleteers whose lives were full of risks. Only senders were threatened.

To protect pitchers but not catchers has ceased to be enough. We know that the right to have mouthpieces on our telephones is equaled by the right to have earpieces. A receiver's problem used to be a chance to learn to read. Now he passes through an endless gauntlet of menacing or beseeching expressions that besiege him around the clock, invade his home, batter his ears, eyes and brain, prevent him from thinking of anything else. He is hounded by expressions as though he were a Puritan editor pursued by the agents of James II, except that the editors sometimes escaped. Receivers' rights have not yet been widely recognized as essential to the communication syndrome's freedom in general, although we have established particular rights at the receiving end, such as laws requiring information about government to be disclosed to citizens and the longstanding rule compelling a witness to testify in court. In their failure to recognize that free communication concerns arrival as well as departure, our old policies resemble a city ordinance permitting skyrockets to be shot off.

As broker, bringing parties together for mutual advantage, an organ of the media shares the problems of each. For example, access to a medium avails a candidate little if he cannot gain access to the audience when most of its members prefer other material offered by the organ. The resulting low audience level for politicians makes many broadcasters despair of devising means to improve such programs' appeal. If any political program that lasted long enough to enlighten rather than give mere name familiarity or a smack of personality is run in the evening, when many voters watch, both the station's audience and its revenues are likely to sustain a drop. Since every audience for a mass organ is voluntary, subject to no pressures to attend but the moment-to-moment appeal of the material offered, it is futile to offer a cultural or educational tone above what the audience is willing to take.

The media's function resembles that of the politician in balancing initiative and responsiveness, and in that where the line is drawn depends in part on public attitudes. Does the citizen wish an organ to serve as a juke box, as Herr Doktor Professor, or as something in between? For the media, the counterpart of the politician's dilemma between parentalism and opinion polls is how to balance the interests of senders and receivers: a person's need as a sender persistently to solicit attention from an audience that is not yet enthusiastic enough about his thoughts to invite them from him, and the same person's need, as a receiver, to choose what he will receive. A receiver's free choice depends on the diversity of clearly articulated and desirable messages from which he can choose. A sender has greater free choice insofar as he can tell any of his thoughts to all.

Some people think the media to be spokesmen for senders, and others are convinced that the media reflect most receivers' wants. The process is reciprocal. Shaw wrote that if you give the public what it wants long enough, the public will want what it gets. Those who present the TV news are criticized for doing so, and thereby exercising influence, when they have not been elected by either citizens or audience, but in a sense they stand for election every evening. Likewise, real estate mortgage money is lent where the lender thinks the situation offers the best repayment prospects, and the lending decisions help to shape neighborhoods according to resources with which to build.

To allow ample receivers' choices permits airing popular ideas and subjects of interest to many. Unpopular ideas best can be advanced by a strong sender's capacity to obtain receivers' attention. Unpopular ideas can reach receivers only when the receivers' pleasure and approval are neither essential to reaching the receivers nor the sender's principal aim.

Where a receiver (reader, listener, viewer) pays the full cost of what he receives, he may demand more precise accommodation to his tastes than where some or all of the cost is borne by advertisers or tax payers. European newspapers— supported mainly by their readers—have been more partisan than those largely supported by advertising. Where the receiver need pay no more than his attention, he less often conditions his support on the organ not only informing or entertaining him but also advancing his cause, his party or some other interest. When exempt from exacting demands, an organ may be less tempted to distort the truth in order to hold him.

Where receivers dominate they can insulate themselves successfully from exposure to notions that might change their minds. In the seventeenth and eighteenth centuries, publishing a book was a large financial undertaking because the cost of paper was high, the supply of type and presses was short, few titles were printed, and few copies were sold. In England, where patronage was used to cover much of a book's printing cost and thus reduce a publisher's risk to the point that he would publish, sometimes a patron could be found who saw merit in the manuscript or for whom an effusive dedication overcame his dislike for radical proposals. But in the American colonies, whether publication was done on pure speculation or backed by subscriptions for advance copies, the printer/publisher took no chances. He would shun the novel, the unknown, or the threat to his prospective customers' interests or beliefs.

The most popular mass media transmit only popular voices, of course, while making an impact on values and taste. An aspect of free speech is narrowed by shutting out those who would importune large numbers with unpopular messages. Tocqueville wrote that before the Revolution, "France had not yet become the land of dumb conformity it is now; though political freedom was far to seek, a man could still raise his voice and count on its echoes being widely heard." Now an unpopular person or idea—whether disliked or unknown—often is given little exposure by those media that provide the only substantial audience. Accentuated by the news broadcasts' daily focus on the consensus, the result favors those who are in or up—the incumbent and the well-established candidate who arrived long ago—and impedes the dissenter and the upstart. Television handicaps those kept in the outer darkness, leaving them and their ideas unknown, extending the contrast between haves and have-nots of access to the medium. Ezra Pound wrote, "Free speech without free radio speech is as zero."

The media concentrate on accepted views, values and tastes because those in control prefer them, and they concentrate on those that are widely held because the economics of advertiser support call for appealing to such a large proportion of the potential audience. The lack of fundamental differences between the principal decision-makers in government and in the mass media reduces fundamental criticism and consequent temptation to censor. It can be taken to mean no more that we are dominated by a unified power elite than that both political leaders and media subordinate themselves to popular views.

This consensus approach may put a brake on social reform, but it provides cohesion through common experience needed from large-scale senders as well as from the formal school system as a means to keep the society's parts from becoming too disparate for it to serve its members.

As between sender and receiver, free choice is like a seesaw; as one goes up the other falls. One is augmented at the other's expense. Aggressive means—a sound truck, telephone solicitor, bull horn or door-to-door salesman—gives a sender more free choice and denies it to a receiver. A sender may capture a receiver's attention, and thereby expand the sender's freedom of choice, by beguiling and enchanting a receiver as well as by assault. Although a communication, like a caress, is aggressive to a given receiver only insofar as it is not invited, the receiver's favorable reaction does not show that his free choice was expanded because the effort that freedom takes is not always preferred.

Whether a sender (author or transmitter) is identified illustrates the seesaw. If a sender can keep his name off his message, he may be more free to express himself because exempt from the threat of those who would retaliate against him. On the other hand, to know who sent the message gives a receiver more freedom. Where a sender knows he will be known, he may be less likely to make a personal attack which in turn may inhibit the receiver from expressing himself. The receiver is given more of the definiteness factor by a labeled message, which may be more accurately appraised, reducing his risks of misunderstanding and deceit. Likewise, where a receiver is identified, the knowledge in others of what he chooses to receive narrows his choice by exposing his thought, yet a known target better lets a sender train his sights on it and thereby widens his choice.

To shift the balance toward receivers' choices by restricting the force of the measures used by senders to win and hold an audience resembles a game law banning barbs on fish hooks or setting a minimum distance at which hunters have to stand from the game. Such a rule, restricting high-intensity means of obtaining an audience, shifts some free choice from the pursuer to the pursued, from the fisherman to the fish.

The media have become more than intermediate agents. In many cases, balancing senders and receivers is more than a switching or brokerage function. By selecting what voices shall have access to it, an organ resembles an individual deciding what to say and what to leave unsaid. Important organs not only select senders whom they allow access, but choose the manner of sending, and even employ senders, so in a large sense they become senders themselves. This does more to make the media politicians' counterparts.

The organ's dilemma is: how far to importune prospective members of its audience to attend matters of less than their first apparent preference but that may be in their civic or cultural interest to receive? If the audience drops below a certain point, the organ, if it must earn its own way, goes broke. If it is sustained by public funds and no one listens, it is wasting its operator's time and the public's money.

Along with advancing the interests of those whom it represents (sender and receiver), and its own, of course, an organ can, and sometimes does, go beyond the service to society performed by honest brokerage to serve the public interest as a sender. For example, the use of television in political campaigns presents three problems from the standpoint of public interest: how to put the candidates before the camera, put the voters before the screen, and induce the former to enlighten the latter. By choosing the manner of presentation (the format), an organ can provide public enlightenment in a way that does not primarily please or satisfy either candidate or audience. The nature of television, aggressive in comparison to the book on the shelf, makes it a fitting instrument to provide members of the public with some of the things that they ought to have in addition to those for which they ask.

The intercourse between citizen and politician may be clarified by having candidates answer questions propounded without notice by an informed and disinterested journalist. Such a series of examinations may be given over TV and reported in the papers. In pairs, opponents submit to the same questions. The interrogator, firm and, where necessary, relentless, takes the audience on a brief guided tour of each candidate's mind, character, history and views in terms that permit comparison.

If tempted to argue with a recalcitrant candidate and thus turn the program into a debate, if not a quarrel, he is not to yield. To do so not only fails to elicit the answers or to compare the competitors but also presents the interrogator as proponent rather than truthseeker. He must not forget that his role resembles that of a French judge, calling witnesses and questioning them impartially, not that of an advocate.

His fairness is both essential and difficult to ensure because a questioner can conceal a bias more easily than a candidate, who must take stands even if they are vague. He does not let charity stop his questions short of discovering that on a certain subject the candidate is an ass; but once the fact is brought out, he takes no cruel step beyond. (By comparison, an innkeeper breaks the law if he ejects an obnoxious patron by clubbing him when a push would suffice.) No question embodies a rebuke. The Puritans are reported to have opposed bear-baiting, "not because it gave pain to the bear, but because it gave pleasure to the spectators." Here the questions aim to reveal important matters, not to give either pleasure to the interrogator and audience or pain to the candidates.

To watch candidates give unrehearsed answers to fair questions that they tackle together enables a voter to compare them in candor, knowledge, views, control of temper and general nerve under conditions of moral stress. In straight debate, a person with more experience or aptitude may have an unfair advantage, and one or both debaters may so cloud the air with impassioned double talk that the audience is left in frustrated ignorance. With a set speech, in the absence of audience knowledge that the speaker prepared what he said, the only things tested for sure are his choice of speech-writers and his pear-shaped tones. In a panel show, with several candidates and journalists, evasive answers are safer because the next questioner is unlikely to repeat a question evaded. The lack of protecting rules tests some people's tempers by straining them but fails to test self-control properly because here that quality has doubtful worth. Free discussion exaggerates the importance of conversational aggressiveness and the trick of cutting someone off as he enters his windup or starts his punch line. Interruptions by him, rather than of him, may reveal bad manners; evasiveness may reveal ignorance, cowardice or clever disingenuousness; and failure to complete an adequate answer before the subject is changed may reveal inarticulateness. The confusion, however, does not let one display his merits and it permits him to hide his defects.

Observers of the judicial process have agreed with Wigmore that cross-examination constitutes the most powerful engine for eliciting the truth from a person. Cross-examination combined with television contributes to the electoral process. The presence in voters' minds of a rational basis for their choices reduces the appeal of slogans and softens the impact of incitements to suspicion, doubt and hate.

For a given organ, its emphasis in service as between senders, receivers, and the public varies according to its size and source of support. Where the programming decisions must suit a controlling public body that pays the bills and need be based on pleasing neither large masses of people barely enough to make them watch (and thus generate advertising revenue) nor a small group of people enough to induce them to commit themselves in advance to payment, the senders' choice is especially wide. Such an organ, able to disregard commercial considerations of revenue, though not of cost, is chiefly needed for benevolent parentalism: unresponsiveness to popular tastes coupled with a concern for some aspect of the public good.

Essentially, the profit requirement forces every business dependent on the favor of many people to practice cultural democracy. An organ that derives its revenues from its audience grants wide receivers' choice as it practices a form of democracy in serving minority tastes and interests. An organ that depends on advertising, which in turn depends on delivering an audience to the advertiser, is democratic in the sense of making a sensitive and obedient response to what appear to be mass tastes. In its undivided effort to meet many people's desires, management is incessantly preoccupied with how to please "them"—invisible, manifold, perplexing. Those broadcasters who thoughtlessly scheduled the first moonwalk for the hours before dawn had to be prepared to listen politely to angry telephoned rebukes.

On the other hand, an organ supported from a source independent of audience size or satisfaction has wide freedom of sender's choice. It can afford aristocratic (or representatively democratic, if one dislikes the term *aristocracy*) programming, in the sense that it can provide what it thinks the audience ought to have. One more reminder to look at results as well as labels is provided by how the most directly democratic practices toward their audience are conducted by organs that seek financial gain.

The pattern of large-scale sending organs probably will continue in screen communication as it has done in print: a few senders with a big audience and many senders, each with a small audience (e.g., a few big daily newspapers and national news magazines among many small special-interest periodicals). A cause of this pattern is many people's tendency, perhaps from habitual effort to simplify their lives, to confine most of their attention to a few things.

A stronger cause is that although advancing technology is reducing distribution costs of large-scale communication, production costs of material that can collect and hold a crowd continue to be high. To develop such material, one cannot depend on the cheap labor of electronic circuitry. Human skills that are demanded yet scarce remain expensive. Conversely, the high production costs of appealing material can only be paid for by attracting a big audience, whether payment comes from the audience, from advertisers who address a commercial solicitation to the audience, or from some other group that delivers a thought or sensation to educate or propagate beliefs.

Although unlimited competition may promote the greatest freedom for ideas and for the retail sale of some goods, the free exchange of ideas may be best assisted by limited competition among those organs that primarily depend on an audience. A pattern of a few big senders may represent a civic asset as well as an economic necessity. Imperfect competition among a few competitors, by reducing the intensity of the scramble, may enable higher standards of what is sent. Where the audience for all organs in a given market is fragmented beyond a given point, competition for survival drives certain organs to shift their balance so far toward what pleases and away from what has importance that they jettison standards, offering cheap thrills in ever louder tones to catch part of the audience, as when the starving fight for scraps.

Beyond a point in size, an organ gains power to constrict free trade in thought. It acquires so many ties to the surrounding society that in its news operations it may be inhibited from criticizing as it should. But at a lower limit in size, an organ has so few ties to the society that it lacks the self-sustaining independence that enables it to speak out.

The media have acquired such power that without being treated as such they have become transformed into an element of government, insofar as government means the power to influence events on a large scale. The label "Fourth Estate" (applied originally to the press alone, without its since-added components of show business and advertising), borne since 1828, has shifted from rhetorical courtesy to fact.

The media change people's behavior through their rational faculties by simply observing events. When the Greeks and Jews started to write history, they changed its course. An abstract example is publication of a social theory that explains an aspect of human activity, such as an economic process. Once most people come to know and understand the theory, then—especially if it is true—they tend to act according to it. A common consequence—so powerful is this process—is to change the conditions to the point that the theory ceases to fit, for example, Keynes's portrait of economic operations. The original creative thought is not part of the mass media's process, but the impact is.

As they inform, interpret and criticize, the media influence people not only by the thoughts presented but also by moral and intellectual authority and by feelings that they stir. The sight on the screen of Alabama police dogs and fire hoses inflicted on well-behaved people provoked public sentiment supporting passage of laws to keep states from denying some of their citizens the vote. The sight of Chicago street violence during the 1968 Democratic convention is thought to have turned some voters away from the party's presidential nominee, with conclusive results.

Provoking the audience is a process as old as the transmission of news. But a new phenomenon is the impact striking not only the viewers but the viewed. The process of covering events influences the behavior of those observed. This resembles the Heisenberg principle of quantum mechanics: measuring tiny particles of matter changes their behavior from their common practice, as flashlight beams may give a mistaken impression that cockroaches always are running for shelter. Where a person engaged in significant action finds himself in the presence of reporters, cameras and microphones, the process is direct and strong. At a demonstration in the street, news cameras may restrain the police from brutality yet encourage demonstrators to riot. Publishing another's confidential advice to an executive may inhibit later offers of advice. When a deposition is taken, the silent presence of a court reporter bent over his recording machine in a corner makes a deponent weigh his words.

The formal political process is legitimate and has control connections with the public but it is bogged down from lack of adequate communications. The media enjoy communication with the public but lack a control connection. The overall system suffers from insufficient living, feeling communication. The complementary changes— reduced satisfaction from the conventional means to exercise political liberty (voting, public meetings, etc.), decline in resonance of the political process, and rise to power of the nonresponsible media— have increased the need for the media to acknowledge their function as in part a coordinate branch of government, legitimate and responsible, an independent branch, not an arm of another branch, and intended to help the society govern the rest of government.

Such a change would be more of outlook than of function, and citizen attitudes would be the largest enabling cause. Those who operate the media would not find it difficult to alter their performance in the ways required because already they have shared with politicians so much experience, such as two-way communication and measuring the audience (balancing the significance of a small, intense, largely negative group against a large more positive and passive one). Churchill, Mussolini, John F. Kennedy, Jean Jacques Servan-Schreiber, and Willy Brandt are among the capable men who have made an easy transition from journalism to politics (publishing contributed Adam Clayton Powell and William F. Knowland). Many in each vocation have been engaged in competition, ranging from stiff to desperate, for support that is not numerous enough to sustain all the competitors because it is sought from the puddle that remains in the center of an almost dry water hole. A few have enjoyed sinecures. Each has the problem of ghosts, stand-ins, copies of copies and all the other elements of unreality created by modern technology and the graphic revolution. Each has problems of relating reality to entertainment and dealing with communication breakdown where the material becomes unreal because too contrived and therefore dull; and each must face the fact that entertainment alone may fail to satisfy because it is exclusive, and the problem of advertising which, to be effective, must be backed by a competent product.

Chapter | 6

CAMPAIGNS

The continuing process of change in campaign methods has speeded up in recent years. Campaign efforts get less mileage than they did, and less than they will when the rate of change declines, permitting their comparative effectiveness to be better known.

A party apparatus counts for less. The last machine has gone. What remains is only accusation in the mouths of ardent partisans who charge others with possessing one. A campaign staff is the most important instrument because, besides the actions of the candidate, campaigns are now conducted largely by means of professional specialists who fabricate speeches, leaflets, news releases and spots on tape. Money raising and advice on strategy are the only important functions that remain in amateurs' hands.

The party organization used to fulfill the two purposes of persuading people to prefer one party label over another, and then of leading people to the polls. In 1840, "fifteen acres of men and 6,000 females" were reported to have attended a rally for Harrison at Tippecanoe. Now the candidates or the media's agents do the persuasion through the media. People are induced to vote by many factors. A party organization is in most places a minor one, sharing influence with the leadership of other organized groups of which the voter is a member, such as labor unions, PTAs and single-issue groups, and with unorganized groups to which most voters belong.

Parties are still organized on a geographic basis, which no longer conforms to the operation of American society. Improved communication and transportation allow each person to select his companions from a wider circle around his home. Except for farmers (a small minority), some elderly people, and young children without civic responsibility, we no longer associate with each other primarily within our neighborhood.

The party animal has lost not only its strength but also the carrot and stick that induce it to work. Civil service has made campaign activity unnecessary to keep a job and unavailing to get one. For those who work for Uncle Sam, the Hatch Act has converted campaign work from insurance to a risk. Accurate audits and efficient law enforcement have stopped the payment of campaign workers from public funds.

As party activity has become less important the number of party workers has declined. Some old people enjoy the social aspects of taking part and treat the organization as a club. Especially in campaigns, college students take part for a while as an experiment or adventure. The largest and most effective new group is the women not otherwise employed whose family responsibilities allow them free time and who wish to do civic service. Among all ages, prosperity enables participation by more persons in whom idealism is a major motive.

In most places the party organization is a pressure group with more of a power to veto than to select. Although for a governor or partisan mayor to disregard his party organization is difficult, some members of the Senate have almost nothing to do with it, yet do not seem to suffer for their independence. Many organization men and women resent this attitude but realize they cannot replace such a person for renomination, and in a general election they grudgingly give him support.

Formerly, an organization had the sole selection of nominees and often was conclusive in deciding the election. Now people are given a genuine choice, although not always a good one. Many of the best men and women do not run. One can dispute some of the values of many voters. But the voters now tend to choose and elect candidates of their personal preference, independent of an organization's influence. Why politics in the last sixty years has attracted to Democratic tickets more candidates of a quality to win public preference than it has to Republican tickets, despite the higher average levels of education and some kinds of ability and intelligence among Republican voters, goes beyond the scope of this book.

Sometimes a person is elected without spending. However, his success is not owed to some clever trick of campaigning without using money, but rather to the fact that to win he did not need to run. It was enough to stand. A campaign is a means to win only where the net result of all other factors will put within a narrow range opponents' totals of prospective votes

The cost of a campaign has risen because so many more votes have been put at stake. In 1972 Nixon received as many votes from Louisiana as Andrew Jackson did from all the states either time he was elected, and George McGovern, losing, received more than did FDR in the biggest of his four wins. In 1956, the man elected governor of Ohio received more votes than Lincoln did from the nation in 1860. In losing a race for Congress, I received 10,000 more votes than John Quincy Adams did when he was elected President. But the common remark that campaigns have become far more expensive is a misleading truth. In relation to the national economy and the cost per vote, campaigns do not cost much more than they did twenty or one hundred years ago. The difference is that the work used to be done by an organization, and in the main the cost was borne by an indirect and unofficial public subsidy (the spoils system), supplemented by a few men, often senators. A campaign was conducted by a band of workers impelled by hopes and fears that jobs would be won, kept or lost. The candidate gave only his spare time. Today, however, the mass media, TV above all, have become the chief means by which he can influence the reason or passions of the electorate. In campaigns, the media and the related services necessary for their use must be paid for much of what they do.

This increased emphasis on cost does not mean that as a ticket for admission to public office the gifts of political leadership have been superseded by the ownership of riches—Pericles replaced by Croesus. Nor does it mean that campaigning skills have given way to the skills of making money—the replacement of Gladstone by Crassus. It does mean discussion of public ideas is narrowed, with a concentration on the proven, the popular and the previously successful.

The burden of a campaign's cost, which used to rest on the taxpayer and a few rich men, has shifted to the candidate himself who must pay from his own resources and what he can collect from others. He is either pressed or compelled to enter Faustian bargains with persons and groups to which he should wish not to be beholden. Like one in business for himself, a politician sometimes feels as though his life were a continual process of incurring obligations and repaying them, but the oppressive difference from business is that these obligations are located on the fringes of his work instead of at its core.

Few contribute much from friendship or public spirit. Small sums come from patriots, partisans or persons who enjoy being identified with a celebrity, like an alumnus who keeps an athlete. A one-sided majority of the dollar volume, given by a minority of contributors, comes from those who wish preferential treatment—or insurance against adverse treatment—by government in rates, rules, contracts, licenses or loans. These larger "gifts" impose an obligation to do those requested favors which, by definition, are against the public interest because, without any contribution, the contributors might expect to get what they deserve, so far as democratic government is just.

A limited allowance of income tax credit might reduce the proportion of large gifts by raising the volume of small ones. A partial public subsidy to certain candidates for certain offices may weaken big contributors' power to induce partiality but it creates complex problems of fairness. Legislation limiting campaign spending on those methods that are directed at the irrational faculties can cut the total campaign cost, relieving contributors and tax-payers of expense and candidates of pressure. These bought services are directed mainly at fears and appetites. A curb on slogans, scare ads, catchwords and name-familiarity ads (intended to implant the memory of a name without offensive associated meanings) would expose the voters to more clear light, fewer refracted images and less heat.

The most effective measure to reduce the thralldom of politicians to money raising, and to liberate citizens from representation by politicians in such bondage, is public disclosure of contributions, those who make them, and those whom they benefit. As an aspect of how justice depends on certainty, keeping records and making them public have done much to increase human liberty. In the Roman republic the recollections of a privileged oligarchy had preserved the law in a biased de-pository. According to Sir Henry Maine, the recording on tablets of the Twelve Tables raised the level of Romans' freedom not by the quality of laws or any symmetrical classification, "but in their publicity, and in the knowledge they furnished to everybody, as to what he was to do, and what not to do." In Western Europe the development of public records of private ownership made it easier for a comparatively poor man to keep his property without having to fight for it. Keeping a daily log of a ship's voyage has protected the rights of those whose interests (as sailors, shippers, owners or underwriters) are affected by the ship. To remove the lid from the underground roads along which private money passes to influence politicians' decision making enables the citizen to make better-informed, and thereby more rational, decisions. Compelling disclosure of the contact, and inferentially the impact, satisfies not some private interest (as when Menelaus intercepted his brother Agamemnon's letter to Clytemnestra) but a public need. The recipient can be measured by the financial company he keeps. By ending its invisibility, most of the harm done by this private money is prevented.

> Publicity is justly commended as a remedy for social and industrial diseases. Sunlight is said to be the best of disinfectants; electric light the most efficient policeman.
>
> BRANDEIS

The drop in prospects of material gain, caused by general knowledge of this information, dries up the flow of money from venal sources. At best, disclosure of contributions would shift their nature from implied contracts toward true gifts of the kind made by Justice Holmes when he named the United States the residuary beneficiary under his will.

Another important change in campaign methods has taken place in the operation of national conventions. They have become tame and polite. The public-address system makes shouting unnecessary, and, without a mike, the size of the crowd makes it futile. Conventions used to be stag. Now the presence of women improves the manners of the men. Air conditioning makes a convention so much easier on nerves and tempers that it might be impossible now to nominate a candidate under the former two-thirds rule because the delegates would not become so desperate to go home that most of them would be willing to agree. Television encourages the wish to show off but inhibits some vulgar deviations in behavior. In the convention hall, fist fights and drunkenness have almost disappeared. Delegates are circumspect for fear they may be seen back home. During invocations men even stop smoking cigars. A counter factor is the increased social and ethnic diversity—with consequent abrasiveness—among delegates.

The strongest cause of better manners at conventions is the higher quality of delegates. Civil service and the Hatch Act have withdrawn most of those with primarily venal motives from the group available or willing to go. Because so many more people now can afford to make the trip, delegates are elected from a larger, more competitive field.

On the other hand, in some places, selection as a delegate still rewards faithful labor in the party vineyards. This system results in delegates who neither represent the best of their party's sentiment in their communities nor respond to the community's wishes, although by trying to pick a winner they seek to meet the apparent national choice. Some political institutions are becoming overly responsive, but some conventions are whimsical and sluggish, neither exercising an independent will nor reflecting the home folks' taste.

Although not every delegate may listen only to his public spirit, delegates are now more free from boss control. During the Democratic conventions of 1932 and 1956 I watched Jim Farley and Carmine DeSapio, respectively manage the campaign of the current governor of New York. Conditions of the time allowed Farley to act as a general and required DeSapio to act as a salesman.

Conventions have become so big that the crowd is docile, because with unruly behavior the process could not work. It is easier to preside over a national convention than over a state or county convention. A delegate seeking recognition cannot even be heard unless the chairman tunes him in.

No one forgets that his family, friends and enemies may be watching through the eyes of the TV cameras, which are pointed down on the crowd like machine guns around the walls of a prison yard. Awareness of this inspection checks the spontaneity of the proceedings. It cuts the time taken up in bickering and debate and produces designs to contrive dramatic effect. The focus of the gathering is shifted from within to without. Television has increased the emphasis on entertainment at conventions; it is speeding the trends in politics to separate the producing functions of work and entertainment, to hire outsiders for the latter, and to increase the consumption of entertainment with political work.

Even a peaceful convention is exciting. This is inevitable where strangers from diverse backgrounds are thrown together, where a substantial proportion are energetic, intelligent, articulate and interested in ideas, and only a few have a mainly frivolous intent; where, despite their disagreement, their thinking is not too far apart to justify conversation and argument; and where they are stirred by animosities within their delegations, among people who know each other and resent the enforced company. An open convention has the tension of a sporting event. One's own propaganda is exciting even when only half-believed. For about a week, several thousand people churn together in a few downtown hotels. Once every four years this process, partly mechanical, partly chemical, temporarily makes a national party out of a loosely connected assortment of state and local groups.

The faults of the presidential nominating process lie more in the method of selecting delegates than in the national convention system itself, which is true representative government, providing the discussion and personal knowledge essential to sound judgment. (These are practiced and acquired, respectively, not on the convention floor but elsewhere before and during the convention.) It is a good device for selecting nominees for national office in a country as big as ours. Still, a national convention's atmosphere is given by the closing lines of "Dover Beach":

> And we are here as on a darkling plain
> Swept with confused alarms of struggle and flight,
> Where ignorant armies clash by night.

A minor device to give more understanding of issues and wider participation in making policy is the medium of state and county party conventions at which many of the delegates are offered an opportunity to take part in considering a platform. At these smaller conventions, run by anarchy or despotism, items of business wallow in confusion or click off according to a script. The main value of a platform is the education received by people who make it; but this chance rarely is afforded because so little time is allocated to it. Speeches are many and long. Prompted by slips of paper sent up to him, the chairman introduces worthies in the crowd, and each feels impelled to say some words of greeting. The keynote speaker often thunders on until he squeezes the platform against the closing time. Soon after debate gets underway on fish versus dams or highways versus schools, the chairman interrupts to say he must entertain a motion to adjourn because this hall has been rented by Johnny Cash for use since half an hour ago. To justify cutting short the platform debate, preliminary greetings and battle cries have to be more inspiring or illuminating than they usually are.

Forgetting that they themselves compose the jury, people sometimes regard their favorite candidate as their champion engaged in a trial by combat to vindicate their principles and interests. To describe a campaign as a "race" or "fight" is inaccurate because the efforts of a competitor seldom are decisive. If his opponent has played the better game, a tennis player almost never wins. But an election does not measure the opponents' comparative campaign performances. A candidate cannot even be sure that his campaigning will change the election result, while a lawyer knows at least that a diligent pursuit of proven methods of preparation and trial will raise the odds of success, even if the outcome in an evenly balanced case may hinge on blended images of half-forgotten experience in a judge's mind.

A candidate cannot experiment. He must act promptly on limited information, as though he were an officer in battle, taking his troops over a hill when he does not know what is on the other side.

Because no one knows what works in a campaign, money is spent beyond the point of diminishing returns. To meet similar efforts by the opposition, all advertising and propaganda devices are used— billboards, radio, TV, sound trucks, newspaper ads, letter writing or telephone committee programs, handbills, bus cards. No one dares to omit any approach. Every cartridge must be fired because among the multitude of blanks one may be a bullet.

Some urge an attitude of Olympian reserve, a few sonorous pronouncements of fundamental principle. Some claim a catalogue of documented facts is just the thing to woo the inscrutable voter. Others insist the only way is to put a hammerlock on the opponent and roll around in the sawdust. A state senate leader, who for many years never had lost an election, told me how he campaigns in his district door to door: "You tell your host or hostess who you are and declare in forthright tones, 'I'm here to talk with you about our state government; you may not agree with me but at least you will know where I stand.' Then you sit down in the living room, listen and agree!" When a fellow named Gillespie Craighead ran for Congress in Seattle, he asserted he was the only man in the race who could prove he was sane; then he would display his certificate of discharge from a mental hospital. In losing to a former U.S. senator, he received several thousand votes.

Many think a speech should be what Napoleon said a constitution should be: short and obscure. Citizens inflict harsh judgments of cowardice or opportunism on candidates for expressing their positions in equivocal terms which citizens themselves compel as a condition of their vote. In the period 1949–75, among those who spoke forthrightly on the issues, only three were even nominated for president, and all were buried by landslides: one lost to a man whose prepared addresses recited platitudes and whose unprepared speech was artlessly ambiguous; Senators Goldwater and McGovern were rejected in favor of men not noted for straight talk.

To avoid being misunderstood is often hard. Once during a race for Congress (already having signed an oath of loyalty to the nation as a condition of filing), I was asked by a heckler at a public meeting to admit or deny Communist Party membership. The crowd applauded my response that denounced the question and declared unwillingness to submit to the degradation of denying treason to my country. But the newspapers declared only that I had declined to answer.

A rare candidate has judgment that shows him better than most the true odds on the prospects of a pending cause. He often receives, but seldom deserves, low grades from citizens, idealistic about personality, who dismiss him from their gallery of acceptable leaders for making speeches that they think expose him to insufficient risk. To back measures that he favors but foresees will lose, even with his support, is not taking a risk, it is paying a price. If he has much at stake, the price takes heroic generosity to pay.

Because his mechanism for measuring prospective consequences is so accurately calibrated,
his willingness to act as he does is morally impressive:
the difference between crossing a field you think
may be mined and one you know is mined. In the fall
of 1813, when Tecumseh, the great Shawnee, discerned that the Indian cause east of the Mississippi
would be lost, he advised his followers to quit the
war and go home, losers but alive, yet because he
was unwilling to leave those warriors who stayed
and whom he had recruited, he made his farewells to
friends and to life, and the next day, after his British
allies had surrendered, he took up his war club and
charged the advancing Kentucky frontiersmen to
his death. To judge our candidates by the standards
of Tecumseh leaves us either with none or with a
purist whom the rest of us will not elect.

Because a candidate who cannot so accurately
calculate impending events does not know when he
is betting on losers, he need exert less moral effort
to speak out for all he thinks is right. Except where
a cause can justify a sacrificial public stand as moral
testimony, that politician whose penetrating and
unclouded realism concentrates his efforts where
they can do most useful good should be considered
not a craven opportunist but a constructive civic
instrument.

In assessing an election, a common mistake is
to assert that a certain event or a candidate's man-

nerism or stand caused him to win or lose. Often no one knows whether its effect was plus, minus or zero, whether the election result was because of this factor or despite it. Spectacular events, whether an attack, a dramatic proposal ("I shall go to Korea"), a sensational story about the candidate (like Grover Cleveland's bastard in 1884), or something in the news outside the campaign (when the Soviets detonated an H-bomb in 1956), are like a revolving door. They win some votes and lose others. A report that a candidate's brother committed suicide upon arrest for some disgraceful deed may cause some voters to doubt the candidate's own strength and health, while others may be drawn to him by sympathy and repelled by his opponent to whom they attribute the cruelty of the supporter who disclosed the fact. When I spoke out against the War in 1966, the public reaction was explosive; some people castigated me as yellow, while others applauded me as brave. In these cases, the effects remain unknown in both direction and amount, and even if correctly estimated, such a factor still could not be considered the sole cause of the result. It was merely one of many causes of which the vote margin is the algebraic sum. Where the margin was close, this factor could be called the cause only to the extent that the result would not have happened but for it, like the horseshoe nail that caused the kingdom's loss.

Each voter makes up his mind by the delicate resolution of several factors, some unconscious and all variable. No test has been devised for campaign methods or strategy, and little can be done to measure other factors. To know the effect of each thing he is doing and saying is a candidate's dearest wish. If he knew where pay dirt was he could concentrate there instead of digging all over the countryside. But he proceeds in ignorance. Not even his friends can be relied on to tell him all they know, which is less than the opinion polls reveal. They suffer from a time lag, and their precision belies their accuracy. A person may freely tell which fender styling he prefers. Often enough to be statistically useful, he will say for whom he plans to vote, and then do so. But often he will not or cannot tell why. The interviewed voter may not have been affected by any speech or slogan, yet may feel that unless he says he was, he will be thought an ignoramus. He may have been affected by a certain campaign act but when asked about it he may forget either the act or the effect or both. He may or may not still be affected by it on election day, and he may not vote. The effect of what one side does may be cancelled out in his final decision by what the other side does later. He may not be able to sift the campaign acts that repel him or attract him. Like most people, when he speaks to a stranger about some deep and subtle thought within himself, seldom is he articulate enough to say what he means or candid enough to mean what he says. He may try to tell the interrogator what he thinks the other would like to hear, or he may refuse to talk at all. A candidate does not know whether he is throwing balls or strikes.

By their impact just before an election, poll figures sometimes bring to pass their own predictions. As polls become more accurate about opinion, as distinguished from voting intention, where the margin of error is already small, not only do they directly affect the result, they also alter campaign methods. Candidates watch the reports and try to reflect them.

If response to public wishes expressed in the reports were the only action taken, candidates would be left even with each other. So candidates try to think up an appealing novelty, guess the errors in the polls, or forecast opinion change between the sampling and the election, and try to express it first. This resembles playing the stock market in trying to anticipate the trend or to outguess the experts, although the game is even more elusive because it rests on slippery elements of opinion, while in the market the starting point, at least, is measurement of economic fact. A market speculator first will guess the future effects of economic forces, then what other speculators think about these forces, then what may be the expectations of other speculators about each other. Keynes wrote that some imaginative minds carry this process to the fifth or sixth degree. By contrast, a candidate's duopolistic relationship with his opponent seems to call for simpler calculations, especially since he can predict the other's actions more accurately than he can discern an unknown voter's thoughts. Polls and other studies are starting to give him glimpses of current attitudes above or below the surface of many voters' minds. But they may avail him little because voters are becoming more like speculators in basing their opinions on the attitudes of others, who do the same. Instead of splashing around in this quicksilver he may resort to asserting his own ideas again.

Voters do not know as much as they need to know in order to make wise decisions in the matters that they are called on to decide. They have enough general knowledge of politicians and enough details of information about issues but not enough of the converse of either. A way to win a voter's favor may be to press his flesh, and a candidate may gain by knowing many people, but few people know any candidate well. Each voter has many offices to consider, and each candidate has many constituents to reach.

People seem to feel more concern about politics than they did earlier in this century. Although many are dismayed by the size and remoteness of government, and many are less agitated by feelings of public insecurity, they nevertheless have more time to give to politics and realize that government has become more important to their welfare. But the irrationality and confusion of the campaign process alienate politicians from the people. The main defects of this process are its expense to candidates, deception of voters by platitudes and slander, failure to join issues, and failure to reveal the nature and capacity of candidates.

✧ ✧ ✧

The time when a politician should be most responsive is during a campaign and the period of warming up to it. Unpopular stands are better made long before, and soon after, a campaign. A short period limits the chance that events will prove the soundness of an unpopular action, and a candidate's courage will receive little acclaim unless and until his decision has become accepted because generally regarded as having been right. If you are going to oppose the wishes of the people whom you represent you had better not go before them for endorsement until either they have had a chance to forget the apparent injury or circumstances have been allowed to show that you never injured them after all.

The tumult and passion of adversary proceedings make a campaign an unsatisfactory occasion on which to win acceptance of a new idea, although it will do to introduce one. Original proposals are hard to get accepted any time. And in campaigns the natural resistance to a new idea, rational disagreement based on its defects, and opposition hostility and ridicule unrelated to its worth, combine to place a burden of proof too heavy for an advocate to overcome. Idealists or those who favor affirmative thought are often disappointed with candidates who do not go beyond a few of the genuine issues of the day except to criticize persons or to argue issues that would dissolve if only both sides would drop them. In fact, a candidate who proposes something new is often irresponsible or visionary. If he proposes an original, creative plan, no matter how sound, he is likely a dreamer to think he will get anywhere with it in the campaign. If he makes out that he has invented some inexpensive marvel that will bring joy to all, he is either a fool or a fake.

Because a campaign makes impossible a dip beneath the surface, any complex explanation is more effective between campaigns. To paraphrase Mark Antony when he knocked on Cleopatra's door, a candidate says, "I didn't come to teach." In a campaign, people are not interested in theory. The lessons are more often moral than intellectual. People want to know *what* a candidate proposes to do about pending, specific problems (and what the candidate himself is like). In quiet times, one can descend to fundamentals and tell *why*. People then will listen longer to a reasoned explanation and apply a smaller discount to the speaker's words as colored in a way to serve himself. But despite the fact that teaching is less efficient during a campaign than at other times, the value of education and the audience's large size justify making education a campaign's main function, provided this emphasis will not cause defeat—that is, provided one is either way behind or way ahead.

On occasions when there is no real contest except in measure of disagreement, if a candidate is an odds-on choice to win, he can transmit his ideas effectively. Little opposition interrupts him; he receives respectful attention from those who know he is going to be an officeholder and thus important, and from those who admire winners; he can raise funds enough to satisfy quite avaricious dreams. But if he is expected to be a sure loser he can reach voters only with his own resources, for others will give him little. Even if he is thought to be both noble and eloquent, those of the idealists who have money to give prefer to help a candidate of equal merit who has a chance to win. Lovers of lost causes feel that they have done their part if they deplore his plight.

Among those who run for office, it is widely thought that negligible good can be done one's fellows unless one wins. What General MacArthur said, "There is no substitute for victory," is only half-true. Some candidates aim at both halves. So far as he is heard, seen and understood, a candidate is a moral and intellectual teacher for better or worse. Like most means, a campaign is also in itself an end. It gives a chance to demonstrate virtue, to declare, defend and illuminate the truth, and to do the statesman's duty to guide, to elevate and to instruct.

Chapter 7

CANDIDATES

When a person runs for office he anticipates two discoveries with nervous excitement. He begins to find out who are his friends, many of whom turn out to be people he did not know; and on election night he learns how much he has appealed to the enigmatic voter.

The decision when to run for office, or when to run for a higher office than one has, is taken partly in the manner of a surf rider, who bides his time until the right wave looms, then coasts upon it to the beach. A race for office and a ride on the surf differ in two ways. In a campaign, a propitious wave is only one of several elements of success. And unlike a swimmer on the reef at Waikiki, poised to mount his board, one who plans to run at an undetermined time cannot be sure that a reasonable wait will offer him a ride that he can recognize before it has passed. As we sat in a boxcar doorway, westbound through Montana one spring night, a fellow traveler told me how he could have wed a girl worth half a million but delayed too long and had to marry her poor aunt instead. Sometimes a man will plunge because his nerve or patience fails for fear his place upon the slowly turning wheel may not come around to him in time. Others, driven by appetite or deluded by conceit, neglect the factor of a seasonable moment.

A politician jumps across the party organization through the media to reach the voters, for whom the sensation of his personality has become almost decisive. In the past a man had to impress the leaders who would cause his election. His assets might be skill in maneuver and intrigue, judgment, vision, or administrative competence, and various moral qualities. Those leaders, who knew him and appreciated his talents, would not much mind if he was distant or peculiar. Now a candidate's appearance has to please, reassure and satisfy a host of strangers from far off.

Aside from party, class, race and other group motives, most votes are cast, not on some specific issue connected with a candidate, but rather by selection from a gallery of candidates in the voter's mind. The mental pictures represent every school of art except the photographic. In the booth a voter sees in his thoughts the pairs of candidates for each office across the machine as though they were the animals passing two by two. A candidate should aim to use a set of simple strokes to create a favorable portrait of himself set against the surrounding shadows of the persons and issues with which he may be identified: an image in the voters' eyes that combines identity with the voter, through sympathy and common experience, and a superiority that does not stoop but beckons grandly from above.

For some offices a certain type of person tends to be expected and preferred. A rough-and-ready outdoor sort may be preferred for sheriff but go nowhere in a race for city council. A bloodless

Yankee may lose when he tries for mayor, yet get elected county clerk.

In some places a certain past experience may be a bar to election or a condition to success. Depending on constituents' likes, a candidate's having been an Oxford scholar may be a help or something to be hidden. After independence, a senior diplomat from India remarked with scorn for the rabble that recently had entered his country's parliament, "Why, some of them haven't even been to jail."

Enough voters used to give enough weight to a war record to induce some politicians to exaggerate or even, as in the case of Senator Joseph McCarthy, fabricate, hardships and brave deeds in their country's uniform. Tradition, running from the long period when an aristocracy stood at the forefront of the battles, connects public leadership with war service, recognized by everyone as a benefit to all and seen as proof that one was loyal to the state. Some people think of public office as a reward for war service, like a veteran's bonus. By custom in the Roman republic a consular candidate would expose his wound scars to the citizens. When he harangued his discontented Macedonian veterans on the Tigris, Alexander reminded them: "There is no part of my body but my back which has not a scar." Seen as reassuring evidence of simplicity and candor as opposed to bookishness and cunning, war service makes it easier for a candidate to be depicted as "bluff" rather than "glib." When a politician addresses his constituents, a war record may let him affect the manner of Othello to the Venetian lords. Unlike some other forms of public service, it does not offend as many people as it pleases. Yet the new process of war and the sour taste from the Vietnam war have made war service a lesser factor in political choice, to be replaced by other considerations, perhaps a candidate's scholastic record or behavior in some "moral equivalent of war" that may be developed. A convenient marker for this turning point is the career of Marshal Zhukov.

In disgust for politicians, and forgetting that democracy must have them, some angry citizens long to liquidate the class or to restrict its members' tenure, leaving the field to greenhorns. Faced by this hostility toward those who have eaten of the fruit, a candidate may hesitate to display knowledge of the functions that he is proposing to perform. In contrast to how members of other callings seek patronage, a politician sooner may conceal than advertise his professional skills and experience, professing himself an untainted novice to propitiate those in whose eyes a candidate's lack of exposure to politics confers on him an immaculate conception of his role that more than offsets his ignorance of what it's all about.

Woodrow Wilson pointed out that the public leader of men, that is, one who induces prompt action by large numbers of persons, has a comprehension of mass thoughts, responses and aspirations, while a leader of thought—who may induce action but indirectly and after a delay—may have a deeper knowledge of the individual.

Advances in knowledge of psychology have extended the capacity to manipulate groups, formerly confined to a few leaders possessing singular insight. Their effectiveness in this respect is further declining, absolutely as well as relatively, by reason of the drop in their station's symbolic significance which causes others to heed them. Power to manipulate is coming to depend less on personal insight (combined with the social status for its exercise) and more on skills that give access to the media and skills of predicting changes in taste.

With the mass media, politicians have less need to grasp the interaction of persons on each other in a crowd. About one-and-three-quarters centuries—from Danton to Nasser, during the period after people collected in large cities and before large-scale broadcasting—was the day of the mob. People affected each other by personal propinquity, and the mass affected events. It still does, of course, but without its members' personal and simultaneous effects on each other. The crowd does not gather in the plaza to cheer and throw hats in the air when you come out on the balcony. As much as ever a politician needs to know the factors in common among members of the multitude, the current, commonly held thoughts. And he needs to understand the interaction between each citizen and himself and between each citizen and the forces that influence public opinion. Although changed, the skills a politician requires continue to differ from those possessed by leaders of thought.

When he considers where he is to make his home, one who aspires to a political career must consider the location's effects on his prospects. The strength of the competition varies. The shifting class system is eroding the American tradition of a politician's identification with the community that elects him. The top talent has become concentrated in urban and academic centers of thought, renown and wealth, while Congressmen are still elected according to population on an even geographic spread. Before the turn of the century, in *The American Commonwealth*, Bryce observed this condition, which ever since has grown less useful and more acute.

The dissolution of roots in the community of one's birth has refined and accelerated the sifting process. While the magnetic force of urban centers has drawn able men on a small scale for centuries, only since they could support themselves there have talented women been free to go; now to the gifted of both sexes the big cities are like the sea to the lemmings or the Gadarene swine. In his *Memoirs*, U. S. Grant recalled that his boyhood village of one thousand in Ohio had "furnished the Union Army four general officers and one colonel, West Point graduates, and nine generals and field officers of Volunteers." Furthermore, seven of them had been "residents of Georgetown when the war broke out, and all of them who were alive at the close, returned there." It is hard to conceive of any small town today producing several outstanding persons, and even harder to conceive of them living there after they had made their mark.

Because the talented have migrated to certain neighborhoods of the metropolitan centers in a higher proportion than the untalented, the merit of the average officeholder in relation to the importance of the office is lower in the U.S. House of Representatives than in any other public employment, possibly excepting some police forces. By custom, though not by law, a well-established residence in the district still is a condition of election to the House, even though the conflicts of regional interest have relaxed, and each cluster of communities no longer preserves in isolation a distinctive nature calling for loyalty and understanding which can come only from a deep attachment. The rise in the rate at which persons shift their homes has contracted the period required to establish enough local identity to qualify for Congress. However, the wait still is substantial in all districts and longest in those long-settled, half-deserted areas where the supply of talent is most short.

Every state has urban centers which, in a lesser degree, stand to the rest of the state as Paris has stood to the rest of France. The Senate does not have to take a crop from many barren zones. But many congressional districts have no large town and no college that deserves the name. Young men and women of worth depart when done with school, returning only for outdoor recreation or visits of sentimental condescension. Left behind are those short on education and imagination, indifferent to the world and how it works. One of them, perhaps the best, goes to Congress to shake the earth. In most of these districts voters receive little chance to choose excellence. The country stands to gain if more young persons equipped for national problems take the gamble of settling in the provinces. If they do not, either the customary residential requirement will be removed, as in England, or the authority of the House will not rise above the point to which it has dropped.

This irregular distribution of talent combined with the loss of geographic identity of interest suggests a need for more representation according to occupation, ancestry, economic interest, etc. Already, as people are coming to associate more according to compatibility and shared interests than to place of residence, so administrative units of government are shifting toward jurisdictions defined by function.

On the other hand, to represent residents of a geographical district keeps a person responsible to a substantial cross-section of society. For part of the process of reconciling differences to take place in his thinking may be more efficient than for all to be loaded on the dealings between him and his colleagues, where each represented a homogeneous group with a sharply separate interest or outlook. Almost all testing of ideas must rest on debate, but some of the negotiating and compromising can be done in one's head.

In state legislatures, for other reasons, the situation sometimes is reversed. Leading men and women in rural areas go to the legislature, while many of the most able people drawn to the big cities disdain such offices. Those whose employment follows the farm work cycle are free to serve in wintertime sessions, and so a larger proportion of the capable people are available for such service. People in thinly scattered areas often are more discriminating in their choice of candidates for the legislature because they know them. By contrast, where population is dense, few of one's acquaintances may live within one's legislative district, and candidates for the legislature are overlooked at the foot of the ballot. Despite these variant factors, the legislatures themselves, like the House, are harmed by geographic disparity in apportionment between offices and talent.

General elections for important offices tend to be close. Often the margin of win does not exceed the opinion polls' margin of error, so that there is yet no certain way to foretell the result. Until the moment of truth, a candidate does not know whether he is the bullfighter or the bull.

Politics' uncertainty dismays a person used to systematic plans. The loss of spontaneity through thinking of the next thing is a defect of modern life.

Everyone has to consider the morrow. No one can do as the lilies of the field. Foresight is compulsory because one falls by the wayside if he fails to use it as everyone else does. Yet in a campaign to plan is difficult. One is denied both the carefree joy of spontaneity and the security of foresight. Politics is an art and it is played by ear, though politicians often wish that they could use with profit more scientific method in the conduct of their work.

As generals are said to prepare for the last war, so election campaigns are planned with excessive attention to undigested history lessons. The thinking of a candidate's advisers resembles that of scholastic philosophers: long on speculation and short on verified facts. Members of a strategy committee tend to be boosters rather than detached critics, a command group instead of a staff. Sometimes a candidate feels like a steer being groomed for a 4-H Club contest. His council is more likely to give him encouragement than guidance. For example, once in the Bronx Coliseum a powerful Brooklyn black was hitting me hard; I clutched him and looked over his shoulder at a spectator who pounded on the ring apron as he shouted, "Pretend he's a Harvard man!"

For candidates, campaigns are like a war. With dirt and expense come comradeship, sacrifice, warmth of loyalty given and received, and moments of fulfillment and fear. Absence from home strains domestic ties, and clan ties are strained by taking sides. When it is over, this alien experience drops quickly out of mind, despite the remaining scars and debt. The heat of battle intensifies a candidate's combative spirit. Exhaustion weakens his power to decide. The necessity to act in haste under conflicting pressures and on confusing information makes his decisions less the result of reflection or belief than of character, habit and chance. Unless his friends restrain him he may throw away both his purse and his good name. His friends' advice colors his acts more than when he is not on such a headlong chase. The counselors of even the most obstinate candidate do much to set a campaign's tone. The choice of levelheaded, honorable advisers improves his chances to finish the race without regret or shame.

The hardest campaign is the first. After that the path is familiar, and one has momentum of supporters, friends and a known name. For candidates before a campaign starts an eager, apprehensive wait is full of hurry and busy strategic moves offstage, like sailboats tacking and turning behind the starting line before the gun. As a poker hand is played, the response and strength of possible opponents and the presence of support are tested by experimental bluffs. Next to the wait from the closing of the polls until the returns begin, the highest suspense in a campaign comes when a candidate declares himself. He climbs to the battlements and blows his trumpet, then peers out to see how many men at arms come running to rally around his flag.

He has to be alert to tricks that can have serious consequences even though in form they resemble practical jokes. When Ed Munro, a high-principled politician, ran for county commissioner, an Indian by the same surname filed against him in the primary. This tactic might have split Ed's vote enough to give the nomination to his chief opponent (who one supposes had induced this filing). Before the names had been put on the voting machines, the second Munro withdrew when told that such a deception was a felony, and that if he stayed in the race he would be the only candidate guaranteed to spend some time in the county courthouse. Ed's friends had found this man after a desperate hunt. He was hard to find because he had been sleeping in a tree.

At the start a candidate's efforts are concentrated within the groups (including his party) with which he is most identified. As the scale and formality of the campaign increase, the target shifts to the general public. Like opening in New Haven before New York, on these early occasions, before his audience is critical and large, a candidate's material is tested, giving a chance to sharpen gags, expand lines and cut what falls dead.

At repeated meetings, the candidate grinds out his stock recital to a crowd whose members know him well. Many could prompt him if he falters. Attendance gains him little except to invigorate his followers' working spirit and to avoid provoking their hostility by the appearance of a snub. Senator Jackson, who spent more than half his life in Congress, adopted the sensible practice of saying goodbye to his friends at the beginning of a campaign, after telling them that he loved them but that he would be busy for a while in their common cause. Some candidates take the easy but ineffectual course of campaigning mainly within groups closely associated with them. Like salesmen who cultivate their friends instead of making calls on strangers, these candidates either fool themselves or yield to the temptation to stay where the going is smooth.

Meetings held to enable the community to hear the candidates often waste the time of both audience and speaker. Each candidate is stalled for part of an evening waiting his turn to speak to a few people. Sometimes he finds that most of those present are other candidates. He faces an audience numbed by the beating of incessant waves of oratory. A succession of brief individual interviews is more effective in enabling citizens to know something of his opinions and catch the flavor of his personality. Despite the wasted time, public meetings are justified in the case of candidates for some of the smaller offices because these meetings furnish almost the only means for voters to observe them.

On cold nights a man of lukewarm faith was wont to point to a framed prayer on the wall and say, "Lord, them's my sentiments," as he jumped under the covers. By this means a candidate can declare his platform when allowed only a few minutes to speak.

He states his accord with what another politician stands for. He names the one whose platform is more like his own than that of any other among those whose platforms the audience already knows. An even more common practice is for the candidate to try to identify himself with a victorious figure who sometimes blesses his party mates who are reaching for his coattails from lower on the ladder.

In the campaign, personal contact inspires those who meet a candidate to recommend him to others. To use this multiplier principle, the rings spreading from where a stone fell in a pool, timing is of the essence. Contacts made in the days just before election have slight worth because time does not permit the multiplier to operate, and without the multiplier's effect the number of persons a candidate can meet even in a whole campaign is too small to matter in a large constituency. Early in a campaign, except for an incumbent who is news in himself, public interest has not developed enough intensity to make the multiplier go. The candidate is less a subject of interest and may be less well known. People have less desire to talk to others about having met him. In most cases, therefore, shaking hands with a multitude is most effective during the month before the week before election day.

A wide acquaintanceship acquired before the campaign is a help. "My sister-in-law is a friend of Blank who's running for the legislature. She knew him even before he went into politics"— magic words.

Probably the most effective campaign acts

are those performed between campaigns. The volleys and thunders of a campaign raise a voter's resistance and obscure his sight. A chief justice of the Alabama Supreme Court kept on his office wall pictures of George Washington and John Marshall and an autographed photograph and letter from Jim Farley, congratulating him on his election. It was the only congratulation he had received after the general election, an uneventful day in those parts, as all the other attention had come when he was nominated.

The functions of some offices fail to inspire ardor, either sacrificial or pugnacious. One who runs for governor or mayor is surrounded by many whose assistance is given on condition of an implied reward. But a candidate for the U.S. House has so little patronage in prospect that few self-seekers (except some contributors) repel him by their presence or embarrass him by their efforts. Many people uninterested in favors from him warm and uplift him by faithful work on his behalf.

Several satisfactions invite volunteer campaign work. Some fulfill a wish expressed through a conviction, that is, an attempt to assert or defend a principle or advance or protect an interest. Other satisfactions are directly emotional: sharing an adventure and a common effort and the purgative from close observance of dramatic conflict.

A further motive applies to people below

voting age. They do unexciting work such as handing out folders but they get to hang around the
headquarters and consort with the candidate and
some of his/her lieutenants. Their own views on policy
may be heard and sometimes even listened to. They learn
plans before their execution and feel themselves
participants in matters more important than would
be allowed them in the ordinary course of life. They
are more flattered than older people to be allowed
to fraternize with these men and women. They
finish armed with anecdotes to entertain their peers.

A campaign is a churning circus that bewil-
ders actors and spectators alike. Blocks of votes are
cast against (or for) a candidate for contradictory
reasons, sometimes both wrong. Candidates who
succeed in their effort to please everyone may get
some votes because they are thought to be for the
common man and others for being against him. The
same things may be thought of their more clumsy
opponents with the opposite results. In one campaign
I was attacked as both a Bourbon and a Red. As a
member of the commission that had drafted the
proposed county charter, which was on the ballot, I
supported its adoption in unison with the solid,
"good government" elements of the business community. I was called a reactionary, both for the
stand itself and by reason of the syllogism, common
in campaigns, that since things equal to the same
thing are equal to each other, persons who take the

same side must be alike, making an identity out of what may have been merely a shared antipathy. In a conversation overheard on the bus a man told another he was going to vote against the charter because Bullitt helped write it, "so probably it's a leftwing document."

The ferocity of a rough campaign generates rancor in a candidate's heart and inspires gratitude to those who bear arms in his cause. The rationality of a campaign tends to vary inversely with its length. Candidates may have much in common, but it is on the basis of the differences that the voters make their choice. The sides start close together. They are driven to magnify existing differences and to invent new ones. As they draw farther apart verbally they provoke each other to greater excess. The separation grows by geometric progression until each side approaches nonsense land.

In contrast to an average citizen, a candidate is too busy with detail to be aware of an election's historic import. He is too elated by enthusiastic treatment or too concerned with what to say to a hostile or indifferent audience to think of community or national destiny. In a speech he may say "the world (nation, state) is watching what we do here," without realizing that this may be the truth.

A candidate may see that he is going to lose, if he does not delude himself and the margin is wide enough to be discerned. His helpers can drop out and cut their losses, but, like a player far behind near the end of a game, he is obliged by an unwritten rule of sport to keep giving the old college try.

He must go out to meet people, yet try to reserve time to rest, relax and think, so that his performance before the mass media can be lively and fresh. Long campaigns make this impossible.

Like a prisoner, the candidate marks off the calendar squares until the day when he is to be executed or paroled. On election day he feels like the man who had to open one of two blank doors; behind one was a maiden, behind the other a tiger. To the candidate's friends, however, the contrast in alternatives may not be sharp. Often they are uncertain what fate to wish for him, whether to win or to be spared the pains and, to them, degradation of public life. Thinking of him as though his body were to be tested for service by the Army or as though his mind were to be examined at a sanity hearing, the friends are in doubt whether to support his hopes, his vows, his rights or his welfare.

A politician is almost by definition one who enjoys people. But near the close of a campaign he has been surfeited by them. He resents his enemies. He is exasperated by his friends' proprietary demands, irritated by the importunities of his acquaintances, and weary of his own persistent approaches to strangers. He has had enough of the human race. He does not become a misanthrope but longs to be a forest fire lookout. He would rather be rude than president. But after the election his enjoyment of people soon revives when he is rested and free from such compulsion to persuade, impress or please. Although spent, some defeated candidates begin to think like a losing team's fan—"Wait till next year."

For certain happy warriors, many of them celebrated, campaigns are not nights in a cement mixer but trips to the country. Like Antaeus when he touched the earth, these buoyant spirits, by contact with their fellow men, are strengthened and refreshed. On election eve they turn in with dark-encircled sparkling eyes.

A winner may have second thoughts. He is surrounded by well-wishers, many of whom already seek favors. He may not feel satisfied or elated but he is sure to feel relief. During the campaign he asserted his capacity to solve the problems facing the office he has won and, whether or not he volunteered any answers, he let on that he had them. Now he sees that some of these problems are insoluble, and others would baffle Aristotle. Yet the presumption that it took for him to run is enough to make him feel adequate to handle his job on the level expected of him. For a while no personal problem is likely to dismay him.

A loser in a race for high office is on the whole better off than one beaten for a lesser one. He may feel more disappointment at having missed a bigger prize. Whatever he turns to may seem petty and unfulfilling. But his prominence and known abilities almost assure him an opportunity to make a good living. He is cushioned by the presence of friends and comforted by sympathetic letters from supporters who remind him they are for him still.

One beaten for lesser office is more likely to have a young family which his defeat gives him time to enjoy and serve. He may find work that challenges and satisfies as much as what he lost or did not get. But having gone without pay, borrowed to the limit, and spent beyond his means, he may finish deep in debt, with no prospect of post-election contributions to offset any of it. Having quit or jeopardized his job, he has little or no present income and cannot be choosy about what he undertakes. He is not asked to head a college, invited to become an officer or partner of a substantial firm, or appointed to a presidential commission. His gloom is deepened by the thought that his friends have deserted him. He forgets that those who worked for him for friendship's sake, who have gone back to their private concerns, would have disappeared as fast if he had won. The prospect of snug domestic warmth offers him the cheer that Radames may have felt on finding Aida waiting for him in his tomb. No one calls him except the ad agency's bookkeeper who reminds him of his balance due. Nothing sustains him to counteract the memory of opposition slurs. By the standards of success the opposition has been proved right.

More often than a failure in private life a losing candidate can console himself by cursing fate. An election does not prove that the loser's grasp fell far short of his reach. But when one has been rejected by the voters and also sees no recognition elsewhere, unless he is an egotist or more indifferent to worldly success than most office seekers, he feels himself a flop. However, as a winner's elation soon is cooled by the problems put before him, so a loser's depression is dispelled as he reflects that although he pressed by his creditors and finds himself sentenced to involuntary solitude, the man who beat him is called by his constituents in the middle of the night; his change of weather from storm to calm lets him relax; and sometimes he plans to run again.

Chapter | 8

SOME PERSONAL EXPERIENCE

Each election year the ways by which candidate and voter best can come in touch sustain a minor change. A campaigner experiments or suffers from a time lag. As two means to approach the voters in person while running for Congress in 1954, I attended "coffee hours" and accosted people one by one in public places. I met about 9,300 (count kept by numbered bundles of folders) in five weeks, or about one in sixty-five of the district's population. The following observations were set down at the end of that campaign. They are consistent with my experience in half a dozen others before and after it, in two of which I ran and the rest of which I campaigned for other candidates.

Most of the time it is delightful to sit in a big chair and stuff yourself with cookies while polite guests treat you as a universal expert. In the homes of supporters who had invited their friends and neighbors I submitted to questions but gave no set speech. Because free interrogation at close quarters is such an effective device to probe the nature of a candidate, these meetings assist guests as citizens. They are uneasy though stimulating periods for the candidate; in the course of an hour some cherished prejudices are likely to collide. The voter may go away shaking his head at the thought of this menace to the Republic whom he has just met, while he still tolerates the others in the race. One does not use these meetings solely as an exercise in civics. In turnover they do not approach waiting in front of a mill through the half hour before the eight o'clock whistle. But each contact is more intensive where candidate and voter meet in a home, introduced by a mutual acquaintance, and where, instead of one greeting the other, who passes on, they actually converse. From this transient intercourse under these favorable conditions, if you are or later become a big shot, the voter may refer to you thereafter as a friend of his.

For personal contacts that are more superficial but faster, you stand each day in supermarket parking lots and outside factory gates, or walk up and down the sidewalks by suburban shopping malls and force yourself upon your fellow citizens hour by hour. I went up to each person and said, "My name is Stimson Bullitt. I'm a candidate for Congress and I'm glad to meet you." (When a man was approached, I held out my hand at his belt buckle and waited to see if he would raise his hand to let me take it.) Then I gave him or her a folder. If there was enough time, depending on the rate and volume of foot traffic, I asked his name. If a difficult name, I asked him to spell it or tried myself to do so and asked him if my effort was correct. Each person had a wall of indifference or suspicion to be assailed. At worse, one first is thought to be a panhandler or pickpocket; at best, a salesman. Perhaps a politician comes somewhere in between.

One makes the strongest impact in front of

an industrial plant at dawn. The people one meets are impressed to find anyone out there to greet them so early, especially a member of a group they consider lazy and aloof. As a common experience, the encounter becomes a subject of conversation during the day with others in the plant who were not met.

Suburban shopping areas are better than downtown. The tempo is not as fast, and there are few offensive strangers to make the others shy. People are less hurried and less averse to being accosted. An easy place to work is a commuters' train or ferry. The captive audience takes its ease in security and comfort.

The most barren soil is the waterfront. Many there are tourists, some are bums, and the rest recoil at your approach. A race track is another waste of time. A low proportion of the crowd votes regularly for any office except the presidency. And like people on other intense group occasions, the spectators resent one who interrupts their close attention. Taverns are unprofitable. The bartender is the only person worth meeting. Sober customers think you are a drunk coming over to molest them. Drunks grab you and hold on. They orate. Some used to entertain themselves with heavy jokes about my name and guns. If you approach anyone as you come out of a bar, he flees.

The best situation for meeting people at random is a small group engaged in idle conversation. This may be on the sidewalk or in a restaurant booth or barbershop. The people are less afraid to be accosted by a stranger because they feel protected by each other. Your intrusion does not offend by interrupting a preoccupation. With friendly banter you can often generate a jolly mood, leaving you the subject of their conversation after you have gone.

Handshakes are various: warm, cold, hearty, firm, flabby, moist. I discovered that my hand did not get tired or sore, although my hands are small and not strong. It was a surprise not to be squashed sometimes by a bully. I was embarrassed to make a few jump with pain, presumably from sore hands.

The range of response was wide: hostile, indifferent, suspicious, friendly, enthusiastic, encouraging. (Since the Depression years, the feelings among voters were strongest in 1952, and 1946 was next.) Some were flattered to shake the hand of such an eminent person; others politely stated that they differed with me in politics. Sometimes a person would show several reactions, shifting from one to another in a few moments of discourse. Some turned away, showing ill will because they recognized me as a person about whom they had read bad things in the papers. Some refused to touch me, then, when told I was a Democrat, reversed their attitude and shook hands with warmth. Everyone who asked, "Are you a Democrat or a Republican?" appeared to be a Democrat. It seemed that the Republicans who cared either knew or preferred to learn by looking at the folder.

A tiny few admitted they had voted Republican in 1952 and then had changed their minds. Probably some among the substantial number who asserted that they always had voted Democratic did not tell the truth. Some declared support for the Republican incumbent. Not one of the 9,300 said that he or she was for either of my Democratic opponents. One accepted my handshake, folder, and greeting in a neutral, noncommittal manner, then drove away in a truck with an opponent's sticker on its bumper. I smiled and pointed to it as he drove by, and he waved and smiled back.

Many would not look me in the face. Some would say they were too busy to stop. Some would ask what I stood for, as though they expected a speech, and perhaps expressing what they thought a good citizen should say when he met a politician. A negligible few would ask where I stood on a specific issue. Another few themselves would advocate a measure. Some would refuse to give their names. Others were unfriendly and rude but still willing to tell their names. Some would say, "I voted for you before and you may have my vote this time, too." In the late stages some would say, "It may please you to know that I've already made up my mind to vote for you." While others would say just before turning away, "I've got my candidate picked out, and he isn't you."

Some thought it silly for me to ask to meet them but took a manner of tolerant amusement and willingness to go along with the game. A few thought I was the incumbent. Others, mainly in the suburbs, thought I was running for the legislature rather than for Congress. Quite a number belonged to that large class who fail to realize that politicians, though sometimes made of flawed paste, are neither useless nor worthless. Some would ask, often in a mocking tone, "What are you going to do for us (me)?" A Navy yard worker on a ferry sneered that if I were elected I never would be back again to see him. At a horse meat market in a Bremerton suburb, a customer said he was a welder by trade and fancied one day maybe he would be a candidate and thereby get some easy work. Out of every three hundred people, about forty would be friendly and one hostile. But the effect of the one to depress or upset would equal the lift from the forty.

A substantial number of older people remembered my father, who lived in Seattle for ten years before his death in 1932. If there was any comment it was praise, often with tender and touching recollections of his character, courtesy and charm. As always, such responses moved me with pride at being his son and discouragement at my inability to capture men's devotion as he had done.

Only a small minority commented on my stands on the issues, from information received either from radio or TV talks or indirectly from others by word of mouth. In the late stages many comments were made on my name-familiarity advertising. The TV spots (a clever cartoon) were by far the most often remarked upon, followed by mention of the ads in other media.

Among those recognizable as a class, the most courteous were the persons behind the counter. They treat you as one more customer. The most universally indifferent as a group were the scavengers, the poorest of the poor. Asians, with a few educated and Americanized exceptions, ran a close second. Among those whom I took to be Jews, not one was indifferent. Blacks sometimes showed indifference, reserved hostility, coldness and suspicion, but none was deliberately rude. All accepted my hand.

My impression was that some of the hostile or apathetic reactions were not personal to me or to Democrats in general but rather to politicians as such. To these persons politics appeared to represent frustration and futility. They seemed to feel that nothing good can come of politics, that much of their troubles and perplexity is caused by acts and omissions of government, and that they would rather not be reminded of this painful and mysterious fact about which they feel they can do nothing.

In addition to these baffled ones who were unwilling to assume responsibility, many others were annoyed to be bothered about politics. It was not the loss of time they grudged but rather the drastic shift in state of mind. In this aversion to the intrusion of politics they seemed like combat soldiers who find inadequate their assumption when they enlisted that only others will be killed, and who resign themselves to die, preferring the feeling of certainty of a short life to the anxious hope of a long one; or like some shipwrecked persons on a raft who are said to jump overboard when they no longer can endure the doubt about their rescue. This insecure contentment of the soldier in the field is disturbed by talk of long-range plans for civil life, recalling things that he has banished from the surface of his mind, things he wants and fears will be denied him. It revives the problem which he had settled by renouncing one alternative. In this temper, many citizens resemble these men who are too close to death to ignore it as other young folk do.

In a restaurant on Queen Anne Hill, a man seated in a booth talked with me but failed to take my offered hand. I thought him rude until I realized that he was blind. In the same way two deafmutes unwittingly misled me. On Market Street in the Ballard district, I met a woman who said she had washed my "didies," to use her word, when I was a baby. On the ferry, I met a man with whom I had been a Boy Scout. On Rainier Avenue, I talked with a man who had watched me box an exhibition with Jack Hammer at an Inglewood Golf Club smoker fifteen years before. In front of the campaign headquarters a woman said that she had voted for me last time and then added "in Kittitas County" (100 miles away). On Pacific Avenue in Bremerton, I ran into Bill Whitney, a logger, who had won a four-round decision from me at Kingston. Many of those I met were attractive people of high quality, whom I hoped to have the chance to meet again, and some of whom I wished to know.

Three days after losing the primary, I ran into an acquaintance in the elevator of the building where we then both worked. He was well dressed and above average in advantages and education. He mentioned that we had met on a street corner about a month before. Then he asked, "Say, how's your campaign coming along?"

When the duty was tedious or frightening during World War II, I kept putting one foot in front of the other by recalling words of Marcus Aurelius: "Every moment think steadily as a Roman and a man to do what thou hast in hand with perfect and simple dignity, and feeling of affection and freedom and justice; and to give thyself relief from all other thoughts." In a campaign, under conditions that are comparable but call for less fortitude and more self-propulsion, a candidate may use another precept to keep himself bound to the task. When he has had enough of hunting strangers in the streets and is tempted to take refuge around the corner with a book or an ice-cream cone, he may think of Zatopek's remark. Before the London Olympics, other athletes interrupted exercise to loiter by the playing fields, available for interviews, but Zatopek doffed his sweat shirt on arrival, stepping onto the track around which he ran until time to board the bus. When a persistent reporter puffed alongside and remonstrated with him for this practice, the resolute Czech turned his head and replied, "When I come to the track, I run."

Two score years later, in looking back at this defeat, and another next before it, I find them neither a landmark nor a shock. (Defeats in personal relationships have endured far longer as a shadow or a sting.) Since the shock of even a foreseen event often surprises me, maybe my emotional memory is as dim as my emotional imagination. But as to the lack of landmark quality to those defeats, perhaps the cause is less peculiar to me than common to us all, for whom few single events any longer loom. Now less often is one's future conclusively altered by a single act, such as to enter or leave school, become apprenticed to a trade, marry, move one's home, quit a job, undergo a maturity rite or take ship for the new world.

Changed conditions have lessened the big moments, the great occasions. Thanksgiving no longer offers an opportunity for gratitude for the earth's bounty and to enjoy the uncommon pleasure of this bounty. A feast is not one of those rare junctures when we get plenty to eat. Leave-taking has lost its pathos along with the risks that those parting will not meet again. The ship does not slowly pull away past the sad and stony faces of the womenfolk who stand along the wharf. Before a trip abroad, people often make a will because of cultural time lag and the habit of cleaning up business but not because their return is in doubt. Although still final, death has become often indistinct. In the Middle Ages the moment of death was defined as that day on which the one who died was living and on which he was dead. Since then science has measured life's presence more precisely, but it blurs the occurrence of death where it sustains the twilight zone of nominal life, linking a spark to the name of one whose powers have waned to just a beating heart.

Not only are fewer decisions final, fewer experiences conclusive, but our awareness of change further diminishes their importance to us. Change in social custom and personal development used to be invisible or overlooked. In their reactions to experience, from childhood to old age, Plutarch's heroes showed one consistent character, as unchanging throughout life as the world in which they lived. To overcome the scruples of his king to a measure that the cardinal pursued for some *raison d'etat*, Richelieu argued, "Man is immortal, his salvation is hereafter; but the state has no immortality, its salvation is now or never." This reverses our present view that an institution can be counted on, for better or worse, to function in perpetuity, while each human is not only mortal but subject to drastic change throughout his/her life. Until the nineteenth-century radical legal scholars observed that the common law was modified by the conditions in which it operated, case law had been thought immutable, as its movement had been too slow to be discerned. The imperceptibility of change as process led us to attribute exaggerated causal properties to an event that was noticed because it concurred with a new condition or course, *post hoc, ergo propter hoc.*

Life as a continuous process has become so evident, and we are so aware of it, that we realize how arbitrary were some of the old symbolic milestones; we see that few events constitute a turning point. Habit, pattern, direction, system now seem all. Events that to us once represented—and in our view often caused as well—an alteration in our lives no longer move our emotions or impress our minds as showing a corner turned. Looking back, we see no corners, only curves.

III | Qualities

Chapter | 9

FLAVOR

Citizens' attitudes determine politicians' personalities, both by the voters' choices among candidates and by politicians conforming themselves to suit their constituents' taste. In time, the kinds of politicians' personalities that citizens encourage and permit partly decide the direction and execution of our public policies.

A politician's personality has become a substantial condition of his success at winning and holding office. One reason is that our election days are set, not by the swelling pressure of an issue but by the orbit of the earth. Political careers often are shortened by the dependence of voters' choices on variable factors of personality, both that of the politician and their own. Unlike many other pursuits, politics provides for comparison no measurable records, such as batting averages, nor does success depend on a consensus among professional colleagues, based on the quality of one's work.

Both historians and citizens have turned their attention away from the politician's personality as defined in the sense of the totality of elements that compose him. Historians concentrate on trends and forces, while citizens give special regard to a politician's "personality" in the narrower sense of his flavor to others, the sense in which the word *personality* is used hereafter. To many people, in measuring an individual's value his manner is becoming more important and his character less. An air of superiority, though supported by the fact, is thought worse than a lack of superiority. Hypocrisy, because personally offensive, is treated as a worse evil than vice. Among the things that are easier in private than in public life are not only action based on independent thought but also conformity to a personality pattern that is either offensive to the majority or common only to a small minority. A politician is exposed to criticism from all points of view, while in private life, by confining his associations to others who are like himself, one can snap his fingers at the rest of the world.

In the importance of his personality both for the level of his performance and for the acquisition of rewards, a politician resembles an actor. The professional value of personality as a vendible commodity, and its importance to people and events, make politicians think of their personalities as things apart from themselves, like a tree in the yard. This tendency is emphasized by the egotism of many of the men whom politics, like the theater, attracts. In most professions, personality—a bedside manner for instance—supplements one's working skills and colors results. But as with an actor, personality may be a politician's main asset and contribution, his stock in trade which he sells as much as he does his working skills. However, like the ability to hit a fast pitch, if the right personality is his only asset, it will not assure success in the big leagues. If he has little from within to contribute he still may make a mark by the impact of his personality. If unconnected with any substantial skill or definite direction in a politician, personality may be a sort of Cheshire cat's smile. To be successful with little inside him a politician has to be in full bodily vigor. But his ideas and character, if he has them, can shine through a frail body with a light of their own.

Now the public eye intrudes into a politician's private affairs, in fact, into all he does and is. Modern urban life allows a private citizen to conceal many things about himself from those who know him. But the comprehensive scrutiny fixed on a politician around the clock, by means of technology and custom, makes him feel as though he lives in Orwell's 1984 and his constituency is Big Brother.

The complete but shallow study of him means that he is known widely but not well. He only halfway feels like the drinker in the cartoon, sobbing to the bartender: "Everybody understands me!" Information about him comes at second hand, and he is observed only while engaged in his never-ending courtship of his observers. Before most impressions of him reach the citizen, they are filtered through an interpreting medium such as a news reporter's mind, modified by the editor's mind, or a TV screen, altered by technicians and producers. When seen in the flesh he is on stage. One cannot know how much of a prepared speech originated in his mind, how far his brain and mouth may serve as a transmission belt for others' completed thoughts.

Many of us now ask for one of certain general personality types in our politicians. With our detailed but imperfect knowledge of a politician's nature and activities we verify the degree to which his performance complies with our request. A politician used to be known largely, and therefore judged, by his work and his conduct in connection with it. Those who dealt with him in person, his colleagues and opponents, were the ones who took his measure. Now it is not enough that one acts right; one must have the correct personality as well. If he wishes, a private citizen can disregard in part the public's gentle, pervasive commands, but a politician must obey them to be preferred and thus to survive. At his peril he bucks this tide. He must keep in mind Stendhal's words that "the approval of others is a certificate of resemblance." Success in politics today, subject to the condition of an acceptable personality type, would be almost as hard for some of the Adams family titans as for the tigers on the Assyrian throne.

Among the elements of the preferred personality type are moderation, sincerity and warmth. None is essential. LaGuardia was immoderate; Dewey and Taft were not warm; politeness and the wish to avoid partisanship forbid me to give examples of those who have substituted unction for sincerity.

The difference between warmth and coldness of personality is superficial as to human nature and invalid as to morals. Many people's manner betrays, not the important quality of indifference to life, but the minor one of habitual caution or distaste for displayed feeling. The meaning of outer warmth, not a virtue but a personal attraction, has been perverted and inflated by popular tastes and falsified by our deliberate conviviality. A cold fish may be sensitive and good. In politics, the lightweight carrier of a warm and friendly heart is not worth a Wilson, a Hughes or a William of Orange.

One can classify mankind better than as faucets on a tub. A division can be made into three classes: animals; persons who, as their own judges, make decisions after balancing the merits of the consequences; and those who commit themselves to follow certain moral rules. Members of the first class pretend that anarchy prevails and obey society's rules only so far as is necessary to their immediate personal interest, while those in the second and third classes have loyalties and good intentions toward persons and principles beyond themselves. A person in the second class treats all norms as issues in equity where the factors must be balanced so that a sacrifice is not made without some compensating gain. One in the third class regards certain rules of conduct as laws having only rare exceptions, so that he will take a risk for a principle or person without counting the cost. Holmes's soldier is an example: "The faith is true and adorable which leads a soldier to throw away his life in obedience to a blindly accepted duty, in a cause which he little understands, in a plan of campaign of which he has no notion, under tactics of which he does not see the use." Other examples are the choice Lee made between the Union and Virginia and the refusal of the Secretary of State to turn his back on his fallen friend. The second approach—called the "computing principle" by Burke and Bickel—permits the highest performance of virtue but only when the performer possesses uncommon sophistication and resistance to self-deception; the third group wins most of the morality contests, although it contains some otherwise admirable natures that are tarnished by timid or cruel rigidity.

The current preference for warmth over virtue has the same root as the preference for sincerity over honesty. Sincerity, the truthful expression of one's tastes and feelings, is one of several kinds of honesty, which is the general truthfulness of one's expression. Friendship depends on honesty but cannot survive without occasional insincerity. Chinese and Russian Communist leaders tended in their behavior as such to be sincere but dishonest. Lord Chesterfield's code of conduct, based on policy and honor, enjoined him to constant honesty and frequent insincerity. Some deep and subtle politicians are more often insincere than other more simple and superficial ones, but they are not thereby inferior in public merit. Both sincerity and warmth improve a personal relationship. Often honesty and virtue do not. Sincerity and warmth have become such political assets that a politician is lucky to have, or shrewd to pretend, two of the traits of a drunk.

While directness of purpose and capacity for superior work are, as always, the main assets required for reaching the top, the lack of inherited gifts of rank and situation is being replaced as a barrier to political success by the lack of moderation, sincerity and warmth. The latter lack makes political 4Fs of some men and women who as politicians would do public good. The decline of parties has made it easier for one to succeed in politics without the skills of working with an organization, yet it has made it harder for him to overcome the absence of the vendible elements of personality. He has to get along with everyone because it is no longer enough to get along with colleagues alone. One result of this is to admit to office politicians who have energy, ability and charm, yet lack purpose about anything beyond their own careers. Leo Durocher said about baseball, "Nice guys finish last," but in politics, below the highest levels, they often finish first.

However, trends are afoot that restrict these limiting factors and put the luxurious virtue of individuality, or at least of differentness, within a politician's reach. Recognition that one's power over, and responsibility for, his fundamental elements has narrow limits is extending to those aspects of personal appearance, beliefs and conduct that derive from family, race or custom. The result is increasing tolerance for those whose differences appear to come from ancestry, religion or national background.

As part of our tradition, behavior is allowed more latitude than belief is. The myth of rugged individualism is more true as to conduct than as to thought. But although people are no longer described as weaklings or sinners or lesser breeds without the law, intolerance yet remains for habits and beliefs that seem outside or counter to a person's background and that deviate from current popular taste. The realization that who and what we are is largely determined by causes outside us has not yet spread to apply to those habits and beliefs which still are thought to be exclusively a person's own so that he can be blamed for them. Because their causes are not obvious to all, they are treated as free will's final redoubt.

This residual intolerance is reinforced by the lack of a widespread wish to be allowed this kind of independence for oneself. Everyone wants to escape the pains and burdens of race or religious prejudice or to avoid punishment for a crime committed pursuant to an emotional disorder, and most people are willing to see the burial of such a sword that can be used against as well as by them. But the desire to enjoy individuality is confined to a minority now. The fear of loneliness if one does not conform denies sympathy for nonconformists. The lack of humility about the possible rightness of others' deviations and lack of confidence in, and respect for, one's own conforming practices make non-conformity appear to threaten and insult one's own beliefs and ways. This intolerance is caused, not by certainty of being right, but rather by misgivings about whether one is right and a feeling that no one else knows enough to justify himself in differing from the crowd. Doubt about one's own role and course generates resentment at the apparent presumption of another for taking a position, and causes suspicion of missionary zeal.

Most people in time may come to regard a

person's "voluntary" singularity as having been shaped by his background as much as were his flat feet or his choice of fish on Fridays. In this event voters would permit and, unless their toleration slackens to the point of indifference, might even prefer the presence of independent ideas and character in politicians. However, even if people cease to blame a person for his nonconformity, they still may suppress it for the general good as they would any tendency thought to be harmful to humankind.

The suppression of nonconformity may be stopped by two things: understanding and respect. Understanding of personal peculiarities may spread to the sources of nonconformity and relieve the fear and suspicion of it by removing its mystery. This understanding of other people is going far. It may become the main cause of the conditions that will "save succeeding generations from the scourge of war." Understanding may in time conquer much, if not all. Once it exists, a sympathetic understanding does not easily stop at encompassing only a portion of its object. In the Leyte campaign our antiaircraft fire hit the Japanese plane that came overhead on Christmas night. I felt a tender pity for the pilot far from home as he and his lone plane blazed in the sky like a great star.

Popular aversion to nonconformity may also be reduced by increased respect for it. Before long everyone may have as wide a scope of freedom as was enjoyed by kings of long ago. These new conditions may generate a taste for certain of the old values that resulted from aristocratic ways. Among them is the individual's importance. In recent years individuality and moral confidence, like good manners, have been scorned by people who resent these qualities because they identify them with a haughty privileged class. When Harold Hoshino, a prize fighter, was boxing a convict as part of a show in the Walla Walla prison yard, one of the crowd shouted, "Knock him out, Pete, he eats ham and eggs!" As the memory of unjust privilege fades, most citizens may come to tolerate expression of a strange idea not only when it remains a mystery but even when it provokes dislike. When the suppression of nonconformity confines its means to public opinion, independent behavior may then increase, as people come to realize that when everyone tolerates them they can get away with a lot.

We will stop suppressing nonconformity only if we extend toleration to intolerant attitudes but not to the ultimate point of acts suppressing nonconformity. Yet some who regard their attitudes as advanced admire tolerance and understanding more than insistence on the rightness of one's own principles. They deny personal responsibility for anything except lack of tolerance. Confusing righteousness with self-righteousness, they hold a pukka sahib in lower regard than they do a squaw man.

In order to represent his constituents well a politician must embody and express much of what they believe and like, but his duty to give his constituency responsive representation is not violated by his having a mind of his own. He may bow down to brazen idols or, like Kipling's lascar seaman, he may worship a low-pressure cylinder, although he may not be a monarchist or advocate the system of a single tax. In matters that concern public policy about which his constituents have definite opinions he may not deviate from the norms of the moment as far as a private person is free to do, but to concur with such a consensus does not require him to be a conformist any more than antagonism makes him an individualist. (Tolerance of individuality or of a direct aim in a politician means not indifference to what he stands for but rather accepting the independence of his outlook.) To lead, a leader must be independent but not eccentric. An extreme non-conformist may lack sympathy for his constituents and cannot inspire their trust. But if he conforms to the point of letting others make all the decisions about his course, he does not lead. He may help people get what they want but he does not help them discover what else better there may be to want.

As Erich Fromm has written, "The right to express our thoughts, however, means something only if we are able to have thoughts of our own." Free speech has little worth to those with nothing to declare except what they receive from others and then transmit intact as though they had not even looked into the box in which it came. When Evers used to take the ball from Tinker and throw it on to Chance, at least he changed its course. Citizens gain only from a politician who gives them something of himself, who transforms experience as it passes through him, who is a prism, not a mirror or a windowpane.

When his freighter was torpedoed near Greenland, my friend Fred Sundt jumped into the lifeboat, where he discovered that the rest had done the same, and so there was no one left on deck to lower the boat. If no one remains for a politician to follow, he may think continued attempts to follow are unprofitable if not futile and conclude that he may as well lead. He may try to assert, rather than suppress, his independent ideas if he himself is bored by his affable blandness, if he feels a duty to exercise leadership more far-reaching than hunch bets on next month's opinion polls, and if he is encouraged by public acceptance of more original fare. Concluding that life's only worthwhile pursuit is pleasing experience, some people confine themselves to hedonism through stimulants, indolence and other passive experience, thereby foregoing much experience that is satisfying and deep. Likewise, citizens defeat themselves when they put much emphasis on how their politicians taste.

Although important, flavor is far from conclusive. At any one time and place, successful politicians share certain qualities but in other respects show a sharp divergence flowing from the diversity of what voters want in their leaders. Inherent in each voter's choice of candidates is an identification that contains three elements: common experience, shared aspirations and vicarious enjoyment of worth. The feeling may be negative, as where an unknown person is preferred to a known. When sympathy outweighs admiration, the voter prefers equals. In the converse case he chooses betters.

The balance of those elements in the voter is the counterpart of a politician's balance between responsiveness and initiative. Without some common experience, a politician may lack touch with his constituents and provide at best a harsh paternalism. On the other hand, one may be put in office despite his lack of the merit that the office calls for, or even sometimes because of it, when the electorate prefers to make its leadership in the image of what the maker is rather than what it aspires toward. When a preponderance of voters' outlooks is disproportioned in the same direction, their choice prevails, and their private errors merge into a single public fault.

When the disparities of comfort and opportunity have further shrunk there will be few politicians from deprived beginnings and few voters awed by the comparative majesty of their leaders' station. People have ceased to idealize leaders as they become aware that human frailties, although not equal, are universal. As no man was a hero to his valet, no politician is now a hero to his constituents because they know that his motives, experience and personality have so much in common with their own.

Among politicians of equal rank the range will narrow in the length and steepness of the ladders they have climbed. (The substantial variations will be not in the outer circumstances of class situation to be overcome but in the inner, and largely invisible, circumstances of the leaders' own personalities.) Voters living in comfort, aware that politicians are not much better off than they, feel a weaker need to live through some splendid figure of a leader. Perhaps people will choose leaders who are more like than superior to themselves, who are of a higher class but not far up. After the 1920 election, Wilson Mizner remarked that he had not realized until then the truth of his mother's reminder to him when he was a child that anyone can be elected president. How maybe both aspects of this double meaning will become the common custom. Or then again, in boredom, feeling their lives to be stale, or in anxiety, feeling the problems to be difficult, and no longer much concerned about social inequality, people may prefer superiors.

Three general categories of voter-preferred leader can be discerned, with most consistent winners falling in more than one. Some citizens prefer the leader who champions the follower's deep-felt cause—Gladstone, Bryan, Wilson. Another is preferred because he is liked, admired, or trusted—Herbert Lehman, Eisenhower, Willy Brandt. Third is one whom the voters employ because he is expected to deliver the goods—Disraeli, Lyndon Johnson. Unlike the first two types or objects of voter motives—when the third type stumbles, he is not forgiven and granted another chance; he is regarded as a piece of machinery rather than as someone with whom the voter feels identified.

The variety to be found in this house of many mansions maybe further illustrated by a pair of complex politicians who possessed contrasting constellations of qualities. Once upon a time two able, energetic, cultivated, socially graceful, charming, upright men of substantial honesty and courage took a large part in public affairs. Both had a sense of history; both enjoyed women and were attractive to them; both were intelligent, but neither was a pioneer in thought. In most other aspects of experience and personality these men contrasted.

The Older was a lawyer. Although a shrewd negotiator, his chief professional gift was as an advocate. He married a rich, ambitious, aggressive woman who gave him pain before an eventual divorce. Once on returning from abroad, he was dismayed when someone asked him if he had been gone. The most celebrated orator of his time (also the great wit of his period), he was noted for his grace of speech as well as for its eloquence and force. His need to be admired was obscured by his nobility of spirit and redeemed by his willingness to raise a laugh at his own expense. Although he could not stay for long away from the city and the company of socially significant people, he from time to time withdrew to his farm. Public life meant so much to him that it could not be said he was a gallant, thoughtful, well-bred man first and a politician second, but these two sides of life in him had roughly equal weight. His conduct was marked by his genuine heart for things beyond himself.

The Younger had a parent whose strong personality, disciplined care and concern for his success distinctly shaped him. Soon after reaching manhood he suffered a mishap on a warm sea, being left on an island in danger from which he escaped by his resourcefulness and cool head. As a journalist he showed skill; with a style notable for lack of ornament, he made personal observations without vulgar display of his own personality. He went to Britain and wrote of it. A chronic health disorder afflicted him. His daughter, to whom he was devoted, became well known.

In his early adult years he played the playboy about whom there was scandalous gossip; few discerned his resolute ambition (or foretold its formation), and none expected his high achievement— saw the Henry V in his Prince Hal. When he entered public life, he joined the party of the common people and remained identified with it. He became both a charismatic leader of crowds and a skilled political intriguer, developing what was called a fine Italian hand. Temperate in food and drink, he was profuse, though controlled, in personal expenditures for political advancement. They were the most lavish of his time, and many persons thought they would defeat their purposes; yet the splendor of his manner of life—both the spending and the magnificent, dashing tone—contributed little by little to create and increase his influence. By a series of bold steps, often close in margin of success and precarious in risk of disaster, he mounted the summit of his country's affairs. His presence buoyed his followers. When separated from him, "They missed the sight of their————, his vigor and wonderful good spirits; he held his head high and radiated confidence."

Some thought his clemency toward his defeated opponents was a shrewd expedient, and others thought it reflected farsighted statesmanship. He knew more that could be done for his country's benefit than circumstances permitted him to undertake. He was forthright in manner, yet personally reticent, neither self-revealing nor self-preoccupied. In him thought and action were closely joined, and causing events interested him more than explaining them. Intrepid as a swimmer and in war, traveling often, far and fast, communicating with many people, fearless, living in and for the moment, he had utter self-confidence and unshakable nerve. At the peaks of his civic authority and most of his personal powers, he was assassinated for a combination of political and personal motives, after disregarding warnings of the risk. He was succeeded by a masterful politician who brought about large policy change after he became his country's first citizen.

Not long afterward the Older died in discouragement. By comparison, the Older was reflective, sensitive, literary, idealistic, loving comfort but not ease. Finding his way along virtue's path gave him agony, and making his way along it required much effort—which he took—while the Younger lived life on his own terms without such a conflict. To make up his mind was hard for him, while the

Younger was supremely decisive. He was upset by his family's disturbances, but the Younger was not bothered by his. At times he chose to support causes that he knew would lose, while the Younger, though he took chances, thought it absurd to adhere to any prospectively unsuccessful course.

The Younger's more intense appetite for success gave him greater willingness to subordinate to it his vanity and comfort. More a man of the future, though no more liberal in spirit, he was less introspective, if at all.

Their personalities (like those of Prince Hamlet and the Prince of Norway) diverged so far that the men had little sympathy for each other. In the Older's capacity as a politician, the Younger regarded him as a liability, although he tried to make him his friend. He disapproved of him for combining a quest for high public place with a reluctance to make every sacrifice and undergo all the discipline to get there. The Older disapproved of the Younger as calculating, opportunistic, guided by prudence rather than principle, and lacking a developed philosophy or even fundamental goals.

Despite their differences, they allied themselves for a period (ended by the Younger's death), induced by mutual usefulness and enabled by respect, not so much for each other's qualities as for his gifts.*

---

*Some will see here Adlai Stevenson and John F. Kennedy; others may see Cicero and Caesar.

Chapter | 10

MODERATION

This chapter concerns three kinds of moderation: in policy, in manner and in character.

Moderation of *policy*—forbearance from extremes, a temperate approach to inflammatory problems, the use of reason that is sometimes detached, an attempt to delay action during heated periods so that reason may be applied before important measures are taken—is essential to the practice of free government but of little use for its achievement or defense. Its value is to keep the conditions in which free government can flourish. Because free institutions are maintained by moderate policies and acquired and protected by immoderate ones, they depend on politicians who have a preference for moderate over immoderate policies but the capacity and willingness to use either when needed. In times of stress, when moderation is inadequate, an adequate politician is willing and able to be immoderate toward the end of moderate government, which in the long run depends on a sometimes fighting faith.

The notion that a politician who has a mild *manner* cannot or will not be tough when the public interest so requires is a folly common to dogmatic fogies of the left and right. This notion is unfair because it is untrue. A person can use violence when he thinks it fitting even though he is humble, reserved, or dignified, like Joe Louis and Robert E. Lee. Often soft-voiced politicians in subdued dress have brought their country into war. Because Benjamin Franklin, prosperous, rational, and habitually temperate, wished to be allowed to continue to be so, and because he had courage as well, he was willing to stake all on revolt. Those who fail to distinguish between a mild manner and a slack or rigid character think that a person whose approach to problems is tentative and thorough is therefore spineless or a fossil. For a while, mild-mannered politicians were scorned by some as craven for not using as their guide the New Deal after it had been embalmed, ratified by the Republicans. Any manner, mild or otherwise, in a politician can be compatible with a belief in freedom and the courage and force to act on such belief.

Moderation as a quality of a politician's *character* has been practiced to perfection until it is a curse. Gibbon deplored immoderation in public affairs as a major source of harm:

> In the tumult of civil discord the laws of society lose their force, and their place is seldom supplied by those of humanity. The ardor of contention, the pride of victory, the despair of success, the memory of past injuries, and the fear of future dangers, all contribute to inflame the mind and to silence the voice of pity. From such motives almost every page of history has been stained with civil blood.

But we now are choked with sympathy and smothered in forbearance. Modern politicians have become too moderate in all aspect of conduct and value except narrowness of purpose and willingness to do hard work. Forgetting the limits that bound the golden mean theory, they treat it as a universal, like the candidate for mayor who promised to tread the line between partiality and impartiality. To put it another way, they fail to apply the theory to itself and so they practice moderation to excess. They try to be only moderately wise and brave, like well-to-do college boys who used to think it vulgar to become learned and aimed for a "gentleman's C."

Free government depends on a type of politician whose character is equipped for going both rough and smooth. He can handle the daily low-tension problems with restraint, yet his preference for life in a free climate is so strong that to restore it if it is lost or to defend it if it comes under fire, from within or without, he is willing to kill or die. His balance does not leave him stalled at dead center on an occasion calling for immoderation, whether such occasion be a radical reform to hammer through or an invasion to repulse. A Communist true believer, for example, having none but the martial virtues—courage and loyalty to the authority that he obeys—lacks the temper to operate free institutions and the inclination to make them his goal. Even if he cared about freedom he would be useless for its practice. Such was the history of some Resistance fighters against the Nazi rule, first in war but last in peace.

Among those American politicians who cannot perform this dual function the common type is
neither a bigot nor an enthusiast. His whole nature,
not merely his manner, is so moderate that he can
behave in no other way. Although this type's predominance is preferable to the condition of some
unstable democracies where extremes attract more
of the support, leaving a weak center, so that the
shape of politics resembles a dumbbell, a citizen
may wish for better than one whose moderate attachment to constitutional liberty makes him a fair-
weather boat.

Tacitus wrote of Agricola, "It was a case of a
lofty and aspiring soul craving with more eagerness
than caution the beauty and splendor of great and
glorious renown. But it soon was mellowed by reason
and experience, and he retained from his learning
that most difficult of lessons—moderation." Several
conditions cause this moderation of character, to
learn which no longer is difficult. In the field of
managing affairs, although mobility of status has
increased, risk of disaster and chance for supreme
eminence both have narrowed. As a child I listened
to reminiscences of the Alaska Gold Rush, colorful
accounts of men putting themselves through prodigious exertion and submitting to danger, loneliness, hunger and cold, because success would so
transform their lives to comfort and security from
the condition of a laboring man before the turn of
the century—only a little better than that of a gold-
seeker on the Yukon.

Enlarged opportunity has lifted the limits of

achievement in certain fields, as admission of Blacks to competition has raised the levels of excellence in athletics and popular music, and the increase in the proportion of scholarship students has pushed up the average quality of honor graduates. But as to status and power, as distinguished from achievement, the range has narrowed between ordinary failure and success. The floor has risen, and the ceiling dropped. How many politicians now seem to make their secret motto "Aut Caesar, aut nihil"? Desperate effort is no longer called for by ambition or fear. The struggle has abated as we have grown more tame.

Moderation is increased by the complexity of social organization and the need for trained minds to operate it. Within both organization and minds the paths of action are obstructed by screens, blocks, settling basins, corners and red and amber lights. This raises the threshold for action that is intemperate and sudden. Contributing to moderation is the effort to improve the adjustment between the individual and society. If fewer citizens were on discordant terms with themselves, politics would be a more attractive occupation because a politician would not be afflicted by so many corroded souls who now give him much grief. But if everyone is going to be so well adjusted to society that he is contented with it, few may hear a call to enter such a singleminded life as politics. Churchill observed,

It is said that famous men are usually the product of an unhappy childhood. The stern compression of circumstances, the twinges of adversity, the spur of slights and taunts in early years, are needed to evoke that ruthless fixity of purpose and tenacious mother-wit without which great actions are seldom accomplished.

More than ever, the politician's attention is fixed, exclusively but not intensely, on his relationships with his constituents, rather than on history, posterity or God. The shift of attention owes partly to the constituents' new power and to the respect to which they have become entitled for their own worth. No longer a mob, "a great beast," most of them now are educated and disciplined in the practices of citizenship. The term "public servant," once less fact than blend of self-serving deception and polite ideal, has become an accurate label. But increases in life expectancy and in self-awareness are the chief causes of this increased attention to personal relationships, which in turn is the strongest cause of excessively moderate character.

In the past, when a person spent his life in the shadow of death he was more aware of the power of chance and the supernatural, and he thought about an afterlife. He knew neither philosophic doubt nor economic hope. We now feel assured of the use and enjoyment of our allotted span. We know that there has come to pass a chance to enjoy true and sustained well-being on earth. People have forgotten they are going to die. Death has been hidden from our sight. Only undertakers touch or care for bodies, which are taken promptly from the place of death. Brief ceremonies for the dead are held in a commercial parlor instead of in the building that was one of the central places of the mourners' lives. Evidence is lacking that widows no longer honor their husbands' memories or sooner cease to miss them, yet now the period for wearing black is short. Like sex in the Victorian age, death's discussion is shunned, and its existence concealed from children. In contrast was the action of the people of Messena, who believed it instructive to see a tyrant punished. When they overthrew Hippo they took the children from school and gathered them in the theater to watch him beaten and put to death. Perhaps because few people believe that any part of themselves is immortal, most refuse to remember that the only parts of themselves that they are sure exist are going to rot.

The rise in the average age at which death occurs has changed the significance of death and life. Because longer, life is made more satisfying. When the one who dies has endured enough years to have shot his bolt, death is less bitter to the dying and less painful to those who lose him than it is when a person is denied his chance to put out what is in him. Death is less dramatic when it arrives at the end of a gradual decay of powers than when a person is shot down in flight.

Although a life's significance can be changed by its length, the tragedy of mortality cannot be altered by age or achievement. Nevertheless, our concealment of death from ourselves takes away our sense of the tragedy. When we not only remove from our presence the horror of a corpse, but draw a curtain between ourselves and all aspects of death, resulting ignorance leads us to underestimate the level of that high plane on which life can be taken. To ignore life's tragic element is to forget its exalted dimensions, of which mortality is a partial proof.

Years ago, near where I was working on a farm, a lad climbed on the freight train as it passed each afternoon and rode it half a mile to the pasture where he would jump off and drive in the milk cows. Once, when he made the mistake of grabbing for a rear ladder instead of a front one, he missed and fell between the cars, and the wheels ran over his thighs. A man who had seen him fall got off his horse, pulled him a few yards up the hillside and got a doctor, who tied off the bleeding and gave him an injection to numb the pain. The lad could see his house from where he rested on the bunch grass. He looked across alfalfa fields to the burnt hills, to the green timbered slopes behind them, and to the snow peaks on the horizon under the fall sky. He smoked as his family and his nearby friends came to stand around him. Little was said, but the living and dying exchanged goodbyes. When he was dead his brothers took his body into the house.

Longer life expectancy has raised life's value by raising death's price, which is reckoned by the lost years of life's expected remainder. A soldier, once he has a mortal wound, has no more chance to make himself a hero. The life of Pertinax compels our admiration, but not because when he died at sixty-seven he faced his assassins calmly and did not try to hide or flee. The same goes for Abraham Holmes, who amputated his own arm after the battle of Sedgemoor. During the Bloody Assizes he was brought before the king, who gave him the choice to recant or hang. "I am an aged man," he said, "and what remains to me of life is not worth a falsehood or a baseness. I have always been a republican, and I am so still." At seventy, when Socrates and Seneca drank their hemlock with dignity becoming to the elevation of their lives, they proved their wisdom rather than their courage. It is said that when a weatherbeaten soldier of Caesar's guards came to ask leave to kill himself, Caesar, noticing his decrepitude, replied, "You fancy, then, that you are yet alive."

One result of the probability that one will live long is to make a politician less independent of his constituents, more cautious, less reckless with his life, more inclined to make long-range plans for himself and wait patiently to harvest them, less willing to start a war, less willing to play for high, immediate stakes. And in this attitude his constituents back him up.

Assumption of carnal immortality makes humankind seem even more important in comparison with whatever he/she may revere. It centers the politician's attention on the people, judged by their own standards. There is little thought of eternity in time or space except among a few who may reflect on some of their kind setting out for the planets of Alpha Centauri on a journey several generations long.

Some members of Congress used to keep

their seats until they had reached an advanced age. What kept them there—the combination of secure one-party constituencies and the heavy weight that the rules gave to seniority in assigning influence—has gone. But even with the passing of these factors politicians' average age may be expected to rise, within Congress and without, along with that of their constituents. This change, combined with increased life expectancy, may increase the proportion of politicians who are moderate in character and raise the degree of their moderation. In policy, this moderation of character among the old takes the form of conservatism, as in the case of European politicians after the world wars, which few young men survived. T. E. Lawrence wrote, "When we had achieved, and the new world dawned, the old men came out again and took from us our victory and remade it in the image of the former world they knew."

On the other hand, if older voters feel less need to treat a politician as a parental image, a larger proportion of younger people may be elected, and thus the spread in age by which politicians exceed the average of their constituents would shrink. Also, the number of beats allotted to each heart is being increased more than is the span of capacity for hard work. A person can pull the levers on a voting machine a score of years after he has lost the power to give effective service as a politician. Some men may have cast a vote for both Washington and Lincoln and others for both Grant and Eisenhower, but when they voted last they could not do much more than blink their eyes and state a simple choice.

The increase in self-awareness has become so great that it can be classified as a difference in kind. The Greeks stepped beyond prior peoples with greater awareness of causation and of the individual's capacity to cause events but they were not self-conscious in the continuing awareness of their personality as a mechanism. Now one dissects not only himself but also the culture of the society in which he lives and his relationship to the society and some of its members. He is aware of the marital relationship and discusses it with his spouse. Our double nature has long been recognized. Pascal said a tree does not know itself to be miserable, Walt Whitman said that animals do not lie awake at night and weep over their sins, and Chesterton said you cannot slap a rhinoceros on the back and tell him to pull himself together and be a rhinoceros. But we have acquired a paralyzing knowledge of the degree to which our subterranean selves govern our motives and conduct.

Another cause of self-awareness is our uncertainty about values, making it difficult or meaningless for a person to pass objective judgment on another person or a human situation. So he considers his experience of the other person, applying not judgment but taste.

Spinoza remarked that a passion "ceases to be a passion as soon as we form a clear and distinct idea of it." Now an educated person often finds it hard to yield to emotion or act on an emotional conviction. When a feeling starts to surge inside he can hardly help thinking of the effect of the emotional process on himself, thereby altering the quality of his emotion and reducing its force. When my father had come and told us children that grandfather was dead, he sat down, put his face in his hands, and cried. I wonder how my children will inform their children of my death. Perhaps their sorrow will make them start to cry. In turn they may be reminded that tears are a healthy catharsis. The comfort of this gain—or awareness of their curative quality—may stop the tears. People used to go to church to worship God. Now when people kneel some remember that prayer is thought to be a therapy. In such self-regard one cannot pray; God goes unworshipped, and the supplicant goes without his cure. If taken as medicine, and with knowledge that it is a placebo at that, the Host becomes just another biscuit. Because he concluded that his contemplated action's purpose would be his self-satisfaction, the central character in Sartre's *The Age of Reason* decided against joining the Communist Party and enlisting in the Spanish Loyalist cause.

In our well-ordered society, politicians, like most other people, have lost some of their former dependence on friends for favor, protection and hospitality, although congenial company is important for politicians' pleasure. Added to this decline in the value of friendship as a means of survival, the new self-awareness has weakened a politician's loyalty to, and affection for, friends. It also impairs the quality of his loyalty to institutions. They now receive less loyalty for other reasons as well. Families no longer invoke a strong sense of loyalty, while in the past they were an object of loyalty even in cases where there was no love. Except in those lands that have not enjoyed independence from foreign rule for long enough to take its merits for granted, the central government in its people's eyes grows vague and far off. The splintering effects of assertive nationalities dividing nations do not seem to arrest the growing remoteness of the government and the symbols of the state for the individual who must share this institution with an increased number of other persons. One's attachment to each is weakened by dispersion among all. Since loyalty, unlike love, does not resemble a gas which expands to fill whatever vacuum it enters, Cordelia would have spoken the truth if she had been referring to loyalty when she told her father that if she married, her love for him would be diminished by the love that she came to give her husband, as though she were dispensing money instead of love.

Another consequence of self-awareness is that a person's inclination to do something for another's benefit is retarded by his knowledge that he is impelled by some irrational frailty within. This attitude abates impulses, such as indignation or pity, to do things requiring effort or sacrifice. The same acts continue to be done, though on a steadier flow and with weaker force. They stem less from impulse than from rational selfishness which looks in turn to prior causes. Under conditions of self-awareness, acts of this kind are done to give oneself pleasure by pleasing the object of one's bounty or by adhering to a principle.

Self-awareness makes it easier for a person to commit small sins but more difficult for him to commit big sins. When tempted to do a minor evil act he expects the consequences to be "guilt feelings." This prospect of a personal affliction like a stomach ache sets a shallow bar to sin compared to the former stern and heavy sense of duty to do right. On the other hand, before committing some dark, malignant deed one may reflect that the source of his intent is a thwarted impulse. Its satisfaction does not seem to be ordained by the Infinite. Its misdirection may be corrected. It seems hardly worth the certainty of anxiety and the risk of punishment. He remembers that the prospective victim's offensive conduct is caused by his unfortunately twisted soul. At this point, he may put away his gun, shrug his shoulders and look up a psychiatrist or take a pill. To tranquilize, instead of exercise, his longing for revenge seems more easy, sane and safe. The result is to diminish the intensity and violence of moral decisions, whether good or bad. Less often does a man become a brute or a martyred saint.

In addition, this awareness checks the pursuit of distant goals by denying a refuge in illusions. The result is fewer drastic and uncalculated enterprises, a skepticism toward effort to achieve what seems to be impossible, fewer great endeavors to win "the true glory," "that good fame without which glory's but a tavern song." We are emancipated from our passions without embracing reason, as we disdain the one but distrust the other. Awareness of our impulses to affect other people as being only impulses, not justified by anything beyond the inner wish for their fulfillment, makes them seem absurd and takes from them their dignity which gives them countenance. In part, the notion of God as an ego projection is both result and cause of our self-awareness. At last, many have come around to the notion suggested by Xenophones of Colophon: "Even as the gods of the Ethiopians are swarthy and flat-nosed, the gods of the Thracians are fair-haired and blue-eyed. . . . Even so oxen, lions and horses, if they had hands wherewith to grave images, would fashion gods after their own shapes and make them bodies like to their own." The loss of illusions, which goes with self-awareness, saves us from some folly while it takes away security and boldness.

If we insist on truth we cannot wish for illusions to beguile us. But the conscious loss of illusions makes people shy away from ideals which they mistake for more illusions. When some people said that John Brown had thrown away his life, Thoreau questioned where they had thrown their lives. Like a race of Sancho Panzas in a world they never would have made themselves, today most persons hesitate to shoot the works.

A thinking person may come to think the notion that the aims, efforts and possible accomplishments of our species are important is only an imaginative delusion, just as many have so concluded as to a belief in a solicitous personal god. He may conclude from this that humankind is a joke or at most a mistake. Even if he does not go so far, his aspirations may be dulled by his belief that they are no more than impulses to be humored and indulged, yet without meaning or value other than providing personal satisfaction. However, the impulse to pursue aspirations seems strong enough to endure.

We may be in for a long period during which man cannot possess himself, cannot merge his two selves, cannot put down his looking glass. Our public leaders may be more artificial in their displays of passion or conviction. They may be more reflective, less ready to adopt a hypothesis for radical change.

People have come to look deeper in placing responsibility for human acts. At first the offending thing itself was blamed. The ox in Exodus was to be stoned. Then the act's effect and the actor's identity were the only things considered. Later the question of criminal intent came to matter. Then the motive behind the intent. Now investigators go hand over hand far back along the causal chains, looking for the sources of conduct. If the synoptic Gospels were written now, the authors would not think to call the men who were crucified with Jesus "thieves."

It is coming to be thought that human actions are the product of genes and experience and therefore not a proper subject for praise or blame. Moral responsibility is narrowed to a necessary fiction. People understand all, so forgive all. Moral qualities are treated less as universal norms and more as building blocks with which personality is constructed. Children and old people do not seem to admire or scorn as do people of ages between. Taking people for granted as part of the scheme of things, children like or dislike according to the effect of the person on the child's feelings, but they do not judge a person's merits. Unlike adults, they do not distinguish between inner and outer gifts, but treat all assets as gifts. Old people also refrain from passing judgment, not because they take things for granted but rather because they realize the narrow limits of human responsibility, which makes them skeptical of merit and tolerant of sin. Many of us are coming to resemble the young and old in this outlook. In an after-hours joint, as middle-aged men and women drink in silence, "dismally contemplating the wreckage of their destiny," while deafening music is played, an observer may scorn if he judges, be saddened if he sympathizes or feel nothing if he fully understands.

Security, mobility and prosperity make everyone an actor who can pick his part, and create it from diverse elements. About the time that we are forgiving everyone his total personality as being the product of causes beyond him, we invent means by which he can conceal his background and fabricate his personality by altering the details that compose his appearance and flavor to others. There is release from the moral rules that were embodied in traditions and in the need to make a living, rules that have been only partially replaced by the duties of citizenship in its broad sense. Aware that they are free to manipulate their own personalities, politicians may assume such virtues as they choose. But these qualities are more likely to resemble items of taste than obedience to commands from On High. Exercise of this expanded range of choice is tempered by the growing doubt that a person is the godlike originator of his acts, despite his power to look at the sky and read his destiny in patterns made by celestial bodies that he himself in less than seven days may have constructed in a shop—and despite his share in mankind's choice of making planet Earth resemble either Heaven or the Moon.

On certain idealists in politics the effects of self-awareness have been incomplete. A man of this kind holds tight to his independence in order to escape the risk of turning into an opportunist who scorns and follows his fellow men. He reminds himself to be detached and humble to avoid the mad belief of thinking himself destined to command. He keeps his high principles but may come to cherish his integrity as a pearl of greater price than its true worth, just as the value of any gift can be exaggerated when treated as an independent end.

These factors are changing politicians' mental habits less now than those of their constituents because politicians, inclined this way by their profession's emphasis on shifting personal relationships, were affected first. Three centuries ago Dryden observed that "politicians neither love nor hate."

For ages, the folly of soft blows has been warned against by wise men and avoided by the shrewd. Machiavelli observed that failure to con-

ciliate or destroy enemies was to court loss of office
at least. Emerson reminded the young Holmes, who
had shown him an essay on Plato, that "when you
strike at a king you must kill him." When the
Samnites had surrounded the Roman army, they
could have put its members to the sword or mag-
nanimously set them free. Instead, the Samnites let
the army go, after leading it under a yoke as a
gesture of disgrace. It marched back to Rome, smart-
ing for the revenge that in time it took.

But in the dealings with each other political
enemies have grown less hostile, less capable of
great harm, and less susceptible to be won over as
trusted friends. One's antagonists—the word *enemy*
is too strong to be accurate—are less often individuals than groups. A politician no longer can deal
with an opponent as though he were a wild animal.
For a politician to destroy an opponent is a function
that modern ways have made as out of date as for a
businessman to ruin a competitor. Now halfway
measures are the sensible and customary course.
And halfway measures have become composed of
persistent, smiling pressure, instead of blows that
wound but do not kill.

People have a softer shell and a more im-
permeable core than they once had. Despite their
closer surface contact with each other, their relationships are seldom deeply intimate or ardent,
although a degree of intimacy is given by the new
candor of personal style. Of those who now make
personal relationships the central aspect of their
work many come no more to grips with other people

than did those persons in the past whose attention was fixed on the ideas or things that were the subjects of their work. People erase gradations of familiarity by addressing each other by their given names after a slight acquaintance. Going in the same direction, all people now are coming to resemble politicians in these attitudes. Citizen and politician may give each other greater sympathy because they share some of the same problems and experiences resulting from a multitude of superficial relationships. The diminishing difference in attitude between politician and private citizen and the merger of the politician's functions with those of business and military leaders, making the subject matter of their work more alike, bring their outlooks even closer. Politicians' present attitudes are being adopted by other leaders and by Everyman as well.

Now politics and private life are not so far apart, and a politician's mental adjustment is relatively slight in passing back or forth. The transition in and out of marriage illustrates a similar trend. The distance between the single and married states has narrowed, and the step across is less abrupt.

The modern American politician has the qualities of caution, discretion, tolerance and moderation. Nations are shifting from war to other means to get their way. Politics displays a similar decline in the use of tooth and claw. Personal ties are bent but rarely broken. Elastic negotiators take the place of implacable foes. In contrast to the Emperor Otho, "who acted the slave to make himself the master," a modern politician is a good fellow both before and after election day. In character and attitude he is the opposite of those mailed and clanking knights of the Crusades who fought for God, for glory and for fun.

Chapter | 11

HONESTY

A politician rarely is diverted from the path of right by pursuit of immoral pleasure or illegal gain. His weaknesses take other forms. Standards of money honesty are higher than in business because making money is not such a compelling motive among politicians, and a larger proportion of their financial transactions is subject to public scrutiny. One does not enter politics if his chief aim is to get money for nothing, or even for something. The most able politicians, though stupendous blends of energy, purpose and brains, have been uninterested in money and did not make much. The greatest political leader produced by the Medici family left its riches much reduced.

Money honesty in politics is less important than it was. Society is richer, so it more easily can afford some loss by theft. There is less temptation to steal, and less theft, than when it was harder to earn a good living by working for it, and before thorough record keeping and efficient law enforcement methods increased the odds of being detected. The penalties are not as severe as in the past, but one still is ruined if caught.

A politician has several ways to steal: Take bribes, take from the public treasury, extort money from subordinates whom he has the power to fire, pocket the excess of campaign contributions over sums spent, and engage in speculative trading based on his knowledge of future governmental acts. None of these crimes but the last, which is detectable in other ways, can be committed without the help of other people, whose knowledge increases the risk of his being caught, and whose apprehensions deter them from taking part, and thus make it difficult for the politician to find his indispensable accomplice. Like illegal gambling, the principal vice of politicians' money dishonesty is its degradation of public officials and the consequent loss of confidence in government.

As they have reduced the public injury done by a politician's theft, modern conditions likewise have increased the harm done by his untruth. American politicians' chief moral problem is maintaining intellectual honesty. A free society cannot operate unless leaders tell the truth to the led, and when they cease to be honest with each other as well the fabric of organized society dissolves. For the wheels to turn words have to be trusted. Life is too short for every statement to be put on paper before a notary and under oath. Thomas Browne wrote, "Do the devils lie? No; for then Hell could not subsist." And Montaigne:

> We are not men, nor have other tie upon one another, but by our word. . . . Since mutual understanding is brought about solely by way of words, he who breaks his word betrays human society. It is the only instrument by means of which our wills and thoughts communicate, it is

the interpreter of our soul. If it fails us we have no more hold on each other, no more knowledge of each other. If it deceives us, it breaks up all our relations and dissolves all the bonds of our society.

For the process to succeed, not only must truth be told but the listener must accept it as such. A story introduced by "A funny thing happened to me on the way here" misleads nobody. Nor is the truth expected from one who is offered the indulgence of departing from it. After the Battle of the Granicus, Alexander visited his wounded soldiers, "asking each man how and in what circumstances his wound was received, and allowing him to tell his story and exaggerate as much as he pleased." But in contrast to statements made for entertainment, sympathy or therapy, where not expecting truth does no harm, the value of serious words by or to a politician is impaired by a recipient's disbelief, because truth is useless if offered but not taken. A political speaker often is disheartened by his sense that his listeners may give him their attention but not their trust.

Alexander declared that a king "is on duty bound to speak nothing but the truth to his subjects, who, in their turn, have no right to suppose that he ever does otherwise." Although this aristocratic attitude no longer will do, since the equality of conditions that we achieve for our society probably should not except moral standards, nonetheless the conformity of moral norms to degrees of influence suggests the utility of expecting much honesty from those whose words so deeply affect our lives. Although average levels of honesty among people are higher, the public need for it from politicians has grown further than the standards of practice have gone up.

Among politicians the principal means of deceit are promises, charges of crime and manipulating to substitute pleasing diversions for truth. Failure to keep a campaign promise is not a serious wrong where it reflects no more than some unexpected change of circumstance or the difference between capacity and hopes. But to assure a result in the knowledge that it is unattainable is a fraud. An example is to promise in the same breath a balanced budget, lower taxes, full employment, and enough armed force to intimidate the strongest foreign state.

In the name of patriotism, some leaders in and out of government abuse their power and the leverage of the public trust by accusing people of crimes they did not commit. Such were the charges that China was given away and that Dean Acheson and George Marshall were patrons of traitors. In addition to the wrong suffered by the victims, these injuries done as official acts shake public faith that our government is just.

The third form of deceit uses group suggestion to instill false beliefs. Like other kinds of dishonesty, it impairs freedom. In the past, the phrase "free thought" meant little because government was irrelevant to it, social practice did not impair it, and psychology was not known. Whatever value it deserved, no one trespassed on it. No risk arose until the thought was expressed. Dr. Johnson said, "Every man has a physical right to think as he pleases; for it cannot be discovered how he thinks." Now, however, free thought has become an issue because much can be done to interfere with it. We have learned the falsity of the old assumption that everyone is unfettered in his thoughts, no matter what restriction may be imposed on his rights to express them. No longer can a person reassure himself that "come what may, I shall be undisputed master in the castle of my skin."

Slogans are used as substitutes for policy or masks for lack of policy. One slogan is picked up when the last wears thin, as in jumping from log to log across a mill pond. The fault is not in the use of symbols but in their falsity. The system is to lull or excite fears, reiterate plausible fictions until they seem true, and omit important facts. It turns attention from rather than toward problems or makes people content with what is. The result denies citizens the understanding they need to pass the judgments that are essential to the democratic process. In the past, leaders tried to solve public problems, even though with a class bias. Supplying illusions instead of solutions, the new approach lets a problem lie and induces people to think it does not exist or that things are better as they are. In case of a fresh water shortage, instead of trying to convert salt water to fresh, the preference would be to convince people that the sea had the better taste.

The growing appetite for entertainment in politics and education may soften resistance to being deluded while amused, because when we are entertained we enjoy, or do not mind, being fooled. Many of those engaged in making taste and opinion, except for a few old-fashioned publishers, so dread being disliked that they would be willing to tell the truth in trade for love, but there is little evidence that many people dislike them for their deceit.

Yet government of the many by the few would not be a oneway street for long, because the few would become conditioned by their own methods of control. In the past, thought and immediate power were separate. The training of manhood for violent force excluded thought, while beyond a point cultivation of the mind made one less willing to face a gleam of steel. It is said that when the Goths were sacking Greece they decided not to burn the libraries because they thought that reading books would keep the Greeks from the practice of arms. Now, for a group to be strong and effective its decisions must be made by persons who think. The men and women who have the skills to make and use dreadful weapons, to manage big organizations, and to suggest taste and action to the multitude all think. Their own routines, propensities and values inhibit them from bloodshed and coercion. Today's most powerful Americans have been produced by a training system that would never make a Mucius Scaevola or a Mohawk chief.

Control at first might be attained by

hardboiled gangs. But the nature of the work is such that their members would become, or be succeeded by, affable and sympathetic types engrossed in their relationships with others. Hardly anyone has strength enough to combine ruthlessness with sensitive concern for others' tastes and wishes. Desires and thoughts would be passed back and forth between the many and the few, and altered by each group during passage of a circuit. Dropping the role of parent and assuming the role of pal, the few would cease to be operators of an engine and would become influential players in a serious game. They would deal with the many as a chess expert takes on several players at once, each move he makes being partly determined by his opponents' preceding moves. Like advertising writers, and some teachers of English, who prefer to reflect rather than correct their audience's grammar, these persons would conform themselves to others as much as they would mold them. As to what might happen after that I dare not speculate.

A concerted policy of deceit has the safety for us of being conspicuous. If the worst comes, it may be some other evil. After a while perhaps the pragmatists will recognize honesty's value in their own terms. Intrepid skeptics guard against invasion of our minds. There are more among us than is apparent, because those who cannot speak well or do not care to talk fail to reveal their defenses to a selling pitch, although among persons who proclaim their doubt of authorities, some of those who think cynicism a more sophisticated pose than enthusiasm are guided easily by suggestion toward unreasoned beliefs.

Problems too big to be avoided by pretending their nonexistence provide another limit to this dangerous trend. To hurdle such a problem a politician requires skills for more than tranquilizing the masses. Consent cannot be obtained for sacrifice unless people are told the bad news. When at last the facts reach them through insulating layers that have been put around them, people often replace politicians who have failed either to meet these problems, which cannot be exorcised, or to tell people the truth about them.

In politics, the truth is violated by three personality types. To ideologues, truth may be something to be bent or brushed aside in the cause of an allegedly "higher" truth. To opportunists, without the ideologues' parentalism and often without their arrogance, truth is irrelevant. Advertising and public relations agencies have been among the chief institutional exponents of this attitude, treating public problems as soap to be sold rather than knots to be untied, handling the issues of employment and peace in the way they push the sales of ointment to make hair come off or oil to make it come in. The occupants of the Nixon White House were concerned with what was called credibility but what actually was obtaining credence. Of Lysander it was written:

. . . not judging truth to be in nature better than falsehood, but setting a value on both according to interest. He would laugh at those who thought Hercules' posterity ought not to use deceit in war: "For where the lion's skin will not reach, you must patch it out with the fox's" . . . he who overreaches by an oath admits that he fears his enemy, while he despises his god.

The third type is the self-deceivers. Because it takes less effort to pretend that ours is a splendid world than to make it so, many people have taken comfort in shaping their beliefs to conform to their tastes rather than to their observations. In the absence of accepted values another motive to manipulate oneself is the growing reluctance to pass judgment on other people, a preference to pluck (in a painless way) the mote from one's own eye. A century ago, although scattered philosophers believed this the best of all possible worlds (and everything in it only a necessary evil), although Mary Baker Eddy and her disciples refused even to believe that evil existed, and although Tom Sawyer's Aunt Polly believed in health-fad pamphlets about "what frame of mind to keep one's self in," the stern conditions of existence made such magic tricks difficult, so that many people who found the world hard to swallow resorted instead to belief in an afterlife. Now that earthly distractions and sophistication have dulled the hunger for pie in the sky, and yet few are happy, self-deception concentrates on the here and now. The moral uncertainties with which a politician must forever deal make self-deception insidiously seductive, and one of its most pernicious aspects is to confuse the meanings of "is" and "ought." This lazy equation supports the philosophy of power for its own sake, the belief that might is right.

Courage is a condition not only to taking the right action but to the preliminary step of facing up to the truth in one's mind. As one of Stendhal's characters is described: "Sometimes her ardent imagination concealed things from her, but never did she have those deliberate illusions which cowardice induces."

The aspect of truthfulness embodied in fairness is important and attainable, although it matters less for a politician than for a journalist or a judge. Not everyone now is convinced that such a goal can even be approached. Concern is shifting from the measurement of actuality to the alteration—or "correction"—of the audience's feelings about it. In a sense this corresponds to a broader shift of attitude. We always look at life as a relation between ourselves and the things around us. Of late the main attention has been shifting to our own reactions to things and away from objective truth about the world, so that an individual's attitude toward his experience shifts from whether the thing was right or wrong, true or false, toward whether it pleased or disappointed him. This point of emphasis may be as sound as tilting it the other way.

Some people, however, carry this view to solipsistic error, licensing themselves to practice, in Burckhardt's phrase, "unbridled subjectivity." They conclude, "Fairness is impossible; everyone is so sunk in subjectivity that he never expresses more than his own personality; when people make a declaration of asserted fact, they no more than sing a sort of song that can be enjoyed as art, but no matter how beautiful cannot be characterized as true; therefore I might as well drop fairness and let loose with polemics to make myself feel good by combining a sense that I am candid with a sense that I am right." This is not so. Although absolute truth is unattainable, certainty hopeless to yearn for, and philosophic truth perhaps an empty conception, practical truth about things in the world is possible, and a free society depends on its diligent pursuit. For example, in June, 1950, an invasion took place in Korea. Some news reports claimed it went from south to north and others that it went from north to south. One set of reports happened to be true, and the other happened to be false. They were not to be dismissed as simply expressions of personal bias. A comparison between Saint Louis of France and Richard I of England as to which was the more valiant can no more be determined than an argument about whether Stanley Ketchell could have beaten Ray Robinson, but some things can be verified with enough certainty to justify asserting them. Egyptians did build pyramids. The Plague raised the wages of English farm laborers who survived it. Adoption of the stirrup shifted power from a large number of foot soldiers to a few men on horseback by giving them leverage to swing a heavy sword. It is hard to think that the Union would have survived the slavery crisis if John Marshall had not served as he did.

Among scholars of jurisprudence, some of the realism school, in pointing out that the law is shaped by judges, frail mortals all, have gone so far as to claim that a decision may depend on what the judge ate for breakfast. But although total detachment is not possible, fairness is, in both politics and the law. Justice Frankfurter wrote:

> There is a good deal of shallow talk that the judicial robe does not change the man within it. It does. The fact is that on the whole judges do lay aside private views in discharging their judicial functions. This is achieved through training, professional habits, self-discipline and that fortunate alchemy by which men are loyal to the obligation with which they are entrusted.

Like a judge who does not believe the common law to be a brooding omnipresence that he thinks he applies mechanically, yet who decides cases justly, a journalist can abandon the pretense of pure objectivity, yet be fair in what he reports and interprets. Knowing he is not a machine need not sap his zest and confidence to seek, discover, select, clarify and explain, and to do all as a servant of the truth.

The politician's function does not call on

him to exercise the detachment of a journalist or judge. But he can and should be fair and level with the people who look to him, helped to do so by his sense of his professional role and by citizens who remember they can learn more from him if they let him know they will tolerate straight talk. When a messenger brought Tigranes word that Lucullus was advancing at the head of his army, the king had the messenger's head cut off. After that, since no one told him further news of military operations, he suffered the consequences of his ignorance.

Churchill wrote that in 1940, at the end of the day when he had been appointed Prime Minister, as the concentrated might of German arms descended on his island, he lay down to dreamless sleep, because "facts are better than dreams." Will enough people, exercising their finer hours, insist on facts instead of dreams. To multiply this vital number what should honest men and women do? A condition of honesty is the practice of rationality. In this perplexing time, the pendulum first swung far toward authority, and many sought shelter in some absolutist creed. Lately it has swung toward the other end of its arc, an uneasy agnosticism and unwillingness to be committed, varied sometimes by peevish nihilism. Faith in rationality will be required to steer between the comfortable certainties of ignorance and absolute belief. But "our prejudices are our mistresses; reason is at best our wife, very often heard indeed, but seldom minded."

Among those who expect little of reason, a few are in desperate earnest like Pascal, overwhelmed by a universe not much of which reason can comprehend, but now some people go much further, claiming that rational approaches to the truth and to other people are futile because our minds are governed by mindless inner forces. These people are characterized by snobbery or by romantic savagery. The snobs manipulate others by irrational means, while they use rationality in writing what they publish and in directing their lives, thinking it fitting that they guide their own course with clear thought, while those folk whom they manipulate bumble around without it. The romantic savages try to live according to impulse without reason. They abdicate, letting others carry the burden of operating the society with all the powers of reason allotted them. Perhaps a third group will try to go a step further by living the life of spontaneous impulse and trying to apply it to others as well. The snobs are disgusting and menacing, the romantic savages are pathetic, and if the third group failed it would be funny, but if it succeeded, it would not.

In seventeenth-century England, belief in witchcraft and magic was widespread. The world was bewildering and starting to change fast; one did not need wealth or status to have visions. Perhaps now the more ignorant people will turn to forms of magic and other irrational means of predicting and explaining life. Although for the well-educated, the causality of physical process is more observable (except for atoms), and predictable than it was, for the rest it is not. Because the faster change in social practices baffles most of us, many wish for guidance. Irrationality offers current appeal to some in the middle range of brains and education, more sensitive than able, who turn away from rationality. Joined in popularity to the old favorite alcohol are other drugs and astrology, the occult, undirected meditation, Eastern mysticism, ad hoc Christian-type evangelism, the politics of violence, the politics of abuse. An understandable reaction against an arid rationality that guides the practices of some powerful men and institutions, it is mistaken, I think. Others may be equally in the dark, but they know enough at least to see the impotence of the irrational as a tool to solve our problems or a lens through which to see life properly explained.

If rational thought has no more use than these people think, what are we to do, stop thinking? In dealing with other people— whether through a mass medium or person to person—should we (like the snobs) use an irrational approach, giving others no credit for ability to reason or to appreciate reason? If we use reason to develop our irrational approach to others, how do we justify the inconsistency? If we cannot, should we act consistently and practice irrationality (like the romantic savages)? At what point, if any, does thought belong?

We do not know whether the truth will make us free, or even whether personal freedom exists, or, if it does, what it is, or whether it is what we think good or can attain. However, we will deny ourselves a chance to find out about these things unless we order our society so that minds can be open and in touch with each other for the production and exchange of thought. It is given to us to perceive such a small part of what is. Although our minds are subject to distorting (sometimes illuminating) pressure from passion, interest, appetite and habit, and from civil war with the subconscious, I still would place my bets on rational discussion as our best hope and as essential to what we want, although not the only path to some of the things we seek.

Chapter | *12*

AN ARSENAL OF CIVIC ASSETS

Here is a catalogue of virtues, skills and attitudes that an American politician needs in the late twentieth century in order better to lead a government of free people. The possessor of all these assets is the answer to a good citizen's prayer and would fit the terms of a convention nominating speech. Some of our politicians have many of them in high degree, so this ideal does not insult the real. Although some of these characteristics may help a politician toward success either through personal satisfaction or through rewards from others, the common element of the items on this list is that they enable her to do good works.

A politician needs a sense of history to avoid living only in the present and therefore assuming either that his own epoch is eternal, that it is easy to transform, or that it can be insulated from change. Without awareness of the past and future he lacks the standard of judgment that can protect him from measures that are excessively radical (does he know how many just or happy commonwealths have been brought to pass by slaughter of leaders or enactment of a new code of laws?) or reactionary (will he be like the trembling purchasers of full-page ads proclaiming that forty days remained in which to save their country's way of life?). To the sense should be joined some knowledge. No one with knowledge of our country's history could have thought, as some prominent men at the time declared, that our greatest constitutional crisis was presented by the problem of devising prompt but constitutional means to extirpate the Nixon gang.

Toward the same end of perspective, a politician needs an inner life with a system of principles for his direction. This is both important and rare. The intensity of contemporary stresses makes some sensitive and thoughtful persons crumble or turn inward, leaving the field to nimble men who are directed by ambition and the pleasure of their peers rather than by constructive guides. They are undented by the forces to which they yield, unaware of the strains, and indifferent to the public good. To be wiser and more effective, a politician has to take pains to be a whole person. To keep an outlook of freedom and wide horizons, he must do three things: At intervals, he must take time for reflection under conditions of peace and leisure; he must have a few friends who care neither about politics nor about his personal success; and he must practice some diversion unrelated to his work. Unless he exists as a distinct person he cannot be much use to others or much pleasure to himself.

From Moses to Mohammed to Nehru and Mao, few leaders have struggled to success and had a broad and long conception of the world who did not first pass through a period of forced and painful solitude in adult life. This element of growth is harder to acquire in the United States than abroad in conjunction with success of a kind that depends on concentrated activity. One who stops to reflect may not catch up, and if he does resume the challenge round of competition he needs an excuse for his quiet time, such as an attack of polio, to save him from rejection for being odd.

In the course of a political career several returns to private life will disorder a politician's routine yet offer him a chance to give better service when he is in office. The result is to follow two careers, practiced in alternation, one public and one private. These latter sojourns, which do not have to be in obscurity but should be free from pressure, enable a politician better to contend with the present by not having to live in it continually. Charles de Gaulle observed that men in power tend to be denied time for more than a few minutes' consecutive thought. Living a hopped-up version of what E. M. Forster called the "life of telegrams and anger," a politician finds his reading time is short. Because he must concentrate on immediate problems, almost all his study is consumed by periodicals and technical and staff reports. (Politicians who read more broadly, like Churchill, Theodore Roosevelt and Lorenzo the Magnificent, are exceptions too few to matter.) He lacks time to digest information and conclusions about longer periods when he must bolt each day's raw facts.

A philosopher-politician is a personality of which I cannot conceive and for which I therefore cannot hope. But a politician enabled by periods of tranquillity to improve his perspective and retain his identity is both possible and to be desired.

A sense of history, an inner life and periods free from responsibility for daily decisions all give a politician sounder judgment; they moderate his policies and help him to make their direction definite and realistic. A person who remains in the commotion of meeting daily problems cannot be committed to anything but action for its own sake or a temporary survival on other people's terms. One can be aloof without ever being committed but one cannot become committed to any significant end without from time to time being aloof.

Shaw called democracy a device that insures that people are governed no better than they deserve. Whether they are is no business of a politician. He has no right to say to people, as though he were a fireman standing with his hose and looking at a burning house outside the city limits, "Everything I give you beyond this point exceeds my duty and puts you in debt to me." A deserving constituency should get a politician whose ego is in close balance, with that self-esteem that a person must have to act with his full force, yet without the notion that he stands at the center of the universe, a notion that distorts a person's judgment and morals by fixing his eyes on himself. He has a will to win, but curbs his thirst for glory and crusading spirit to permit the detachment necessary to act in a way that is wise and good. While speaking about John Marshall, Justice Holmes said:

A man is bound to be parochial in his practice—to give his life, and if necessary his death, for the place where he has his roots. But his thinking should be cosmopolitan and detached. He should be able to criticize what he reveres and loves.

And Learned Hand wrote:

And what is wisdom—that gift of God which the great prophets of his [Cardozo's] race exalted? I do not know; like you, I know it when I see it, but I cannot tell of what it is composed. One ingredient I do know: the wise man is the detached man.

But these two judges were discussing two other judges. Regardless of his aptitude, a politician's working conditions probably bar him from becoming truly wise. No one wants him to become wholly detached, nor is there a risk that he will. But such detachment as he can attain may help move him a few notches from shrewdness toward wisdom.

This imagined politician does not forget that, as Dr. Johnson wrote: "In political regulation, good cannot be complete, it can only be predominant." He/she does not enter a suicide pact with a lost cause, but will submit to humble compromise to trade a halfway measure for half a loaf. His attitude contrasts with the adolescent martyrdom of one who suffers total defeat by inflexible devotion to his plan because he puts his pride or self-pity above his conception of the public interest, while pretending to put principle first, pretending he would rather be right than useful, though in political terms he is not even right.

This imagined superior politician's own mind directs his acts, yet like most men he is a political animal, not a member of a more solitary species, like the great cats. The public opinion polls are not his compass needle. His constituents influence but do not own him. He does not think he is the Great White Father figure leading the scorned masses beside the still waters of social security. He may prefer three cheers to three meals, but he is immune to that pernicious disease that attacks an otherwise able leader whose outlook is immature and woolly: First worshipping the cheering crowd; then, as he sees himself reflected in their eyes, coming to believe himself the proper object of their worship.

A politician should be able to reach a decision and stick to it long enough for the people whom he affects to act on it. For the process of compromise to be a constructive element of democratic government a politician must interrupt it periodically and steer a straight line which enables other people to take directed action. Otherwise they cannot know where they stand or what is practical or safe to do. Whether his problem is a budget, an arms control plan or a zoning code, a politician should know when to halt deliberation and fix his course. Only if others can count on him to hold fast once in a while can they proceed in reference to him, pick up speed and make some distance before his course is changed again. That part of government touched by a politician suffers if he never ceases to alter his position according to the moment-by-moment resolution of forces upon each other and upon him.

To do justice, government must combine certainty and continuity with adjustment to clashing interests and shifting conditions. A politician ought to alternate between sensitive responsiveness to changing needs and wishes and a firm course with a measurable bearing and rate. The pressures upon a politician join with lack of standards, much less rules, to bear upon his decisions, making this alternation difficult to do well. It is less difficult if he has an integrated personality, free from irrational fears or prejudices. One who has what we call integrity seems to be more free than the rest of us. Unless armed with inner security, a politician reacts to the pressures—turbulent, shifting and strong—in one of two ways. Either he swoops, careens and swerves or, to stabilize himself, he builds walls through which the pressures become faint enough not to jostle him, but in his hermetic cell he loses that intercourse essential to his function.

A character that is distinct and firm reflects as well as causes a free and independent course. Once wooden ships helped make iron men, but today's mild conditions do little directly to shape an aimed character. Circumstances now are easier to bypass and softer when struck. We avoid them when we can, and sustain more gentle bumps when we cannot. Upholstered boulders in the path must be hit harder now to raise a welt.

As always, a willingness to follow a collision course with other persons and ideas, and to proceed on it with vigor, is the only means by which a straight course can be achieved. The clemency of our surroundings has not eased this task, because it lets our skin stay thin. Opposing pressure from other people has remained relentless, although it is more smooth. To plow through ice floes of circumstance is arduous and painful still; they are softer, but so are we. Not only were former circumstances more harsh, but one was driven against them by his impulse to survive and live in comfort. A man used to collide with circumstances by trying either to master them or to avoid others. They resembled a spinning grindstone against which one had only to lean in order to acquire an edge. Modern conditions are more like a whetstone, sharpening character by the same clash but receiving their force from the person, who is impelled by other voices which he hears and heeds. Their own scarcity raises the value of those people who strengthen their characters by generating their own adversity, those whose own direction and efforts take up the slack left by their forerunners who have made our living soft and safe.

If a politician has no loyalties, he is useless. If his loyalties do not relate to the real needs of the day, his quality may be touching but not useful. In a scarcity economy Lycurgus ceased to eat in order to achieve his death by means of service to the state; but now such abstention would not make one's memory revered. He gives better service if his loyalties are divided and if they are graded in order of their value to the public interest. If his loyalty is attached to a single object, he is likely to do harm. His first preference should be to his principles and to all the people to whom his unit of government is responsible. This group should rank above his constituency if the two are not identical; that is, if his constituency is a part of the larger whole, as is the case for most legislators. If he loves his policies as himself he may ignore their defects and continue to cling to them after they have become obsolete. On the other hand, the public interest suffers if his friends come first.

But for his decisions to be untouched by friendship impairs his service. The supporters of such a politician may be fewer in number, and therefore as a unit less effective in his cause, than the group surrounding a politician who cares enough about his friends to stand by them to some extent. At the same time this smaller group of supporters is composed of a larger than normal proportion of fanatic types who adhere to him, not from affection but from devotion to his policies and devotion to him for his attachment to his policies. Their backing and counsel warp his judgment.

✧ ✧ ✧

He needs to remember the excesses of his own approach to public policy, so he can counteract them, like a golfer aware that he tends to slice. A liberal should resist the "tyrannical tendency of ideas," while a conservative should stop short of the "suicidal emptiness of a politics without ideas," to use the phrases of Alexander Bickel. If he is a liberal he should try not to overlook the complexity of circumstance which must be recognized if he is to be effective and fair. If he is a conservative he should remember that just because the totality of circumstance constitutes a realistic postulate for his thinking it does not follow that nothing can be altered. If he is conservative, he should not try to respond to a modest proposal for action by heaping concrete, technical objections until everyone gives up on the matter. If he is a liberal, he should abjure the counterpart vice of sweeping aside details, abdicating from the hard and limit-acknowledging process of thinking through a solution that will work.

For the headstrong, in Kingman Brewster's words, "Ambition shifts into the high gear of arrogance." And for the unprincipled, excessive ambition can lead to unchecked ruthlessness. But as a support or substitute for character in politicians, a moderate ambition has value that a voter should not scorn. It makes a man assume some virtues that he lacks. An ambitious politician knows that his practice of them does more to advance or support his success than mere verbal tributes to good. He knows that honesty is a good policy. The wish for future

trust and recognition spurs him to work, and re-
strains his grasp from exceeding his legitimate reach.
Unless he has exceptional strength of character, a
politician without hope of some reward beyond that
which inheres in virtue is likely to be dangerous or
useless. As a marriage can be held together by
character in the absence of love, so by moderate
ambition in the place of character the commonwealth
can be assisted, if not sustained.

A politician should have a conception of his
office that is both clear and high. Harry Truman
and Louis XIV offset deficiencies of ability with
their awareness of what it meant, respectively, to
serve as president of the United States and to rule as
king of France. Alexander's elevated conception of
his role as possessor of genius and a crown was his
principal protection from excesses of prodigious
success. His aim was not to do justice, please the
people, right wrongs, maintain tradition, defend
liberty or uphold the laws. Nor was it much for
aggrandizement, although that suited him pretty
well. It was to fulfill his self-image of nobility. As he
blazed his dazzling course his treatment of the
power that he gathered to himself was tempered by
his pursuit of glory. At every step of conquest his
actions were made more constructive and enduring
by his resolve to behave not as a conqueror but as a
noble king.

On entering the presidency, a man will raise

the level of his performance unless he does not clearly understand what is expected of him. (The rule is tested when one comes along who is so insensitive, insecure and insulated that he is untouched and remains a swine.) Not only is he inspired to surpass himself, he is freed from concern for self-preservation and, on the whole, from temptation to promote immediate selfish aims. This owes to the warning that could be displayed above the White House door: "Abandon hope of further advancement (except in history books) ye who enter here." As John Kennedy was leaving a room with a former occupant of the house, he stepped aside with habitual courtesy to allow his venerated guest to precede him through the door. She stopped and told him, "You go first, you are the President." He smiled and acknowledged, "I keep forgetting." And in her humble, unmusical voice she reminded him: "You must never forget."

A politician ought to educate. Powers of advocacy are needed, of course. Mr. Truman's conduct of the presidency suffered from his lack of them. Despite his "bully pulpit," some of his best proposals failed because he could not convince his constituents of their worth. But such powers are not enough. They can achieve superficial persuasion but not enduring understanding. Sometimes eloquence lets you carry people away against their better judgment. By teaching, you make them harder to deceive. Unless you plan to fool them, for them to be sophisticated is no threat.

In order that they may comprehend their society and deal with it as citizens, people need facts. Rebecca West wrote:

> It is the presentation of the facts that matter, the facts that put together are the face of the age. . . . For if people do not have the face of the age set clearly before them they begin to imagine it; and fantasy, if not disciplined by the intellect and kept in faith with reality by the instinct of art, dwells among the wishes and fears of childhood, and so sees life either as simply answering any prayer or as endlessly emitting nightmare monsters from a womb-like cave.

But although politicians must learn facts, they need not convey them to their constituents. Insofar as the media tell the truth, citizens are better informed about public affairs than ever before because the news is more thoroughly covered and widely distributed. People are offered more facts than they can consume. When scattered, facts do not educate. Holmes wrote to Harold Laski, "A fact taken in its isolation is gossip." When a politician teaches, the only information he needs to supply is what has been omitted by the media that his audience receives. It behooves him not to inform but to interpret: to marshal facts, digest them and relate them to his community, showing how events and conditions there relate to the world, outward in space, backward in history and forward in possibility.

Some politicians ignore their teaching function and do not try to exercise it, but, regardless of intention or awareness, all teach something by example of character and conduct. A politician can teach at least as well as schoolteachers those things that are within his experience. In a single talk on television he may reach a larger number than Mr. Chips taught in his lifetime.

Citizens' comprehension may enable them better to form the basic policy which is passed back to the politician to be translated into legislation or administration. For a person to favor another's action—and thus support the actor—he must think it will satisfy some want, whether material or emotional. Insofar as his constituents understand what a politician is trying to do (provided they like what they learn) the more willingly they may support him. When he seeks to serve his constituency by indirection, aiding outsiders or the unborn toward the end of benefits flowing back to his constituency in a circular process, he remembers that he never can win a single vote from anyone but his constituents, who are here and now. People may know what they like, but a politician can help them comprehend those long causal chains through which doing things for impact far away in time or space may satisfy their long-range wants.

The value of intelligence and education in

politicians is more clearly established than some people realize. The risk of mob rule is mitigated by organized society's need for superior thought. In the past, although intelligence and knowledge were required for advances in knowledge, what it took to make the world turn were capacity to lead, force of character, valor and fortitude. "In heroic times, the general was the strongest man; in civilized times, he is the most intelligent of the brave." And the value of intelligence has risen since Napoleon said this. Now, day by day, society must have first-rate thinking and will pay for it with almost all the rewards for which an intelligent person may ask.

Popular hostility to trained minds is reduced as hereditary privilege declines and education spreads. In 1968 and 1972 none of the major party nominees for president or vice president had failed to earn an advanced degree. The cadre of Rhodes Scholars in Congress and the electoral successes of foreign leaders like d'Estaing and Trudeau show further acceptance of educated politicians. Many people in the advance guard of thought are overly pessimistic because they do not appreciate the prospects for further decline in fear of (as well as reverence for) learning as the masses free themselves from ancient superstition, as their leaders have done. As the mystery disappears, the fear and awe tend to be replaced by respect, although scorn for disinterested intelligence and resentment of evident brains have not abated. Politicians will continue to deal with scientific matters that most people will not understand, but a politician will not be resented

for these arcana because they will be no more compre-
hended by him than by any other people who are not
scientists; he merely will use them, knowing something of what they can do though not how they work.

Imagination is an important quality in a
politician. In public affairs, all things under the sun
have been connected in a causal web. Not long ago,
if a politician could understand what was before his
eyes and within his experience, he could handle his
job. It stood within these horizons. Now he must
see far beyond.

In one type of public man vision is short,
although his sight is clear in the clean, well-lighted
room of his philosophy. He sees government in
terms of administrative competence and the balance
sheet. Another type sees it in terms of each person's
dignity, singularity and capacity to exceed himself.
One bases policy on hopes, the other on regrets. As
a symbol of political outlook a rainbow is better
than a ledger. Politics needs both.

A politician need not be an original thinker,
but a new idea should not make him flinch. In
proposals for action, his thought need be only just
far enough ahead of his time to be within the understanding of his constituents, yet beyond their natural
vision. Any more is a dangerous adornment of little
use and likely to frustrate him, while to fall short
keeps him from being a leader, although he may be
a success. He should not be a "pioneer of pioneers,"

as Parkman described LaSalle. If he should come to believe the wisdom of some advanced idea for action he should keep it to himself until the time comes, if ever, when he may advocate it without making too many of his listeners angry, bewildered or afraid. He ought to propose an attainable end, one to which the voters probably can be persuaded to go. When Solon was asked if he had left the Athenians the best laws that could be given, he replied, "The best they could receive." Woodrow Wilson wrote of Burke, "He went on from the wisdom of today to the wisdom of tomorrow, to the wisdom which is for all time; and it was impossible he should be followed so far. . . . If you would be a leader of men, you must lead your own generation, not the next."

The intellectual abilities of a nonpolitical manager of affairs are mainly ones of judgment, the accurate prediction of events, that is, accurate measurement of *probabilities*, while the creative thinker's intellectual abilities are mainly discerning in nature and humanity what are the *possibilities*. Creative thinkers shape more than their share of history, but judgment is what the world pays for and what it looks for when it votes. The manager's work is governed by his worst moments as in the case of a golf or chess player, while the creative person's work is governed by his best moments, since he has only an indifferent universe as an opponent, one which will wait for him and when he stumbles will not pounce. A politician's role belongs on the boundary between the two types, since his power of decisive social action and power to intrude—if not impose—ideas on people is joined to an indirect creative process upon ideas that he arranges and selects.

A free government requires that some of its politicians be willing to try new ideas. Some intellectually mature politicians are indifferent to new ideas for action, even though unafraid of them. Their freedom from illusions about the nature of the world is often coupled with a reluctance to experiment because they doubt whether a proposed change of course will work or do good. Among some politicians this common distaste for trying new ideas is partly inherent in maturity and partly because to obtain mature politicians people often elect old ones; age and maturity combine to strengthen the preference for habitual patterns. Old, mature men who have lost passion, vigor and illusions tend to be not only temperate and sensible but also bound by a taste for the tried and, so far, true. Even more than most old men, temperamentally disposed by age to favor (or at least accept) things as they are more than young men do, an old politician tends to be averse to novel policy. He has a reputation to lose, and it may be lost less through inaction than through committed mistakes, while by some daring action a young man's reputation may be swiftly made.

A politician should be able to combine his measures for immediate action with a glimpse of long-range goals. The "conquest of space" is one target that may be erected. In logic this phrase, which calls on us to dominate infinity, is of course absurd. And yet if taken as a direction, one which is not to apply to any sapient beings whom we might meet in outer space, and to whom we would not wish to play the conquistador, this phrase seems merely presumptuous, like every admirable aim. After all, a worthy challenge to the human race may be to conquer something that it cannot even comprehend. When a politician points to far-off realms of gold, he must make clear that he is aiming at ideals, not calling for immediate action, that he is urging a course or a change of course, not a running jump into the distance. He may and should hold up a star for his constituents, but he has to leave no doubt that it is a long way from his and their wagon.

He dare not propose, or even reveal that he foresees, a state of things that contradicts the hates or fears of the moment, such as friendly equality with some current enemy race or creed. For example, Isaiah safely prophesied that "the leopard shall lie down with the kid," but an American politician during World War II could not predict that shortly his constituents' sons would be bringing home brides from Japan, and until some years thereafter in some states a politician would as soon lie down with a leopard as foresee that the races would mix.

A useful end for him to urge is a tentative ideal pattern for society. This is not to propose a single step ahead of the existing path of progress, it is not to recommend more consumer goods and services for less work and with more security to maintain this condition, but a whole new framework for a way of life. A politician is both necessary and well fitted not to invent or discover utopian goals

but to proclaim and explain them. He can enable
people to evaluate their present way and, if they
find it wanting, to decide on the best alternative
target. Political talkers have long been chewing a
stale cud. In America politicians are needed who
will spell out brighter, better worlds and show us
roads for their approach. "The environment of the
twentieth century," wrote Barbara Ward Jackson,
"is designed for the men who dare greatly and
dream greatly and let their work catch up with their
dreams."

At the proper time and place, a politician has
the duty to discuss with his constituents every item
of policy in his program. But although he should
propose utopian public ends, he is wise to say nothing
of the lifetime goals he has set for himself. Who else
is much interested in them? They look grandiose
and improbable for a callow lieutenant of artillery
who has not even taken Toulon, yet if he is old, they
may seem too dampened by prudence to inspire.

In directing another person according to your
own principles, to expound your philosophy to him
often gains advantage. He can better follow your
directions if he knows the reasons on which they
rest. The importance of this process increases according to how much discretion is granted to his
role. But to proclaim to the public your personal
chart hinders you in attaining your ends. What you
say may strike some people as pompous, naive,

cynical, self-righteous, or stupid. If you later should change your mind and express your new beliefs or act according to them you may be more embarrassed by the inconsistency with the prior public declaration than you would have been by the contrast with your prior conduct alone. Montaigne wrote:

> You never speak about yourself without loss. Your self-condemnation is always accredited, your self-praise discredited . . . if I say what I plan to do, it seems to me that I prescribe it for myself, and that to give knowledge of it to another is to impose it upon myself. It seems to me that I promise it when I mention it. Thus I seldom air my plans.

To declare one's own philosophic interpretation of life's meaning may contribute to knowledge or truth. But to proclaim the principles that guide your life resembles boasting about what you are going to do. It predicts your actions—whether their achievement or their quality. A boast about the past—if a statement of fact rather than self-serving opinion—may be useful self-advertising. But because futile, a boastful forecast is childish and therefore not only useless but harmful to oneself to practice.

A politician has to take more pains to keep the remnants of his privacy than one whose daily life is less exposed. He fittingly may leave it to his conduct, insofar as it can, to reveal such ultimate, unattainable ends that he may have. He need not affect beliefs he lacks, like Henry of Navarre who decided Paris was worth a mass, but taste and discretion bid him contain those almost inexpressible thoughts.

Regardless of the end he has proposed, whether a far-off comprehensive scheme or the location of a bridge, the politician should take a stand, not confine himself to fearless endorsements of completed public works, praise of great dead men, or pronouncements like the Aztec lords' annual vow to keep the sun on its course. Otherwise, he is worth little to his constituents, and politics is not worth its cost to him.

In personal terms the price of political success is so high, and knowledge is so uncertain about its causes, that you might as well enjoy yourself by taking sides. It is not necessary that your convictions be strong. Nor do your stands have to be consistent, either in sequence on one subject or on several subjects at once. And of course you need not take a stand on every issue. But you must stand up for something in order to exist apart from the abstraction of mankind and to gain private honor from yourself. Of the Spartan kings at Thermopylae Demaratus lived longer, but most people ever since would rather have been Leonidas.

If you stand up for something you believe, you may be surprised to succeed, or at least survive. In the mysteries of the political process, the conventional wisdom is often wrong. During the dreary later days of the Fourth Republic, a French politician, tormented by inroads of American culture and Algerian arms, might regret that it would be no use for him to strap his harness on his back, rise up like Roland, resolute before the Saracen host, and sword in hand call out, "Praise God and all his holy angels, France shall never lose her name through me!" Yet one unusual man in substance did so, and did not fail.

A society cannot indulge in rational pretensions to be free unless it is equipped with politicians who seek some form of freedom for all as their fundamental end. To try to justify this proposition would add nothing here. As Fats Waller said to the young lady who asked him to define swing music, "If you gotta ask, you ain't got it."

According to his values, his opportunities, and the needs of the time, such a politician can emphasize one or more of several well-established paths toward civic freedom: preserve public order, protect the individual's property rights, treat people equally, and broaden direct latitude of individual choice. He should not forget that if given excessive scope in relation to the others, perhaps from being treated as a good in itself, each of these means may cramp freedom rather than enlarging it.

This politician so cleaves to civic freedom that he not only will fight to keep it for himself but will refuse others a right to surrender it, knowing it is not ours to give or trade away. Each of us holds it in trust, inherited from his ancestors who won it hard, and he owes a duty to his descendants not to start them off in bondage by dissipating his legacy.

> But do we great-grandchildren of the combatants really deserve to be born slaves? Are we cowards that we fear to die? No, this is a punishment for our fathers' fears.
>
> LUCAN

It cannot be thought that a person can freely choose not to be free. One who relaxes his hold on his civic freedom shows himself incompetent to equate his wishes and his interests, since with a sane awareness of his own interests he cannot wish for the later consequences of his act. I regret to cite Rousseau and Herbert Marcuse as authorities, but candor compels acknowledgment that both wrote that slaves must be made to be free.

> If it is not lawful for a man to kill himself because he robs his country of his person, for the same reason, he is not allowed to barter his freedom. . . . The lawfulness of putting a malefactor to death arises from this circumstance: the law by which he was punished was made for his security. A murderer, for instance, has enjoyed the benefit of the very law which condemns him; it has been a continual protection to him; he cannot, therefore, object to it. But it is not so with the slave. The law of slavery can never be beneficial to him; it is in all cases against him without ever having been for his advantage.
>
> MONTESQUIEU

Every citizen, being accountable for his
life to the state is still more so for his liberty, and
consequently has no title to sell it.

D'ALEMBERT

Political spokesmen for freedom need to
choose between the two principal complementary
aspects of social freedom. One may be called
"freedom from," a right to be left alone, to live some
aspects of your life in an imaginary globe within
which you may rattle around, doing your own thing
according to your whim; an irreducible minimum
latitude of thought and action; a personal zone on
which society regards itself as barred from intrud-
ing, whether to regulate, to influence, or—in some
cases—even to know.

In its modernity, "freedom from," now attracting many people, contrasts with the long history of "freedom to." This latter conception, typi-
fied in the spirit and gifts of the ancient Romans, is
the chance to give one's society direction and shape.
Lord Acton was correct in urging that freedom
depended on the right to participate in all forms of
government, including religious, so that a prohibition of authority in church government denied a
person full religious freedom. Freedom is narrowed
unless one may take part in social action organizations of all kinds by free association, both to influence conventional government and, as forms of
government themselves, directly to influence events.

In his funeral oration over those who had
fallen in the first year of the Peloponnesian War,

Pericles declared, "We Athenians regard a man who takes no part in public affairs not as a harmless man but as a useless one." In each society that had a large nonparticipating class, the society as a whole was unfree and either stagnant or unstable, although the participating class may have enjoyed much freedom. And the result was the same even where the nonparticipating class was not kept hard at work. Bread and circuses for an idle proletariat had only limited and short-run success. And where a large section of the upper class abdicated from a full part in the society, as in France two hundred years ago, the results were even worse.

Where "freedom to" is confined to the government, both "freedom to" and "freedom from" are circumscribed. Acton wrote that the ancients concentrated so many prerogatives in the State as to leave no footing from which a man could deny its jurisdiction or assign bounds to its activity. . . . What the slave was in the hands of his master, the citizen was in the hands of the community. . . . The passengers existed for the sake of the ship."

As a politician shapes policy toward his fellow citizens, he may wonder whether it is better to encourage an individualistic toleration of others and a jealous assertion of private independence or better to encourage one to become a political sort. Both approaches are essential because interdependent; the only way we can assure ourselves of the former right is by exercising the latter. The "freedom to," participatory approach, provides both self-realization as a political animal and the protection of "freedom from," the defensive right. One reason why the Christian church survived and prevailed over other religions is that it developed a widespread organization modeled on the government of the Roman Empire. Yet, paradoxically, by encouraging the disregard of civic functions, it helped to bring about the downfall of effective government in Europe, thereby reducing both kinds of freedom.

To pursue the American Dream of a free society depends on both aspects of civic liberty. The need for belief in both is illustrated by the lack of belief in either. Sometimes it seems as though American society is collected in two groups, neither of which cares to pursue the dream. Some think it hypocrisy and a contemptible deception. For them, the Constitutional Convention was no more than a gathering in which blue-nosed, blue-stockinged Puritans who hated pleasure and attended to money met with ruffle-shirted slave owners who loved pleasure and neglected money; and the two groups exchanged pretentious rhetoric and connived to make their federal scrip redeemable. To some of these people, the music of "John Brown's Body" and the names of Antietam and the Seven Days and Salerno connote only governmental butchery. To them, the building of our cities and what supplies them meant only rapacious greed; and the pioneer experience, pushing the frontier from the Cumberland Gap to the end of the Oregon Trail, was no more than a completed program to clear-cut forests, extinguish the passenger pigeon and employ cavalry to commit genocide.

In the other camp are those who think the American Dream was true, but think it has been fulfilled simply because their own ancestors worked hard and struggled for their freedom; so these folk now, in a sense, have it made and they recline in civic indolence, enjoying their civic inheritance like others who have been given money.

Both sets are wrong, of course. The American Dream is real, good and remains forever unfulfilled. A moral frontier beckons to citizens, and what a shame if we fail to amplify and extend to our posterity the blessings our ancestors have bestowed on us.

If a politician's great problem of self-restraint is to forbear to mold his fellow men, and to forbear to mold himself to suit them, his high duty of positive effort is to be brave. Conditions of modern leadership narrow opportunity for physical courage and reduce its value, although it has not become a dead asset, like a natural immunity to smallpox. But under today's uncertain, thunderheaded sky it is both needed and difficult to let our minds be bold, to act on independent judgment, to live by principles, especially one's own, and not to forget the unceasing dependence of freedom on courage. In some ways bravery was easier in days of old when there were dragons into which you could stick your sword and an audience to applaud. To struggle bravely with formless masses of society is like swimming in the middle of a gentle tropic sea. For this perplexing time when sometimes courage seems futile or unnecessary we can recall the words Pericles spoke at the burial of Athenian dead, "The secret of happiness is freedom, and the secret of freedom is a brave heart."

Unless a politician's courage is exercised as an act of responsibility, its assistance to the cause of freedom or the commonwealth is indirect at most. The public good need not be a motive. Nor does it matter whether the nature of his action is a combative zest, the nerve to confront a danger in order to escape it, or willingness to risk a loss for chance of gain. But the public good is not served unless his intent is the defense of a principle, a policy or at least a portion of the public. Bravery for one's family is a private virtue. If his aim is merely to win elections, a politician's willingness to stand up to angry crowds is gambler's nerve which proves his ambition rather than his public spirit.

Of all the brave actions that support the general good, those of highest worth are efforts that a politician makes when he declares the truth, and next most valuable are those he makes when he fulfills his word. "Bravery means to tell the truth, in most cases, it seemed to me," wrote Milovan Djilas, brave in anybody's eyes. Courage is needed to enable one to tell the truth against adversity. "Metellus, as Pindar has it, esteemed 'truth the first principle of heroic virtue.'" Veracity most helps the cause of freedom at those times when veracity depends on courage. And courage as an element of probity inspires less folly than courage does in other forms. In our era the always high value of these two interdependent qualities has risen even further by reason of their short supply. By comparison, other qualities given higher value by their scarcity were kindness and mercy in first-century Rome, skepticism in twelfth-century Europe, self-restraint in fifteenth-century Italy, and breadth of mind, sensitivity and tolerance of others' frailties and differences in late nineteenth-century United States.

Pride can serve as a useful ingredient of courage—Sinclair Lewis's Gustaf Sondelius says, "I want you to see how an agnostic can die." But it loses its value when turned so far toward oneself that it becomes vanity. Even where the public welfare is a politician's conscious aim in exposing himself to harm, the public does not gain by it when his action is misled by narcissistic motives. The memory of Marcus Curtius was honored for his having caused improvement of his city's central square, whose beauty and convenience were impaired by a gulf that closed as soon as he had galloped into it on his horse. But evidence of the price that divine forces had set for their performance of this piece of public work was thin enough to suggest that substantial elements of his decision were excessive pride and pleasure in self-display.

Although essential, courage does not protect honesty from any temptation except to play it safe. Enemies of truthfulness also include ambition, passion and cupidity. Benvenuto Cellini, a man of unexcelled boldness and nerve and with frankness assured by habit and pride, nonetheless confessed, "I have always been the greatest friend of truth and foe of lies; yet, compelled by necessity, unwilling to lose the favour of so great a princess, I took those confounded pearls sorely against my inclination."

Some wise and truthful people who do not display courage do not seem to need it because they have no beliefs that call for action against powerful opposition. Sometimes, a person's own conclusions like those of Santayana, show him no value in asserting or defending any beliefs. Others, like Morris Cohen, provoke our admiration by their willingness to face the harsh facts of the universe without leaning on a philosophic crutch. But whether he undertakes fastidious resignation, floating down a long river of culture, or whether he pioneers alone, a philosopher need apprehend collisions with nothing but the opinions of other scholars and his own doubts. This exemption is unavailable to those on political battlefields. Whether exercised or not, courage is required to permit a politician the freedom to change his mind and disagree with some opposing force. We all are surrounded by so many threats to our comforts and peace if we assert definite values that we must face fear if we are to act on independent thought. Fear is hard to escape even for one who swims with the current. Dr. Johnson was quoted as saying, "You remember that the Emperor Charles V, when he read upon the tombstone of a Spanish nobleman, 'Here lies one who never knew fear,' wittily said, 'Then he never snuffed a candle with his fingers.'"

Yet for a politician the problem is not solved by any kind of bravery alone. To serve the public interest, or the cause of freedom, virtue cannot be coupled with continual defeat. Popular admiration for success encourages belief in the morals practiced by winners; people often despise the high principles for which a loser stood. If he makes a gallant losing fight, the crowd will cheer him when he leaves the ring, but next week will go to watch the other fellow fight. Many candidates are pragmatists about the ethics of what it takes to win, yet primitives in their assumption, with inconclusive proof, of a causal connection between methods and elections. If a man has been elected after dodging issues or defaming his opponent, he and others will perform the beastly ritual again.

To perform his role as it should be played a politician cannot do without that rare blend of temperament and character that enables one to make his way through the never-ending maze of moral ambiguities that politics presents, and to do so without flagging and with steady hand.

A politician's basic task is to draw the line between the public interest and his own survival. It can be claimed that this continual decision is not moral but strategic, that it is a matter of judgment alone because except in office politicians cannot do much public good. This would be so if man were just a scale. But his judgment is distorted by his hunger for success. Idealism and good sense may cause him to identify his country's fortune with his own, but then, deluded by conceit, he sees their major causal sequence in reverse. (In response to those complaints, a politician may justly grumble that if he did as he was criticized for having failed to do, his only future part in politics would be to write a book about it.) He must have courage to speak about the important things with more honesty than his judgment suggests. Discretion is not worth as much as valor. As he follows the line between truth and success he needs courage to favor the former.

Furthermore, an aspiring mankind should have men and women willing to risk their rank to save their honor. To be a politician of a democratic nation, one no longer need risk his property or life. The public interest is served by the effects and example of politicians who would rather be right, whose "nerve of failure" sustains them on their own way, undaunted by the chances of rejection or defeat. Even if he loses more often than others, a politician who peddles the truth is his constituents' gain. And he strengthens their stomach for truth by often repeating the dose.

IV | Puzzles and Issues

Chapter 13

LEADERSHIP AMONG THE LEISURED

Issues that perplex politicians are the issues that vex us. We all know them. Important problems do not reach the political stage until people know and care enough about them to press some politicians, and permit others, to make issues of them by discussion and contest. (In the 1920s the biggest problem was the menace of economic collapse, but since few people saw this risk, Prohibition and the Ku Klux Klan occupied the scene.) It seems fitting to examine what fundamental questions may come to absorb politicians in the discernible future. They are neither so distant or universal as to be only philosophic, nor so evident that concrete solutions can be sought. A politician may handle them better if we recognize and reflect upon them before they are upon us.

Throughout our country's history the chief boundary between the parties has been changing. Sometimes it has been regional. From 1930 to 1960 the primary fault line ran between haves and have-nots. Since then, it has been hard to find. Political fortunes await the first politicians able to locate the next fifty-yard line. It may divide upon the complexities that we have made for ourselves: Perhaps imaginative versus unimaginative, educated versus uneducated, boldness versus caution, conformity versus nonconformity, closed mind versus open mind. Or the difference may depend upon the window through which one sees the world.

The new main division may result from the condition of a liberal upper class and a conservative lower one. To consider this conjecture, let us examine society's future arrangement and shape. What follows describes and predicts but does not advocate.

The class system is being transformed by changes in the definition of worth. By "worth" is meant that set of qualities and conditions that society values in assigning social class rank. Contemporary opinion both formulates the set and applies it by putting each person in his place.

Worth is what the "electorate" admires, for whatever reasons. Examples of what societies in the past have rated highest are: in China, scholarly learning; in Japan, the qualities of a noble warrior; in some primitive tribes, prowess at killing game; in India, Brahman birth; in Europe, royal birth. Certain moral qualities may be elements in the formula. In the sense that nothing succeeds like success, sometimes a person's skill at getting what he wants impresses his electors as a quality that they value, so his skill is rewarded by elevation to higher rank. Whatever qualities or conditions are valued are embraced.

For a long time, a large element of rank has been one's parents' status, a factor both recognized and resented since Lucifer's rebellion was provoked by God's appointment of His Son to rule in Heaven. The Roman Catholic hierarchy omitted birth status from its ingredients of worth, and so did most of those armies that were both efficient and large. (Efficient only on the regimental level, the Scottish clans were led by hereditary chiefs.) Several Balkan peasants came to rule the Western world by rising through the Roman army. But these institutions were notable exceptions.

Where birth status was a substantial component, it was embraced on one of two rational grounds. First is the logical connection between one's parents' personal worth and one's own. By personal worth is meant the value that society gives to personal attributes—what one does and is, factors inherent in personality rather than elements of one's background. A person's personal worth tends to be closer to that of his parents than to that of other persons. One is more likely to have high personal worth if one's father, by his own merit, was an admired leader than if he was "a servant of servants."

Birth status, then, was treated as a device for measuring personal worth which remained the underlying standard of value (although people in time came to treat the measuring stick as an element of value itself). Even where birth status was a large or even conclusive element in determining worth, no one ever left the class into which he had been born except by reason of his personal worth (or by marriage).

An ancestor's social status, however, does not imply a child's personal worth except insofar as the status implies the ancestor's personal worth. If a man had been made a count by merit, his son might be regarded as more promising than the average for no reason except that his father was a count. But each additional generation that applies birth status weakens the inference of personal worth.

Even when the inaccuracy of this device was observed, if not admitted, birth status was retained in the formula to stabilize a frail social structure. In the crumbling Roman Empire in the fourth century, perpetuation of function—and thereby status—through descent was undertaken to maintain economic production, tax revenues and performance of public responsibilities. A municipal leader was required not only to stay in office with the duty of paying deficits in tax revenues out of his pocket, but to have his son replace him. Likewise, a baker was required to keep baking and to supply a son to succeed him in the trade. Later on, when custom and authority came to let a man both be rewarded with land for meritorious service and to pass its ownership to his children, he thereby was enabled to keep them up on the level he had reached by having earned it. This stabilizing aim was expressed in hereditary monarchy by which legitimate birth status was made the sole condition for membership at the society's peak in order to transfer power without bloodshed and to maintain for a nation an enduring human flag.

Now this component is being discarded. More reliable means of measuring personal worth have been devised than the old inference resting on the German proverb that the apple does not fall far from the tree. By restricting the variance in station between parents and child, birth status made society stable at the price of vertical mobility, the lack of which reduced social efficiency and, once many people began to resent it, reduced stability as well. With a more stable social order, to avert a severe dislocation it is no longer necessary to freeze the classes by remote ancestors' dead hands.

Also, birth status lost political support. In the argument over the relative importance of heredity and environment, persons from privileged classes have emphasized the former, and those from unprivileged classes have emphasized the latter. Because their share in applying the formula was small, and their share in shaping it was even smaller, those who lacked high birth status also lacked the power to discard it as the basis for social rank. Now that broadened political and economic power has expanded the proportion of those who share in shaping the formula, birth status has become a factor that many will not brook.

Starting with Article VI of the French Declaration of the Rights of Man, birth status was taken out of the formula for worth in the requirements for holding public office. Since then, it has been diminished for most other aspects of rank.

Birth status is removed from the formula for worth by the successive removal of different parental attributes from the measurement of a person's worth. One is the parent's own formal rank, title or caste membership. Others are ethnic and racial identity, religious affiliation and social training (gentle breeding or its lack). These attributes contribute to birth status because they measure a person by the performance of those who came before him and are identified with him, whether or not he inherited their blood.

The spread in inherited wealth is shortened by taxes on estate transfers and income, at progressive rates. As the connection between parental money and a person's power, education and refinement has become attenuated, the social importance given to one's parents' riches or poverty has been reduced. The declining necessity of parental money to obtain a good education makes such backing less useful to develop personal worth—in turn the principal means of rank.

The importance of birth status in the formula is further reduced by the present tendency of inherited wealth to impair development of personal worth. On a climb toward high rank, money beyond a certain amount may be no more help than handicap. Heirs of the rich are left with luxury and personal independence but often do not receive the former additional attributes of wealth consisting of responsibility and power offering a challenge to achievement. Causes are the separation of corporate ownership and management and those tax laws that encourage forming trusts that last for a couple of generations. A rich person's child or grandchild who is made a trust beneficiary for all his life is not only barred thereby from managing business enterprises that the trust assets represent, he is denied a chance to employ his inheritance: To multiply, lose or merely save it.

These conditions turn a rich man into a remittance man, like so many American Indians. Disconnection of the property rights he inherits from the levers of economic activity to which property rights used to be attached leaves him tempted more by luxurious idleness than by challenging work. Self-indulgence, indolence and lack of accomplishment induce more of the same by impairing self-respect. Treated as a child, he often behaves as one.

Inheritance of riches, by reducing the chances of developing personal worth, partly offsets the social advantage that the wealth provides. This handicap grows as, among the components of the formula for worth, personal worth rises and inherited wealth drops. The taxes' subtraction and the debilitating tendency of the remaining rights in the property cause some descendants of rich people to end up without either the money, which used to be a large means of rank, or the personal worth, which has become the principal means of rank.

For the same reasons that take from a person the social value derived from his parents' possession of wealth, now a person's direct ownership of money, even if earned, has declined as a device for measuring worth. Although it cannot yet be said that redistribution of wealth and income is compressing to a pancake the stack of economic ranks, the raised floor and the truncated top have reduced economic inequality's political significance. One's worldly goods used to be a large factor in worth by determining culture, comfort, security and power. The spread in comfort and security has narrowed. All four have become less directly related to ownership of money. With a direct relationship gone, money counts less in measuring worth.

What will the new formula for worth contain? Probably personal worth alone. Perhaps this bundle of socially recognized personal attributes may be largely elements of exercised ability and talent, but since to refer to it as "ability" might be misleading, let us hereafter, in considering the foreseeable future, use the more comprehensive term "personal worth." As birth status fades, personal worth expands to take its place. This formula change lets a person rise or fall faster and farther than before. The old observation about "shirt sleeves to shirt sleeves" may be contracted from three generations to one.

Vertical mobility is augmented by reduced expectations that one strive to meet the standards of his ancestral station. Castiglione held noble birth to resemble "a bright lamp that makes manifest and visible deeds both good and bad, kindling and spurring on to virtue as much for fear of dishonor as for hope of praise." The sense that one ought to emulate one's father and grandfather has dwindled to a zephyr on one's choice of course. To remain in the rank of one's birth is no longer a duty any more than it is a necessity.

Each social class used to have a wide range of

personal worth among its members. The weight given to birth status froze people in their parents' class despite substantial differences in personal worth. Boswell's servant "spoke many languages." The highborn idiotic Bertie Wooster was surpassed by his gifted servant Jeeves in all respects but rank. I saw once in a newspaper a photograph of the mother of Frank O'Connor, the Irish author. Her face showed her to be a person of superior qualities. Her life had been spent as a domestic servant.

However, insofar as personal worth becomes the sole standard of worth, then on each social level all persons' personal worth will be the same. The society would be described as a stack of narrow grades, one for each level of worth. Within each grade there would be no range of variation unless and until these thin sheets coalesced into a smaller number of classes.

Despite free mobility, the rate of vertical movement within the society, considered as the distance a person moves from his parents' station to the level reached by him, is unlikely to increase as much as might be expected because on each class level personal worth will be uniform. Where worth is defined as personal worth, everyone in a class has the same amount. Children's variance in personal worth from their parents' class average will be shortened because their parents' own such variance will disappear. The sole cause of movement will be, as it always has been, variance in personal worth from the average of one's parents' class. In a society sensitive to degrees of personal worth, after the inertia of birth status has gone only a minor variance from one's parents' class standard will suffice to take a person out of the class into which he was born.

"Free mobility" permits movement according to any variance, in contrast to the wide one that used to be required, when it was so hard to penetrate the ceiling or floor between which the class of one's birth was fixed. Those differences in worth that were wide enough to constitute a ticket to another class were as common as the smaller deviations are likely to be in the future. Once, without differing from his parents at all, a man's level of personal worth might differ substantially from that of his parents' class. He could break out, if at all, only if the amount of personal worth by which he differed from the class average was sufficient. In the future, however, a person's difference from the average level of his parents' class will be smaller because it will be no more than the difference from his parent's own worth level— which must be the same as that of the class, personal worth being the sole standard. Therefore, with easier movement balanced against a narrowed range of variance, the rate of movement seems likely to be little greater than before.

In the transition period, as the gates open above and below each person, many people may move far from their parents' level, with some ascending or sliding the whole way between top and bottom, like Anatole France's Anchorite and Thais or the weights that hang from a cuckoo clock. Thereafter, when people are settled into the class

that fits their personal worth, their offspring's rate
of movement may decline, although remaining well
above what it was when birth status acted as a drag.

What will be society's new distribution pattern of its members according to worth? The pattern of society's class structure has been a kind of
cone with a concave face in its upper portion and a
convex face near the base. Its point was up. The
small ruling class occupied the upper part. Where
the middle class was especially small, the upper
class was a nob at the tip, barely joined to the rest of
the human race below it, so that the pattern resembled an hourglass in which minutes dripped
into hours. (A vestige of this remains in pockets
such as Manhattan, where the natives appear to be
bankers or waiters.) Most people were located in
the laboring class at the cone's base. The face of the
cone was concave above, rather than flat, because
the numbers of persons in each class level, measured
in upward progression, diminished at a decreasing
rate, since the upper class was so small in relation to
its height above the working class.

The class pattern is likely to have more vertical symmetry than before. Half the population
would be below the midpoint of the vertical axis and
half above. In the old pattern of distribution, most
members of the society were concentrated below its
vertical midpoint. That society's inability to support
more than a small minority in relative comfort

joined that minority's defense of its privileges to make a big, low bottom and a small, high top.

The pattern for most measurable human attributes describes a Gaussian normal curve of probability distribution. In measurements of humankind, the curve does not extend infinitely in either direction. That a coin will come up tails ten times in succession is more probable than that a child will grow to be ten feet tall. It seems reasonable to expect that the personal worth pattern describes such a mathematically ideal probability curve, as skewed by social policies and other circumstances. Where the vertical axis measures worth and the horizontal axis measures the number of persons at each worth level, the pattern's lowest point would locate persons of minimal human capacities, while the highest would locate a genius or saint.

Accurate sifting of abilities will divide society into haves and have-nots of personal worth rather than wealth. A sharp division between upper and lower will be replaced by a scale of imperceptible grades from Newton to Jukes. The pattern will resemble not an hourglass or a cone but a fishing bob, or a pair of coolie hats laid brim to brim, with a spike projecting from the peak of each. In statistical terms it can be described as a pair of normal curves, the bells on their sides, bottom to bottom; the mode will be at the mean and bigger than it used to be in proportion to the whole; the tapering ends (rounded off) will be correspondingly longer and thinner. Since the area (representing the population) remains the same, the pattern becomes thinner if longer and fatter if shorter, like the outline of a necklace made of fine-link chain and spread on a table.

The boundary between upper and lower halves will not run along a gulf but in fact will cross the thickest place. This means that the broadest point of the pattern (largest concentration of people) and the midpoint of the vertical axis would coincide. More of the people will be clustered near the equator which divides the two main classes and perhaps, though probably not, the two main parties. Measured by the terms of upper, middle and lower, the middle class will be much the largest.

Although the shift in the class pattern from cone to normal curve is primarily caused by the changed definition of social worth from birth status to socially desired personal qualities, our new technology accentuates it. In proportion to skilled persons, fewer unskilled ones are needed to build a rocket ship than a steamship. Armies and corporations themselves are swelling in the middle with administrators and technical experts, while simple Tommy Atkins and Rosie the Riveter come to be needed in smaller numbers.

Some factors work the other way. When computers were expensive, their economic use depended on their operation by operators of high skill, who could make the most of the expensive operating time. As these machines became easier to operate and cost less, they could be employed most economically for many uses by lower-skilled, lower-cost operators. But these tendencies are the weaker and shift numbers within the middle range of skills, not from skilled to unskilled.

Whether the vertical axis is extended or short-ened will depend in part on how people on different levels of capacity come to feel about effort for sustained performance as a means to rank. The value put on social status has been driven in both directions by the changes that have taken place. The advent of the chance to rise or fall has increased the value of social status in many persons' minds by coming in part within their power, while it used to be wholly settled by the fate of birth and accepted with resignation or contentment. Like this altered condition was the experience of many people whose industry was increased on coming from Europe to America, where for the first time they could earn a reward for extra hard work. In the last decade of the twentieth century a similar explosion of productive energy may be expected from many American women and Black men.

On the other hand, comfort, leisure and civic order, giving social status lesser consequences, re-duce its importance for many people. We may not so closely connect social status either with longing to rise to comfort, security, perhaps even luxury, or with fear of falling into drudgery, ugliness and indignity. Availability of comfort and freedom to indulge one's tastes without severe effort may make competition for position seem an adolescent pastime, not worth the effort when so much an end in itself. Insofar as people disdain such competition as a game, they may suffer from boredom though not from tensions of the never-ending chase. One's social status may become little more than a kind of merit badge, an accurate label, a correct noun, but standing for something of slight value. We may come to look on status in the way that a man regarded his having been run out of town on a rail. When asked how he felt about the experience he replied that if it were not for the honor of the thing he would just as soon have walked. If this condition comes to pass, much social status may be backed into by indirection, resulting from development and exercise of talent for other purposes. The pursuit of an all-consuming hobby may put one either high or low in society as a by-product of one's efforts.

As old fears abate and appetites are gratified, one's efforts may depend on drives toward less well-recognized ends. This for a while may give a special advantage in the class pattern to those groups that now possess such drives in a high degree; that is, people who, though comfortable, still work hard.

Probably the shape will be longer and thinner at the upper and lower ends, where extending factors exert the most force. For persons of highest potential the factors helping them to rise will be stronger, and for those with the least, the factors helping them to rise will be weaker. It is as though the pattern were spinning on its horizontal axis, and the extending factors were centrifugal force, strongest on those persons farthest out.

The mass in the middle seems likely to be made shorter and broader. For this mass the vertically contracting factors appear to be stronger near the horizontal axis, the line bisecting the middle class. It is as though the contracting factors were a force of gravity, acting with diminishing strength as the distance increases from the center of the mass. (See page 329 for diagram.)

✧ ✧ ✧

As always, the members of the upper spike will have high political significance. Some are politicians themselves. Thorstein Veblen drew ironic comparisons between the habits—such as idleness, corruption from luxury or hardship, and conservatism from contentment or exhaustion—of the top and bottom classes in his day. By contrast, in the pattern ahead of us, the members of each spike will differ more in all respects from the members of the other than from the members of the large middle group.

The lower spike at present is the remnant of the former large class of the disinherited. Vertical mobility is enabling those who can to climb out. At the same time its numbers are being increased by the defective and the feeble old, enabled by medical science to live and enabled by society's wealth to stay alive.

Those on the bottom grades and a few next above lack skills of collective action for political self-defense. Opening the doors of opportunity gives no help to those without capacity to enter. Depending on the rest of society for the quality of its members' lives, this group is weak and growing weaker. Except for those who live in some of the better public institutions and those who are cared for by their families, when their families are better off, the members of this group, dependent for justice on sympathy, often suffer injustice.

> We both alike know that in the discussion of human affairs the question of justice arises only where the pressure of necessity is equal, that the strong take what they can and the weak grant what they must.
>
> THUCYDIDES

When those at the bottom of society constituted a broad base, their vitality and freedom from convention enabled them to be social pioneers in some ways. Their behavior could provide examples of experiments in living and of life not obscured by a glaze of convention. Those novelists who now fix their attention on the present occupants of the bottom either are morbidly preoccupied with examples of human deficiency or they are so blinded by tradition that they do not realize that this class has ceased to be an informative object for literary study, although it remains a proper object for public policy.

To correct the injustice—mainly not enough money—would take little sacrifice from the rest of society in view of the relative proportions of its wealth and the size of this unfortunate class. Where those denied a fair share of the society's material goods constitute a large proportion of the society (the former cone with a concave face) correcting the injustice is harder materially but takes less moral effort than it does where the poor constitute a small minority. For a deprived ninety percent to secure a fair share from an overprivileged minority, they do not beseech; they take.

On the other hand, a deprived ten percent is too weak to enforce demands. To receive their fair share its members must depend on a mixture of benevolence and common sense by the comfortable ninety percent, each member of which must forego only a small amount. One shift requires organized selfishness, the other organized unselfishness. The former takes more daring, the latter, the one at hand, takes more imagination.

Unselfishness and imagination by those on high may not be enough. The have-not ten percent may be called on to assert themselves a bit, and this may be difficult for them. Among other things, they are handicapped by lack of skills to read and write. When the technology enabled the masses to over-come the privileged few on top, sometimes the masses still did not prevail. Their principal im-pediment was ignorance and illiteracy (as well as exhaustion) which restricted potential leaders from developing themselves and communicating with the mob, and kept its members from forming an orga-nized group. Unless self support can be enabled by means provided and methods taught and learned, redistribution will not improve the lot of those who populate the lower spike.

Members of the pattern's lower half, excluding the bottom spike, will not be powerless to try social experiments or press for drastic change, like the more oppressed members of the former working class, who lacked the skills and vigor to apply the necessary force and were resigned by weakness to the fellah's outlook that everlasting servitude is Allah's will. The upper half will allow the lower to assert itself to alter society's rules and shape in every way but one. It will not let the lower put itself on top.

Most societies of which we know have favored some people despite their lack of talent, but it is hard to conceive of a society so irrational or an elite so self-abasing that it would raise people *because* they lacked talent. Although the lower half will be free from the ignorance and lack of organization, leisure and weapons that burdened the former laboring class, the upper half, much larger than the ruling class in the past, will surpass in its members' realized abilities all the lower half, in contrast to the past substantial overlap. When pressed to protect itself against the lower half, the upper could exert preponderant strength.

Although the lower half cannot dominate, it can rock the boat. Yet its members may resist a tilt. In its political attitudes the lower half will be more conservative than the upper half and more conservative than the former working class. Three things will produce this conservatism: alleviated discontent (perhaps only temporary), lack of broadening and enlightening activity (dull work and excessive play), and type of persons in the group. Without a new incentive to replace the spur of want, the lower half may lack both hope and need for fundamental change. Insofar as leisure pursuits do not challenge the faculties, and insofar as in other respects they are fulfilling, and audience participation makes this more likely, more leisure may cause a more conservative attitude. The closer horizons of the less-educated raise their resistance to new ideas and to change that is not the current whim of the crowd.

The lack of that imagination and boldness of thought that characterize a liberal outlook will be both cause and consequence of conservative thinking's predominance in the lower half. Cause because those qualities contribute to the personal worth that puts one in the upper half, to which the more daring offspring of lower-half parents will have been lost. Consequence, because of the company kept and the life led, minds being made more conservative by association with others of like mind.

Those who are found in the lower half may compose a group as torpid in its thinking as the old working class, which had the leavening of the more able men and women who used to belong to it. Manual laborers' residential areas will produce no more folk art. Labor unions already do not obtain leaders from among the ablest children of the younger members. Class loyalty's appeal has declined; so has the goad of class hate. The success and peace of the labor movement have dampened the idealism of all but a few incorrigible zealots. The most gifted of the youth in laboring class families have left for more rewarding work which has been put within their reach by the removal of hereditary bars. If they have the ability, those who want money go into business or medicine; those who want security join a large nonprofit institution, whether an army or a library; those who want mental exercise go into scholarship or science; those who want fame go into entertainment, politics or sport; those who want time and energy for leisure pursuits work for a big company or government at short hours; those who want power can get more for the same price in fields other than union leadership. The union membership has lost not only most of its potential leaders but also many of the more vigilant members, who do so much to select the best leaders and insure that they perform well.

For the converse of the causes making the lower half conservative, the upper will be the more liberal in political outlook and more liberal than the ruling and middle classes of the past. With broader horizons and bolder minds, it will welcome experiment more than the lower half and be less disposed to resist change. As the lower half will have little to gain by social change, so the upper half will have little to lose, little that it will have a strong class wish to conserve. Unlike wealth, whether inherited, earned or won, personal worth neither can be given nor taken by social change. Without inherited titles and with minimal inherited wealth, members of the upper half will not, without a radical reversion to the old ways, be able to pass their status to children except by assisting them to develop their talents (a big except). Nor can these members even keep their status for themselves except by their own continued efforts. They will have no vested interest in things as they are except the right to have worth recognized.

This turnover of outlook between upper and lower has its harbinger in physical appearance. People who were pale and fat once could be identified as belonging to the upper class, while, except for cooks in a great house, members of the lower class were lean and tan. Now the indicia have been reversed.

If the lower half is not adequately supplied with leaders, then by effortless superiority the upper half could partially subjugate the lower by default. Because it holds higher cards, it could treat members of the lower half as pampered animals, protected from hardship and pain, and given comfort but not luxury and little freedom and respect. By conditioning and suggestion, the upper half may cause members of the lower to do willingly that which they would not have wanted if left unmanipulated. From Cromwell to Castro, men of superior capacity have been essential to any successful revolutionary movement. Without able leaders the lower half will not even have a chance to hold its own.

Unlike the way it has been when all classes produced leaders, under the new pattern leaders will belong only to the upper half, regardless of which half they lead and regardless of their parent's class. Leaders may be born of lower-half parents but before they become leaders they become identified with the upper. Formerly, men of working-class parents never attained more than a partial measure of upper-class identification, and then only after they had achieved high leadership (examples are Bevin, Krushchev and Lincoln). In their own minds and in others' eyes, these men's links with the working class to which they had belonged remained unbroken to the ends of their lives and evident by indelible marks.

When a person is a leader of the lower half, in a day when all leaders belong socially to the upper half, his role is something like that of a patrician tribune, though with more than tribunician powers. This undertaking requires that his motives be strong enough to induce him to leave the club as well as to undertake the effort of leadership. It is possible, of course, and has been done—witness Mirabeau, Chou and Cripps.

Three motives may induce people to become leaders of the lower half: preference for the conservative philosophy, a sense of injustice to be righted or needs to be served, and a wish for a leadership position in a field where the number of such positions in both halves is limited and of about equal desirability in each. The first motive will have replaced the personal preference for the liberal philosophy which sometimes tended to induce a member of the ruling class to advocate the cause of the working class. The latter motives always have been present. Injustice and social needs, provoking sympathy, can be counted on, guaranteed by human nature and by the lack of adequate lower-half leadership. The third motive, personal wishes for this role, rests on other motives of the kind by which men always have been drawn or driven into public life. Some will try to climb higher in the upper half by promoting the interest of the lower. Others enjoy conflict and contention and like to engage in it on a big scale, so they look for an army to lead, searching not for a job but for a war.

The working class would still be the working class if it had had to depend on ruling-class persons as its only leaders. However, the larger number of potential leaders in the upper half makes for more who may be inclined to cast their lot with the lower. Saturation of upper-class leadership positions should leave a surplus of aspirants who will have to turn to the lower half.

An irresponsible who undertakes to lead some sector in the lower half may hesitate to venture into the demagogue's role at the risk of unpopularity in the upper half, then overcome his hesitation and defy his critics. His knowledge that his negative merit of not being a bad boy will not suffice to win his fellows' approval may cause him to repress his wish for it by charging them with ingratitude, with lack of sympathy with his aims, or with something else. He might be one who "from Rebellion shall derive his name, Though of Rebellion others he accuse." However, leaders of the lower half are not likely to be treated as traitors to their own upper half. The upper half will be too diverse and im-personal to constitute much of a binding old school tie. Class lines will be blurred by the free flow up and down, and the narrowed range of living comforts and civic rights may soften class antagonisms. Certain common interests loosen class ties by drawing people together along slanting lines that intersect the horizontal planes of worth.

Opposing these motives, other factors will solidify the upper half. Assignment of ranks according to precise measurements of personal worth makes the members of each rank more essentially alike, more congenial, and therefore more influential with each other. Segregation according to talent gives people companions more like themselves than are most of their kin. An example of what may become more common is Harlow Curtice and his brother, who were employed by General Motors, one as president and the other as a machinist. They had little to do with each other, although it is said that their mutual feelings were cordial. In the past such brothers probably would have been engaged in similar work, had closely overlapping circles of friends and often eaten at the same table. This shift in association loosens family ties and puts one closer to his peers. As their attitude moves from awareness of the common denominator to attachment to the group, its members are transformed into a social class that mutual loyalty unites.

However, an aggressive solidarity intense enough to undertake and maintain oppression is unlikely. The prevailing tendency to a liberal outlook in the upper half will cause upper-half members to disagree with each other more often than they otherwise would. More probable is a latent solidarity which comes into being for defense under threat, as when the quarrelsome Greek soldiers composed their differences in Persia so that their army could make its long march home.

Sometimes a group has been kept in servitude through removal of its leaders by death or exile. Our upper half (or the top quarter, to confine attention to the source of leadership) may do the same by making offers too tempting to refuse, but probably it will not prevent the lower from being defended by leaders adequate to maintain it in a position not far subordinate to the upper half.

Although by definition the upper half will be composed of people superior in abilities to those in the lower half, it must not be supposed that the society will be ruled by a committee of natural kings (any more than that the lower half would be composed of those Aristotle called natural slaves). The required superiority for membership will be no more than to exceed the average for all. The bulk of the membership will be close to the dividing line in worth. For the upper half to constitute itself as a royal committee would mean a kingdom containing one subject per king.

The new system's accuracy in personnel measurement and labeling may cause experts to influence opinion about subjects in their own fields more than they have in recent years, when most people have had enough knowledge with which to form a basis for an opinion themselves and yet have been uncertain who were the real and reliable experts, and more than has been done by anyone since the days when ignorance forced most people to form their opinions in reliance on some leading members of the ruling class.

Substantially more than half of the Jews may be expected to be found in the upper half. It is ironic that not until now could the Jews be thought a superior people, whether chosen by God or by chance. In antiquity their contribution to civilization, though substantial, was not comparable to what the Greeks and Romans gave; between then and the recent past they lived in isolation and obscurity, with modest accomplishments for a time in Spain, later in Turkey, Holland and elsewhere. They were outshone by the Normans and by other gentile groups in Italy and France. But the exclusion of non-Christians from land ownership, forcing Jews to live in the towns and thereby to become adapted to urban culture, gave their descendants a cumulative advantage from this head start.

Urban life under persecution made them the only recognizable group in the world that has been subjected to the process of natural selection on the basis of brains for enough generations for it to take effect. Over an even longer period a reverse process among gentiles also has been causing this comparative superiority. Of the best in quality (not necessarily the most fit where survival is the only standard of fitness) of male Jews and male gentiles over the last ten centuries, a larger proportion of the latter did not beget children. From the ninth century to the nineteenth (the process dwindled last in Ireland, Italy and Spain), a substantial proportion of the finest (mainly for qualities of intelligence and idealism) gentiles became celibate priests. From Roncesvalles to Iwo Jima, many of the noblest (mainly for qualities of courage and loyalty) gentiles were killed on the battlefield before they had begotten their share of children. Members of a third substantially large group of superior (mainly for qualities of boldness and vigor) gentiles failed to reproduce themselves because their lives were cut short in the course of travel, exploration, duels and feats of daring. On the other hand, the persecutors did not discriminate on the basis of quality among their Jewish victims.

In addition to their early adaptation to modern living and the results of natural selection, both positive and negative, the Jews retained their straight and narrow outlook longer than most gentile groups, emerging late from their form of Middle Ages, and now are in a delayed renaissance. In most of those areas of endeavor that we think important, there is, and for a while in America there will continue to be, soaring achievement, not of Judaism but by Jews.

Elaboration of our technology and the dispersion and increase of wealth have expanded the demand for skilled services. On the whole, this demand is being met. The capacity to afford them has increased along with the capacity to afford training to perform them. Although some young people prefer to take the ready cash and forego the greater future gain, for many others the willingness to prepare has not declined. The prospect of the first few years' austerity and effort has not offset the appeal of the higher pay and the challenge of the work.

However, for politicians, and for other persons who manage affairs in business, education or philanthropy, the days and months of work will not decline. The demand for their services is high, but the supply will not increase enough to make the vocations less arduous. Higher pay will not help. Where much of the work cannot be done well unless concentrated in a comparatively few hands, a pay raise, rather than easing the work load by spreading it among the larger number attracted to the field, may only intensify the competition that drives each participant to harder, more continuous work. Of course, the public may benefit by attracting more persons to offer themselves to politics so as to raise the quality of those among whom to elect. But if politics becomes even more competitive, the inducements to enter politics may not attract the best people, and in the future a large pay raise is not likely to be powerful bait.

It is difficult to conceive of making politics less competitive without either making it unresponsive or shifting functions to another field, where the problem would be renewed. In some vocations a limit imposed on hours may protect practitioners from the harms of frenetic competition. But for politics, populated by energetic souls for whom rest is penance, hourly limits would be unenforceable if tried and against the public good if they succeeded.

A solution to loss of perspective from long-sustained intense immersion in a vocation that needs perspective would be to interrupt the service by an occasional sabbatical. While it is impractical to blow a whistle, making politicians quit work four hours after lunch, each politician for a year during her term could be prohibited, on penalty of forfeiting her office, from appearing at any scene where public policy is formed or set in motion. If she were sent home to wait, she could not escape from politics, and idleness she could not stand. Instead of fruitful reflection and refreshing rest, her time would be consumed in worry about her state, her country and her career. The sabbatical system could succeed only if she were enabled to live apart from her constituency and to take some employment that made moderate and intermittent demands, such as those of doing administrative or diplomatic service in another country or teaching in another state. Someday, at regular intervals, instead of merely throwing the rascals out, we may throw out the good ones too, inviting them to rest and then come back.

Even if our conceptions of worth stay as they are, the pattern could be reshaped by changing people rather than rules for their measurement. Or society may choose to change the composition of the human race through its power, by influence if not control, to increase the numbers or quality of those thought useful or pleasing or to eradicate types it does not want.

The high proportion of talented people among immigrants to the United States does not elongate the pattern but it adds volume to the upper end, increasing the proportions of those parts of the society that are far apart.

The lower spike will be restricted even if it is not shorn. Composed of those with the least social value and capacity for happiness, its members need not be disinherited by the rest of mankind but will continue, by definition, to be disinherited by God. For even a rich society to survive for long depends on limiting the size of the group below the level of near incompetence, unable to carry a share of civic or economic contribution. Without such a partial Plimsoll line, no society so successful as ours in perpetuating minimal human life can stay afloat. The question is one not of truncating the spike at any point but rather of total area, whether the downward spike is long and sharp or short and blunt.

A society rich enough to support many unproductive persons may be willing to pay for a narrowly restrictive definition of those who are not to be allowed to continue to live. Such tight scope may be thought a price worth paying to reduce the risk of snuffing worthwhile lives. Enough hale persons will come to direct in writing that if and when they later lose their powers their life supports are to be denied, so that the most perplexing questions will be where to draw the line in cases occurring near the time of birth.

✧ ✧ ✧

Let us return to the original question in this chapter, American society's main political division. There may be greater fragmentation of groups in temporary coalitions, perhaps, as in the past, through the catchall means of two major parties (whether organizations or labeled outlooks), but differing in that the opposing alliances will not be dividing along a significant line. The division, which probably will not run along the horizontal axis, could result from either popularity or power.

If the latter, whether the power was raw or polite, the division would be both result and cause of the lower half's subjection by the upper. Because relative strength would be so one-sided, power would be imposed but not contested. This would further decrease the rate of movement between classes. The resulting maintenance of class membership between generations of one family would increase class solidarity which in turn supports the subjection, with each component strengthened by pressure from the one behind it. To have all the strong on one side and all the weak on the other would lead to quarrels among the strong. This impermanence makes it unlikely that the upper half will be monolithic enough to keep leaders from forming alliances between elements of both upper and lower halves. Stagnation's unlikelihood is one of society's few dependable prospects.

For the main line to run along the horizontal axis is as little to be expected if the concentration in the upper half is popularity as if it is power. Even if people agree on what constitutes worth, settled lines will not run between dumb and smart or bad and good, with all wisdom or virtue on one side. Although merit may be confined to one group because we can classify as we choose to define, it cannot for long be confined to one party. Narrow partisans always have assumed a congruence between the line that divides opposing political groups and the line that divides the better people from the worse. When they believe this in the future, they may think that the party division coincides with the division of merit, and that therefore their party constitutes the pattern's "better" class. If this ever comes true it will be brief. As upon extinction of the Federalist and Whig parties, followed promptly by a Democratic Party split, an evident concentration of merit does not last because it attracts the whole electorate, and so the process of division into two disputing parts will have to start again.

So long as everybody is allowed to vote, and if the main party division follows the horizontal axis because power is concentrated in the upper half, there will be a falling out. If the line runs there because all the believed merit is in upper-half leaders or policies the line will drop to the pattern's bottom; the upper half will receive the support of all, its party will capture everyone, and a new separation will be required.

The main boundary, therefore, is likely to cross the class pattern along some angled line. This would be the case if the main issue is liberal versus conservative (distinct from the current secondary division of sentimental humanitarianism versus decayed liberalism and a vision of the old days looking splendid in the dusk with the light behind them). Although most liberals were in the upper half and most conservatives in the lower, both views could be found scattered throughout the society. Perhaps more than half of the liberal leaders will be found in policy-making positions in the executive branch, which has become the main originating source, while a greater proportion of conservative leaders may go into the legislative branch, which in its now reversed position primarily vetoes, approves, adjusts and corrects.

We may divide on defining worth, contesting the rules for going up or down. For those trying to raise the values of what they happen to possess this would be a power struggle. For those concerned with the comparative merits of qualities and conditions without reference to the proponents themselves, it would put ideals in conflict.

Diagrammatic Representation of the Class Pattern of the Future

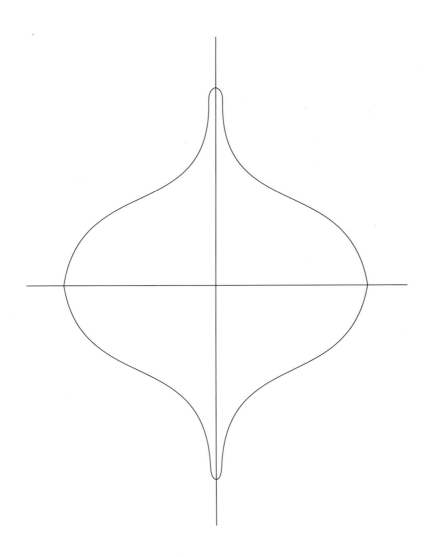

Chapter | 14

BOREDOM

The failure of communication between citizen and politician disappoints many people who feel that something has gone wrong. But this communication has never been good, and it used to be worse. Like Asiatic poverty, not until now has this evil been recognized as such, because in the past the leaders did not care and the people did not hope. Citizens used to be resigned because they felt the failure was ordained; now they are frustrated because they realize the obstacles could be removed. Wishing understanding and appreciation from their constituents, politicians are anxious about their lack of sympathy. Most politicians have acquired an emotional dependence on the people; they deal closely with them, respect them and need them.

This communication failure does not stem from lack of information that citizen and politician receive about each other. Such information is more complete and accurate than it used to be. The vital matters that fail to be communicated relate rather to meaning, significance and purpose. The failure of communication between citizen and politician largely results from politics' unreality which in turn is both result and cause of its dullness.

Among creative persons, neither scientist nor artist has a clearly defined constituency, but each seeks to communicate to others. One may pursue his

vision without need or duty to compromise, but
unless he transmits the fruit of his pursuit to others
he does not affect them. A scientist may mark the
world even though he himself reaches only a small
audience of peers, his own profession. The spe-
cialized communication is sufficient. But an artist—
whose function a politician's more closely resembles—fails unless he relates what he has to say to
a larger group. And part of his function is to determine the appropriate size of audience to seek.
This size determines how popular he must try to be,
how far to entertain and meet others' tastes.

A free society requires communication efficient enough to permit people to understand each
other on the political plane. This depends on political engagement in which some take part and
most attend. Engagement by citizens can become
satisfying experience only where citizen and politician truly come in touch.

Many people push themselves through their
citizenship chores by will power based on an often
exaggerated, and currently declining, sense of duty.
They shun political engagement because they feel it
is a boring, far-off business and they resent their
obligation. Citizens feel they are not players, but
only spectators or victims, and that the governmental
process leaves them out. A healthier climate would
result from a sane and less grudging approach.

Moral entreaties do not induce people to
vote, and voting is not enough either to satisfy the
citizen or serve the needs of the state. There is no
hope to breed in men the sense of civic duty of

Aristides or Brandeis. Among those few on whom such effort may succeed, not all can do and understand what they have been made to feel they ought. Beyond a point, exhortation in this direction does no more than generate indifference and guilt. A person may be driven by shame to vote but not to inform himself or to take part in other ways. And where some informed votes are cast abstention does less harm than uninformed votes.

Yet political engagement, because an essential condition of good government, is a duty, as joining the union is for a person in a union shop. To refuse is to secede from the community. Our purpose in this matter, as in much of public policy, is to make good conduct appealing enough to be practiced, to make the duty attractive enough to be done.

The subject of citizen participation, beyond casting votes, need not be national or international affairs. Some think local politics trivial and vulgar, and that nothing short of nuclear warheads deserves their attention. Others' main concerns are garbage disposal, crosstown transit or insulating walls and roofs. Issues are available for every taste. Needed is not new or more diverse subject matter but new approaches and new objects to be approached.

In some communities, citizen participation in local government has increased, but the action is confined to a small, intense minority. The presently available ways to take part appeal to few. The shift of the campaign process from party organization to media has left amateurs little significant work.

Routine measures, such as handing out hortatory leaflets, leave many cold.

Most people want more than a personal program limited to study that contributes nothing except to the student's improvement. Like other complicated matters not absorbed through experience that either is passive or incidental to some other activity, public affairs require effort to comprehend, and worthwhile political engagement is impossible without understanding. The effort of study nonetheless may be made if other ways to take part are made attractive in the manner of other optional enterprises that require effort yet give enough pleasure to induce it, such as crossword puzzles, bridge and climbing a hill to see the view from the top.

The public's disengagement from the formal political process exposes us to the dangers of doing without democracy: First social disturbances and then we know not what. Already, to use Galbraith's phrase, we follow the practice of the bland leading the bland—interrupted by venomous quarrels. Bringing citizens back into engagement threatens some uncertain harms, but the risk is justified by the chance to avoid certain harms, among them the process becoming atrophied and falling by default to the dreary and prosaic and to the cranks who find the conventional political process to be still interesting, or to the opportunists who find it profitable; and that element of government that has shifted to the media being misused by irresponsibles.

For people to be induced to take part or at

least to pay attention, they must be satisfied. After taking care of their necessities of existence, people now have time left in which to give politics the attention that it needs. Their choice depends on whether politics offers them the satisfactions that they want. Partial political engagement for the chance of jobs or fees appeals to few. It is no longer needed to guarantee security from private persons or from some capricious governmental acts. Nor is it much needed to hold or obtain a substantial class advantage. Compared to the past, politics can appeal to citizens for their attention and participation more insofar as it can offer satisfying experience rather than protection or contractual rewards for what they have done.

In order to satisfy people, politics must induce them to give their attention. To obtain this has become far more difficult for politicians. The shift in medium to a TV screen from a hired hall has made an audience harder for a politician to hold. A TV program must entertain from the start, while in a theater the main entertainment appeal can be delayed without the audience leaving since they have made more of a commitment than turning a switch. The contrast resembles the change in form of the novel, which no longer can afford to follow the nineteenth-century practice of spending its first fifty pages to set a scene.

Citizens' attention to leaders no longer is confined to priests and politicians but is spread among leaders of other groups among which power has become diffused—ethnic, labor, news, commercial, industrial, financial, professional, educational, charitable and cultural.

But politicians' biggest problem of attention is entertainment. As politicians have come to need to be liked, citizens have come to need to be entertained. In their attitude toward politics the mass of people used to be passive because, having little power, they felt they might as well relax and enjoy the stately processions with their banners, embroidered clothes, polished metal and nodding plumes. Now in some ways people again are passive, this time by choice. They want politics to be entertaining as a condition of their attention or activity. They want this despite their present political power with its grave duties, despite the fact that they are literate and better informed, and despite their independence from politics as a major entertainment source. Memory remains of the tradition that politics provides amusement. In some ways people have acquired more of the outlook of the guest or customer, whose function is not to act and to decide but to receive, consume and be entertained.

A taste for pleasure is this demand's main cause. By cultivation, people have developed their capacity to enjoy entertainment. Having acquired the opportunity to obtain frequent pleasure, most people have chosen it long enough to make a habit of this choice. Depending on the individual, pleasure may be his sole end, his chief end or an incidental accompaniment to some other satisfaction. He may take it as actor or spectator. He insists only on a course of experience that entertains enough to please.

People's price for paying attention has risen. Extended access to superior art and entertainment, available recreation and mixed work and play all contribute. Flamboyance, parables and funny stories no longer will suffice. Like teachers, politicians have to submit to the condition that their pronouncements be fun if the audience is to listen. (Yet compared with some teachers, politicians have it soft. In New Haven I coached boxing at the Dixwell Avenue Community House; in Seattle I conducted a Bible class at the Cathedral of Saint Mark. No political situation has been as hard to meet as those tests of teaching adolescent boys.)

As people's price for their attention has gone up, politicians' capacity to pay that price has fallen. Once a major source of entertainment for the public, politics has become a sideshow with loud barkers but unexciting acts. Dealing with a populace ignorant of public issues and whose political power was small and largely negative, leaders used to practice calculated pageantry in order to maintain a passive consent. Later, as most people began to acquire political power, entertainment was used to obtain their attention and approval. With people uninformed about public affairs and not yet inhibited by the "pale cast of thought," leaders approached them largely through superficial appeals. Bonfires, free liquor and bombast were combined in order to please and arouse. It is said that in the back country of Ghana the campaigns consist largely of arguments about the relative merits, as persons, of the elephant and the lion, which are the symbols of the major parties. Until recently it has not been hard for politicians to amuse people because there was less attempt to inject a discussion of issues and because people had little amusement available to them other than to watch a hanging or listen to a speech. Old people who were enchanted long ago when a circus came to town are puzzled when their grandchildren take the circus as a matter of course.

But now people are bored by a politician before he opens his mouth. Rare is the political speaker like Milton's Beelzebub, whose "look drew audience and attention still as Night." When the Watergate constellation of arrogant practices and squalid tricks was exposed, it gave absorbing entertainment of a sort, but only one of the main characters was a politician, and the subject was less politics than scandal and crime. If politics were not so dull for citizens, politicians, to attract attention to their words and to themselves, would not have to resort to hyperbole and noise.

The biggest cause for a politician's reduced capacity to win and hold attention by entertaining has been the rise of skilled professional entertainers. In the mass media, the politician and entertainer directly compete for audience, and the latter wins.

Some people regard as distressing evidence of their fellow citizens' moral decay the fact that politicians have low audience ratings in comparison with the popular culture stars of the hour or (a more enduring object of interest) pictures of well-formed naked bodies. Although our moral fiber may be growing slack, this popular preference is not proof of such a trend. It used to be no more entertaining to watch a juggler juggling fruit than to watch a magnificent cardinal conduct a mass or to watch a duke in a warm and handsome suit astride his well-groomed horse. But now, as entertainment, politics is excelled by the better professional entertainment, construing the term broadly, whether the producers' common label is artist, athlete or entertainer, whether the product is beauty, a win or a joke.

As the size and profits of the entertainment field have increased, it has drawn to it most of those who have a talent to amuse. If they had lived a hundred years ago, probably some of our best contemporary entertainers would have entered politics or the ministry instead.

Although his constituents wish to be entertained, for a politician to amuse them with wit or humor is dangerous as well as difficult. Wit and humor help to hold an audience while it hears the message, and ridicule may come in handy as a club. However, a funny person may be dismissed as a clown; many people equate humor with lack of the dignity that most people demand for all public offices except a few vestigial ones. (In the latter they enjoy a jester because they can afford him.) Wit may win a politician grateful applause from a bored audience, as it used to do for Mayor Jimmy Walker, who once was introduced at the groundbreaking ceremony for a subway tunnel after a long-winded speech by another man. Walker stepped forward and spoke one sentence: "You build a subway with a pickax, not a thorax." Then he picked up a shovel and started to dig.

But wit suggests the brilliance many think incompatible with sound judgment, which most people prefer in their public leaders. A caustic wit may be thought ill-tempered, and an intellectual wit may be thought high-hat. A witty politician is likely to be hurt no matter whom he makes his target. If he mocks himself, people may take his playful self-depreciation as true instead of applauding his humility. In hot dispute a mace or lance that springs to mind is hard to hold in check, and bystanders may worry when a politician's wit is used to scourge another's folly. Bacon wrote, "He that hath a satirical vein, as he maketh others afraid of his wit, so he had need be afraid of others' memory."

As in any mass communication, a subtle wit will not do. Common denominators of expression forbid things meant to be recognized by a happy few.

Unless politicians find some way to entertain their constituents, politics is likely to be sluggish and limp. "Weight without lustre is lead." To jazz up the political process, making politics more entertaining in the terms of the entertainment media, can be done only by shadows of shadows: delusionary and inadequate. In time, facts force their way through, dispelling the temporary contentment, and lack of participation denies enduring satisfaction.

Instead of competing with his superiors in the field of conventional entertainment, a politician can better reach his audience by using art to make politics more real. Art in politics is no novelty. As he was about to return from Egypt, Shaw's Caesar declared that Rome appreciated art. An elegant Sicilian sneered that the only art enjoyed by uncouth Rome was what it bought or took from others. Caesar replied, "Is peace not an art? Is war not an art? Is government not an art? Is civilization not an art? All these we give you in exchange for a few ornaments. You will have the best of the bargain." As an artist's attention swings between his audience and the vision in his mind, so a politician's thinking oscillates between his constituents and his policies. Much art of all kinds affects political attitudes in ways that are pronounced, though hard to perceive, and even harder to measure. Aldous Huxley once advanced the notion that a substantial cause of Germany's political instability was the absence of the novel as a native art form. Wagner's music is thought by some to have encouraged the acceptance of Naziism. Except in Calvinism or Communism, beauty has been used by organized religions to win and hold adherents. Entertainment's increased importance in American society has given more power to the writers of the country's songs over the content of its laws.

In his use of art, a politician aims to amuse and thereby attract and hold attention to his communicated thoughts; to give understanding of the truth directly by making the communication more readily understood; by pleasing, to encourage participation, some of which is a condition of politicians' being understood; and to shape attitudes toward politics.

✧ ✧ ✧

Art can make politics more real in two related
ways: individuality among politicians and pursuit of
utopian goals. A politician bores his observers and
fails to reach them if, like a poor musical composition, he has no direction or if he lacks a theme that
from time to time he can restate. The politician
should forebear to flatten his individuality, while
the citizen should let his politician be himself.
Public acceptance of a wider latitude of personality
among politicians would permit a larger proportion
of politicians with a distinct identity to get by. The
proportions of character and ideas in politicians
could be increased as a supplement to ability and a
substitute for moderation and warmth. Most valuable would be those politicians who incorporate
elements of independence and purpose, who contribute more of themselves, advancing ideas that
they did not necessarily originate but that they
chose. Because each detail of politics is dull unless
regarded as a means to some splendid end, independent politicians with direction of their own
inject into politics a sense of adventure, the tingle
of statesmanship.

Individuality depends on identity, which
depends on a sense of direction, which depends on
goals. One can be identified only by locating himself on a graph having coordinates with which to
determine his distance from other points and his
direction in relation to them. One's identity can
come from a sense of direction that relates to career

achievements, performance of a personal philosophy, human relations, affecting events, exercise of a
talent and so forth.

Widespread leisure increases the need for
new ideals. Even guided leisure is not an adequate
substitute for idealism since it provides artificial
temporary goals but is aimless in the long run.
Marvelous means of recreation are becoming
available but with less effect than intended because
without some purposeful undertaking, whether or
not it is called work, or even thought work, one
cannot be re-created. "If all the year were playing
holidays, / To sport would be as tedious as to work."
The politician who assumes the role of games director at a resort fails to fulfill people's need for
goals.

This need shows itself in the decisions to be
made in bringing up children. In some ways, children today perceive their parents' lives as children
did before the industrial and social revolutions. In
the intervening period the children of each generation expected adult lives on a higher level of
comfort and civil liberty than that of their parents.
Before that era, children could look forward to
living on about the same level as their parents.
Now, too, a child knows he is unlikely to dwell in a
house larger or more elaborate than his parents'
house. The incentive and expectation of effort to
surpass one's parents' comforts and civil liberties
have declined.

What moral goals can a child aspire to except
to be a good citizen so that the institutions will be

efficient and just? He is neither put on narrow roads nor given norms of duty, such as to be loyal or to work. If male, his conception of his role as a man may not be clear. Should he learn to be gallant to women who are as self-sufficient as he? Should this child be taught physical courage if he is not to exercise it beyond the playing fields, if drugs protect him from pain, if police protect him from attack by individuals, and if he is to learn that each major country's force is like a scorpion with others in a bottle? Is there good reason why this child ought not become like that despised tribe of old whose members' "valor had been eroded by prosperity until their cups were heavier than their swords"?

Our old goals of physical comfort, relief from physical toil, dignity and political rights, goals that formerly constituted an implicit utopia, were to some extent afterthoughts forced on us by hunger, exhaustion, indignity and inequality. They have been reached by many and are in sight of the rest. Their attainment calls for their replacement. New ideals, though no more independent of causation than a comet, may be rooted in more exalted desires.

The goals we adopt must be not solutions to immediate problems, but utopian, that is, remote, offering the appeal and convenience not often to be made obsolete by attainment. For a business organization to operate well and to survive, it must have administrators who can solve problems. Doing so is their principal function. But the big successes in business are achieved by persons who pursue a more distant vision—one that turns out to be right—

developing some strategy for the use of economic resources. Likewise, although political problems exist and are important, they do not make politics real unless they are linked to a more far-reaching aim. A large challenge, an impossible dream, gives an inspiring force not only to pursue it but to attain immediate, reachable goals. Excessively easy goals alone sometimes do not arouse enough energy to attain them. If the cup on the green were three feet wide, would anyone bother to putt?

To make our politics real, the ideals we adopt should be real as well, not fabricated images.

> An image is something *we* have a claim on. It must serve our purposes. Images are means. . . . The image is made to order, tailored to us. An ideal, on the other hand, has a claim on us. It does not serve us; we serve it. If we have trouble striving toward it, we assume the matter is with us, and not with the ideal.
>
> DANIEL J. BOORSTIN

To forsake pursuit as arduous and to try instead to impress by transmitting an image entails only a fleeting contact with the people, not a continuing involvement of them. Our ideals should be regarded as a standard of good, not as a sincere person's ego projection and a hypocrite's pretension. We can comprehend our ideals only if we can be enabled to see the world as it is, not as flickering shadows on the cave wall, facing which we sit in chains. Seeing our ideals clearly, however, is less difficult than finding them.

And they must not only be found but publicly considered. For goals to be present in many people's minds is not enough. The political process remains unreal so long as they are not openly discussed, contested, and dealt with in politics. For a society not directed by religious faith, Tocqueville thought that as his foremost duty a politician ought "strive to place the objects of human actions far beyond man's immediate range."

For our goals to liven politics with reality not everyone need have the same set. To hold society together most people must agree on, and practice, certain moral values, and these may stem from utopian notions. But to have agreement approaching unanimity on some goal of action, making it a national purpose for a continental nation, is likely to leave matters as dull as before. The kind of goal that most members of a complete society, such as a nation, can agree on without leaving politics unemployed is a general vision of an excellent life. In such a case the diversity of alternative types and means furnishes plenty of issues to dispute.

Measures alternative to new goals are inadequate. For relief from troubles many of us turn to self-manipulation, which helps to drive away fears and unpleasantness but does little to dispel boredom. The books of self-treatment may teach their readers how to exorcise the menace of some problems, but they look dull. The numbing pleasures of drugs and drink intensify boredom as much as they abate it; sex leaves intervals to be filled with something else. Where people make personal satisfaction their sole end, as where they choose a career only to gratify themselves, they turn much of their efforts into self-manipulation, treating their career the way they treat a health spa, or the way people used to treat the purchase of indulgences before the Reformation. Pursuit of personal satisfaction as an end in itself gives limited satisfaction, without as fulfilling a harmony as where efforts are directed toward a distant end.

✧ ✧ ✧

Utopian goals are needed not only to make the political process a more effective instrument with which each individual can help to manage society and live in freedom with it, but also to prevent the process from becoming convulsed. Boredom starts to stir inflammatory discontent when people cease to treat it as only a personal matter and, as citizens, start wondering what to do about it.

The conditions of American life create a risk of frustration in society's bottom third. Such frustrations, if not relieved by the leadership, may provoke an outburst of cruel and passionate injustice, whether by violence or otherwise. In this event, in a departure from the pattern of a conservative lower half and a liberal upper half, there would be a period of efforts to destroy by the lower half and reaction by the upper.

This danger is caused by resentment at receiving one's deserts and by boredom. First the former. When impediments have been removed from each person's rise or fall to the level that his worth fits, he becomes aware that everyone who knows him recognizes that he belongs where he is, accurately placed with a certain kind of justice, that he has no excuse for his low station or that he is thought to deserve credit for his high one. This condition makes people feel more comfortable with others on their own level. In the bottom third, among those who may feel bashful and lonely among their betters, segregation bears with greater stratifying force. The close association may reinforce the other feelings caused.

A ruling-class member used to excuse to himself his class's suppression of others by the belief that their low birth status proved low personal worth and therefore justified the low rank that his class played such a large part in imposing. For a while in the time ahead, conversely, one who finds himself in a low rank by reason of inferior personal worth and who is born of parents who belonged to a group that used to have low birth status, may assume that his superiors are still practicing the old formula Those who he thinks control allocations to class level he may accuse of using birth status to keep him down. But this belief may not console him for long after it becomes evidently false. In the Soviet Union, suicides increased among those who found that they no longer could blame capitalists and foreigners for their failure to rise in their vocation or advance in their school.

A member of the lower third, who can look a short way downward but a long way up, may think, or feel: "Social inequality remains great and is unjust in itself, I am low on the scale, my small deserts are nakedly exposed, and I am denied comforting indignation at being denied deserts. In time past, those in the upper third would reserve judgment on one in my position because my merit was not proved by my rank. They might hesitate to look down on me because they knew that but for the grace of the social system our positions might be reversed. But now they know that despite the presence of a marshal's baton in my knapsack I remain a private. The former unfair snobbery was *galling*, but this just disparagement is *crushing*. They used to impose social barriers to my rise, but that injury offends me less than their present insulting disdain. (They do not express it—that is part of their lordly arrogance—but I assume they feel it.) I hate them."

Three things may mitigate such resentment. First, most people will have greater understanding, and therefore sympathy, for persons on other levels of personal worth than used to be felt between classes, whose members lived like different species. Formerly the members of the ruling classes, from Marcus Aurelius to slave traders, hardly saw members of the laboring class as human beings. Scrooge's nephew called Christmas "the only time I know of . . . when men and women seem . . . to think of people below them as if they really were fellow-passengers to the grave, and not another race of creatures bound on other journeys." And poor folk used to regard some of the nobility as embodiments of more marvelous qualities than they possessed in fact. To some extent the serf would live vicariously through the lord of the manor his glories and his comforts such as adornment, grace, valor and the regular eating of meat.

Second, people now tend to recognize that rank depends, as always, on background which determines what as well as who a person is; and they recognize that the background factors that determine rank have been shifted from social setting to personality, from outer to inner gifts. People may at first conclude that snobbery has become justified and just, because class superiority depends on personal superiority. Later it may be thought that snobbery, because it inflicts pain and impairs perspective, continues to be immoral and that as a belief it has not ceased to be untrue, since the capacity to make oneself a noble character is derived from one's parents and one's past no less than is a noble title. Walking across the campus of an Ivy League university, you see some of the generation's future top people, just as could be done half a century ago; the ticket then was one's parents' money, and now it is one's parents' brains. For several centuries in England a "great" man was one with a great title and estate, while now the word means a person blessed with another set of gifts. Unlike the dictator Sulla, who recognized the agency of Fortune, yet vainly regarded her as his handmaiden, but like the Paris artist in Camus's story who modestly attributed his talent to his star, we may come to keep in mind that all gifts are gifts. Likewise, things despicable or base we may attribute to damnation by the past.

In time custom and policy may condition people to accept their personal limitations that decide their lot, just as their ancestors accepted their lot when it was set by birth. (When Carlyle heard that Margaret Fuller had said, "I accept the Universe," he commented, "Gad, she'd better.") But now that people have the power to resist the rules assigning social rank they may accept their personal limitations, yet strike out hard at the vertical range of rank.

The third factor to temper class animosity is mental health. As it is improved, this resentment may decline because it is irrational, directed not at injustice but justice. Yet the day seems distant when pain shall cease to be a by-product of the truth.

Among prospective causes of frustration in the bottom third, boredom equals resentment. Boredom and discontent, boredom's companion and sequel, are not confined to the political process but extend to other areas of life. Our achievement of some old goals supplies us with a new ground of discontent: not a barrier to approaching desired goals, but a lack of goals for which to feel desire. Inability to pursue goals is as frustrating if one is thwarted by a curtain of ignorance before unknown goals as by resistance to pursuit of goals that are in sight. Frustration is caused equally by impregnable resistance or by none. Partial resistance, yielding to our assault, is what we like, as contentment comes from the combination of goals and progress toward them. Our present discontent comes less from trying to scale a greasy pole of infinite height than from the absence from our sight of any poles that we think worth a try to climb.

Absence of appealing paths of aspiration causes boredom; this hardens into discontent and then, when unrelieved, becomes frustration, which in turn, when suffered by a group that has power to impose on others, causes injustice. The argument is convincing that boredom was a motive for lynchings in impoverished rural communities; that without cars or movies, and with old forms of self-made entertainment forgotten, one had little to relieve tedium but put a neighbor to the torch.

Boredom with many aspects of life is strong and it augments frustration by government. People's sense of civic impotence is not caused by change in government or organizations of other kinds, since the citizen exercises *more* influence in some ways, as his vote is more precisely weighed, his opinions receive more consideration, and he is better protected. A temporary cause is the growth and rapid change of our society that overload government, making it respond poorly to demands that rising expectations have intensified.

A deeper cause of frustration may be awareness that majority rule, so basic to our present notion of what government should be, is losing force and acceptance. Minorities' power has expanded. The social sciences have thrown light on them, they have a greater sense of their own power, and they are visible to others. Our record-keeping and abstracting powers have grown until they show us the significance (with statistics, trends, classifications, social models) of masses and groups of people. As newly measured, the groups outshine the individual and his particular situations which used to stand in the foreground of attention. Also, the development of flow technology enables a few people to disrupt urban society; for example, to throw a switch, lift a drawbridge, cut a cable, break or plug a pipe, spill chemicals in a reservoir, place a bomb, scatter tires on a freeway. These two elements— group measurements and flow technology—can protect minorities, but they may be used as selfishly as majority methods are, and for smaller numbers. By joining with those who constitute the minorities with which we identify we can veto and obstruct.

The decisive figure of fifty-one percent, its constituent parts unseen, used to seem a solid unit with magical properties. If what we now know had been known before, the proposition *vox populi, vox Dei* would have been recognized as the nonsense that it is rather than enduring for so long that it comes to us in a learned language. But neither no rule nor any minority's rule has been found to be as just or stable as majority rule, limited by minority interests and individual rights. To increase minority power from limitations on the majority toward John C. Calhoun's nullification, even without going so far as Poland's *liberum veto*, may leave government unresponsive. The sense of defensive strength that we may receive from this new minority power may be outweighed by the sense of diminished roles as individuals that emerges from weakened capacity to accomplish united action by the whole.

Social mobility, which enables one to climb or compels him to slide, at each year in his adult life, to the rank that is the reward or penalty of his performance, contributes to our anxieties. They may in time be reduced by maturing attitudes toward status. Ridding ourselves of irrational anxieties is all to the good but does not cure endemic rational anxiety, our bitter discontent that eats us deep.

Chapter 15

ABILITY GROUPING

Two issues over which politicians are likely to struggle for the foreseeable future are ability grouping and conditioning. First the former.

Most people think each person should be allowed to live to the limit of what she has within herself. Thomas Wolfe wrote:

> So, then, to every man his chance—to every man, regardless of his birth, his shining golden opportunity—to every man the right to live, to work, to be himself, and to become whatever thing his manhood and his vision can combine to make him—this, seeker, is the promise of America.

It is thought that to enable fulfillment of personality gives not only justice to the individual but benefit to the society to which he is enabled to make the greatest possible contribution.

> The object is to bring into action the mass of talents which lies buried in poverty in every country for want of means of development, and thus give activity to a mass of mind, which in proportion to our population, shall be the double or treble of what it is in most countries.
>
> THOMAS JEFFERSON

Little dispute remains on the general proposition that society should use its engines of compulsion and assistance to provide equal opportunity for almost everyone to fulfill his potential. (Many would include in the policy those without the potential even to meet the minimum standards of citizenship, a humanitarian measure rather than a means toward a free society.)

This aim to bring out the most and best within each of us, in early years and late, has led to two complementary sets of social policies and practices. One seeks to provide free mobility, both horizontal and vertical, for apparent talent to go where it may be most fully exercised, and thereby further developed and fulfilled in the doing, through employment and promotion according to capacity to perform. The other pushes equal opportunity upstream—roughly, from jobs to education—to enable each seed to become whatever plant its blueprint might provide for it. Erich Fromm wrote, "Education is identical with helping the child realize his potentialities." The policies include measures to improve the care of ill-cared for children, universal public education, scholarships, public libraries, and training programs open to all who can profit by them.

As both a means toward and result of equal opportunity, people are brought together according to their capacities, potential or realized, in all aspects of their lives: education, work, play and residence. The elite schools, research institutes, corporate R&D divisions, residential enclaves occupied by people in the foregoing institutions, all concentrate rich supplies of socially significant gifts. Those of us with more modest endowments find ourselves elsewhere but together. Low income housing projects gather people with a different average level of capacity. One is encouraged to spend his days with his peers, discouraged from associating with his betters, and exempted from associating with his inferiors.

These practices, combined with our complex technology, express our values favoring a meritocracy of socially desired talent, dependent on brains and skills as a new form of wealth and source of power. And they move us toward such a meritocracy. Our direction poses a challenge that combines an appealing opportunity with a perplexing problem.

Ability grouping will provoke controversy, largely expressed in terms of rights and justice, although more fundamental considerations may be the effects on the society's productivity, stability and diversity and on its members' freedom. In ardor and intensity the disputants' claims will be exceeded by the contestants' clash over the policies to be adopted.

Those who favor ability grouping may argue thus. To prevent ability grouping by public policy is impossible except at the cost of measures that also would return us to a level of civilization not far above the Stone Age.

In contesting this issue as citizens setting public policy, most parents will put their duties and interests as parents ahead of their duties and interests as citizens. Most will think that their children tend to take after themselves in level of potential ability. Most of the more able parents will think that their children have above-average potential and that ability grouping therefore would assist their personal development, even though it might harm society overall. Among these more able parents, not enough of them to defeat ability grouping would be willing to sacrifice for the common good even a small degree of what they see as the chances to maximize their children's chances for success in life. Because most of these more able parents would be on the same side, their side would win.

For persons no longer under their parents' jurisdiction, much of this controversial grouping is voluntary. We associate not only in obedience to concerted policies, public and private, that segregate people according to talent; we also associate according to our own tastes, which often fit a narrow range of talent. (My own tastes in people have been more catholic than most and my opportunities broader, yet in later years most of those with whom I associate from personal affinity fall into a fairly narrow range: bright, well-educated members of professions, coming from middle- and upper-class family backgrounds, with ethnic background Jewish or old-stock white Protestant.) The voluntary quality of this grouping makes desegregation difficult.

Even if an effort to desegregate by ability succeeded, the pressures that would have to be applied to induce compliance would violate personal rights to associate and would inflict a repulsive imposition on personal tastes.

To provide equal opportunity to fulfill one's potential, to perform according to one's realized capacity, and to be recognized according to one's performance, all are just. The long-sustained Chinese empire maintained equal opportunity of sorts but confined it to the society's upper sectors. That scholarly meritocracy drew its members mainly from parents who already were well-to-do, since a peasant family rarely could afford to pay for the years of schooling needed to qualify for the civil service. Our extending equal opportunity to education enables more people to fulfill their potential and provides more justice.

Our humanity may make us deny the battle to the strong, but justice calls for an accurate stopwatch, a fair measurement, as the only condition put on the race going to the swift.

A third form of justice is to compensate in part for the range of natural inequality—since we cannot shrink the range—by some degree of artificial leveling, not of opportunity but of result: experience, station, power, comfort, perhaps happiness. Progressive income tax rates, welfare payments and public services available to all tend to equalize the results of economic effort. The universal franchise and legal and constitutional curbs on officials tend to equalize political power. These measures support the bottom and restrict the top. When I was young, social relations between boys and girls during the years from puberty to marriage often were corrupting and cruel. When the wallflower and the belle of the ball made the scene, big losers were miserable, and big winners were spoiled. By custom imposing a floor and ceiling on these practices, the net sum of unhappiness has declined, and outlooks have become more sane.

But to prevent ability grouping carries this artificial leveling a further step. The minor justice it may provide of a more equal fulfillment of potential is more than offset by the major injustice of carrying leveling too far. The natural inequality derived from birth, and more often accentuated than diminished by early parental upbringing, is a stump that we can plow around but cannot remove. Not to admit that below-average people compose half of humankind is self-deceiving sentimentality. To ignore the range of human capabilities and contributions by imposing equal benefits, rewards and authority on everyone would deny more justice than it granted. Our human seeds will continue to be unequal unless we adopt genetic engineering to give our children uniform potential like baby rabbits or seedling strawberry plants. Although our personal inequality makes association with each other more interesting, complex and rich, it is, next to mortality, life's greatest injustice. This fact we cannot change and ought to face.

Social efficiency—redounding to the whole society's benefit—can be increased by maximizing the personal development of those with the most to develop. Unless the upper spike is maintained above a certain size the society will suffer from inadequate leadership and needed superior talent of all kinds. Members of Phoenician society would burn their babies to appease the gods when things were going badly, and Carthage was weakened by its leaders' failure to reject this practice for their own children (although they sometimes tried to escape it by substituting bought babies). We all gain from the contribution made by the best and brightest who are developed to the fullest. We should be allowed the services of statesmen, musicians and surgeons, the realization of whose gifts has not been held back in furtherance of social policy to make things more interesting for their inferiors. Those with highest potential can be developed to where they can contribute the most only if they are immersed in a concentrated solution, undiluted by dolts and drones.

To prevent ability grouping would achieve no compensating social good because the opponents exaggerate the risks that they foresee. Some European and East Asian school systems group their young by aptitude to learn and train, yet do not stint the slow. Our society is not growing more unequal. Even if ability grouping does reduce equality of opportunity to fulfill potential, this reduction is more than offset by what we have done to equalize such opportunity by freeing most people from distracting discomfort and stupefying toil. There may be no longer some who have enjoyed leisure, education and enlightening experience, while others are kept as drawers of water and hewers of wood. When no one must become jaded by long, tiring routine, each person may have more nearly equal chances to exercise and thus develop his or her mind and skills, even though differences remain in the degree to which people's work requires or permits such use while on the job. These conditions contract the vertical axis by removing disabilities from efforts to rise by persons who formerly would have stayed undeveloped and performing at a low level. It lets them catch up with those who, from the privileges of birth, would have had greater chance for self-development. It gives no better chance for self-improvement to those who would have had it anyway in the past. Compression from below is not coupled with commensurate stretch above.

The upper and lower sections of society are not being alienated. In fact, the trend runs the other way. For over a hundred years several movements have been reducing individual differences: travel and communication, the rule of public opinion, the leveling of social classes, removal of inherited class barriers, spreading wealth, and adoption of a uniform system of technology. Common experiences and shared development are bringing a closer understanding between people on different levels of education and advantage.

Each of us is enabled to reach more other persons for exchange of ideas, for personal association, for mating, for transactions of all kinds. Travel and entertainment arouse in the uneducated an appetite for self-improvement. In some respects the media bring each person in touch with all. Although one on the lower levels of capacity will lack personal association with first-rate people, he can obtain through the media certain elements of their company—among the living, some of the upper spike occupants, and among the dead those who, if alive, would be at the pattern's summit whether or not they had been so recognized in their time. Except for intercourse, he can enjoy almost all the best of themselves that these people have to give. Those who avail themselves of the right portions of the media are enlightened and stimulated. Availability invites. The presence under their noses of these opportunities—not merely the existence of the right—tempts uneducated people to take advantage of them. Without intent or effort but by inadvertent exposure, they receive improving experiences such as from an appealing genius, like Leonard Bernstein, appearing on their television screen and teaching them painlessly to appreciate good music.

Some people feel that world culture is becoming a spinning blender, on its way to making us alike, so that we will taste to each other like baby food. Travelers reach for the match book on the bedside table to see in which Hilton hotel they have awakened. The more that presently separate cultures acquire common characteristics, the easier it becomes for people to move freely between them, thereby making them even more alike. The risk of dull uniformity exceeds the risk of excessive differentiation between society's high and low levels.

Also, ability grouping mainly affects people's experience. Such stretching as this may do to society's vertical axis is outweighed by the stronger force of heredity pulling toward the center, so that parents with abnormally high or low capacity tend to have offspring closer to the norm of human kind.

The opposition argument may run as follows: As to the body, one sees little ground for belief that ability grouping causes potential to be realized in unequal degree. To segregate the best athletes by putting them on teams together does not impair other people's chances to develop and exercise their bodies. Nor does teaching musicians grouped according to talent seem to arrest the growth of those whose potential is low. For other aspects of personality, however, convincing evidence shows that ability grouping, although it stems from a policy of equal opportunity, causes *unequal* fulfillment of potential. By stimulating the development of those with higher potential and stunting the development of those with lower potential, ability grouping creates unequal environments. It also fails to enable the maximum possible sum of everyone's fulfillment (approaching full development for everyone).

Helping the high while impeding the low, enabling some to develop themselves to their limits but at the costs of impairing others' development, makes ability grouping unfair. The failure to maximize development for the society makes it less productive. And its division of society into upper and lower sections alien to each other creates risks of social harm. The impending conflict between the rich nations and the poor is a partial model of the problem accentuated by ability grouping and in part results from this process.

People are sorted out, and those with high potential are put among gifted peers, while those with low potential are put among those like them who contribute little to each other. One set of unshaped personalities is surrounded by high standards and models of excellence, while another set, those least able to do things for themselves, is not. We segregate criminals in prison. When we let them out, we segregate them again by not allowing them to earn a living and thereby to live among those who know how to live more or less right. The qualities that they share with jellyfish make them susceptible to their associates who encourage those propensities that they share with a shark.

The process is intensified by treating potential as fate. People are associated according to an unexplained set of measurements that determine their potential and predict their behavior. By indexing, catalogues and so forth, rational organization is given the accumulated data about each individual and the groups to which he belongs and with which he is compared; they are analyzed and interpreted. The statistical probability for most members of the group, given predictive force by newly developed accuracy, is translated into an ineluctable destiny for each. The individual's own conduct is changed both by his own acceptance of this fortune cookie and by the acceptance of those around him, whose attitudes affect him.

The society's vertical extension is further enabled by the new freedom to associate and to differentiate oneself derived from extended opportunities to travel, communicate and choose from among various occupations. When you pick your associates from all the human race you can match up with fine particularity. It is hard to think that the human preferences that determine the voluntary groups will be less various than the circumstances that shaped the lives of the groups that geography used to form and that developed differences in isolation. Affluence enables diversity in life styles. We may have horizontal contests across vertical boundaries: C. P. Snow's Two Cultures head to head, technocrats versus politicians, physical scientists versus social scientists, physical scientists versus the psychologically oriented, artists versus the rest of us. Even this diversion of hostilities from vertical class conflict might not suffice to let society continue to cohere when so many had grown so distant from each other in essential respects.

New patterns of work and leisure string out the procession, pulling the engine further from the caboose. Work is becoming less evenly shared. Challenging and strenuous work of a kind to help one to fulfill potential is more available to those of high potential than to those of low potential. Such self-developing work not only is more available to those of high potential but it has come to exert more incentive to work hard and long and thereby develop oneself further.

By contrast, the abilities of low-potential people tend to be dulled by excessive play and slackened by undemanding work. Compounding this general condition is the wholly involuntary idleness that afflicts more low-potential people than it does high-potential people. Although we have escaped from debasing labor that leaves no surplus energy for self-development, we have not yet learned how to unload our incubus of widespread enervating unemployment that leaves its victims' equipment rusting on a side track, a process almost as disabling as physical exertion that is both excessive and incessant.

Self-development always has provided rewards of self-satisfaction, but in the past one could not change his rank by exercising or failing to exercise his developed talent. Even among those people with the most privileged position, opportunities for self-development were limited by short lives, poor health, lack of communication with those who might stimulate them, and inferior education, training and knowledge. Whatever opportunity one had to develop his potential, this had no effect on one's social position insofar as society denied the second opportunity: the chance to rise or fall to the level fitted by one's revealed talent. Since one's station was largely frozen by birth, development of one's potential, no matter what other differences it might make to a person, made little difference to one's social rank. Now, making rank depend on personal worth offers a further incentive to self-development (of those qualities and capacities that affect personal worth rather than what may give self-satisfaction but not be regarded by society as something important) by everyone who cares about his station in life. Yet the chances are not even.

Those with the greatest gifts enjoy conditions that let them magnify their callings further than was permitted the most privileged aristocracy of the past: fewer hours of narrow routine, good education, and, most important of all, the company of superior associates and models, with no longer lower standards to accommodate well-born second-raters. At the top the cream thickens and genius flourishes, while the rest of the society suffers an ability drain and is left the poorer for it. At the other extreme of a Pruitt-Igoe housing project the social structure crumbles where those with low potential are left with each other to marinate.

Opportunities for human development always have been unequal. In the traditional culture, each class contained a mixed bag of talent. Some children of high potential and low station would be held back by a restricted environment, while others who inherited low potential and high station would be enabled to develop themselves far. The mutual cancellation effects, tending to equalize realized abilities, kept a lot of the society bunched in the middle of the pattern. Samuel Johnson described this when he observed:

In barbarous society, superiority of parts is

of real consequence. Great strength or great wisdom is of much value to any individual. But in more polished times there are people to do everything for money; and then there are a number of other superiorities, such as those of birth and fortune, and rank, that dissipate men's attention, and leave no extraordinary share of respect for personal and intellectual superiority. This is wisely ordained by Providence, to preserve some equality among mankind.

Now the removal of most of the inequality of opportunities for fulfillment of potential that the hereditary class system had imposed has stopped the process by which some people with high potential were held back and some with low potential were allowed to make the most of it. None of us wishes to return to the barbarous conditions to which Dr. Johnson referred; few of us wish to restore hereditary impediments to talent; and most of us wish to assist Providence to ordain maximum fulfillment of each person's potential.

Any human development stretches the vertical axis because some people can develop much and others not at all. A primitive society has a short axis. Lessons and practice offered to everyone leave people farther apart than they were when separated only by their undeveloped differences. The higher that talent of genius can be developed, the further the top of the pattern is extended from the vegetable anchored at zero.

Realization of everybody's potential, by ex-

tending the differences in realized capacity between groups at the two ends of society's vertical
axis, may impose social strains equivalent to those
strains that have been imposed by barriers of hereditary social classes. Most people think that the
human ends attained are worth the price of these
new strains. However, this extension is so long that
a further stretch creates severe additional risks without compensating gain. The practices and conditions that we all support and wish to keep make
ability grouping a threat by substituting for the old
hereditary inequalities its own unequal effects, so
that the opportunities and potential reinforce each
other, rather than offsetting by the random operation of the past, so substantial numbers either go
way up or stay way down.

What is significant is not the total length of
the axis but rather the bulk in the top and bottom
ends. To avoid risk in a policy of universal opportunity for self-development, both spikes must be
kept from growing too heavily populated in relation
to the balloon at the middle. The remoteness of
these sections, augmented by radically divided
outlooks on life, could divide the society in ways
that all would regret. The alienating gulf put between the enriched rich and the impoverished poor
may so curtail the mutual sympathy needed for
concord and justice between the two groups that the
one's resentment and frustration and the other's
disdain and repulsion may increase the centrifugal
forces to the point that the unstable society first is
separated, then cemented together in unjust, unfree

relationships of leader and follower, master and servant, guardian and ward. With a sufficiently elongated, narrowed pattern, the top people may acquire such power over the rest of mankind that they could not resist the temptation to behave as temperate Spartans, Mongols, Normans, Incas or Haidas, while the others are subordinated and overlooked. The former dominant groups were not invulnerable because they lacked a monopoly of talent, but it is hard to see how an elite with their weapons in their heads could be dislodged by an unarmed class.

To restrict ability grouping would not restrict competition. In fact, reduction of ability grouping, by enabling more people to develop themselves more fully, may enable them, if they choose to compete, to do so more effectively. Nor does restricting ability grouping eliminate inequality of capacity, performance, worth or social rank. Equalizing opportunity to fulfill potential enables performances that differ in vast degrees. It does not level but merely limits the stretch.

The word *homogenization* has received a bad name from comparison with the flatness that some features of our culture have acquired. But for a just and free society the model of a cup of cream beside a glass of skimmed milk may be worse than that of homogenized milk. In the former model the whole is divided into separate orders, while in the latter, despite its dismal uniformity, its parts are left related.

To enable the greatest human fulfillment demands a compromise in extent of development between those on different levels of potential. Some of the most gifted have to be offered less than fullest development of their abilities (on the other hand, their social sympathies may be enlarged) in order to enable those of middle potential to develop themselves more than they would in the absence of such stimulating models among them. And the same goes for the middle folk as to those below them. Such policies may give the pattern of society a shorter vertical axis and a broader girth. Even if the more compact pattern fails to increase the resulting sum of everybody's development, it may be justified by protecting the human race from a split into two societies. The whole society profits if the leaven is mixed through the loaf.

Chapter | 16

CONDITIONING

Public policy toward conditioning personality is the other fundamental issue that will cause a continuing political struggle. Society has used three methods to influence its members' behavior. Physical and material measures (force, pain, help and reward) were supplemented by moral sanctions: praise, blame and reverence for the titles of authority, and by belief in divine punishment and reward. Now we can adopt a fourth method. Its vehicles include education, training, the mass media, our new powers to affect behavior by predicting it, and the old methods applied to establish habit by legal and moral deterrence and reinforcement.

Compared to the long-used physical, material and moral measures for influencing behavior, conditioning is efficient but complex. Like preventive medicine it does its task in advance, and less rescue and repair work are required. It complements the other methods by succeeding where they fail. Its influence is stronger in many respects than those external devices aimed at a more immediate external response. The conditioned person is induced to want more wholeheartedly what the policy aims to have him do. An external offer or threat—whether physical, economic or moral—offers a rational choice to a divided mind. One course earns you a reward, which you want, but makes you forego something else you would like; the other may offer to gratify a different desire, yet at risk of the stick. A conditioning process may make your wishes more one-sided. Instead of a conflict between appetite and conscience, with an even chance that the former will win, the process may both strengthen conscience and alter appetite to make it consonant with the conduct approved by conscience. Conditioning may make all your conscious aspects want to be what the makers of the conditioning policy regard as good.

Whether to adopt a concerted public policy of conditioning has been made more important by the increased consequences of the decision. The foremost contributing factor is that we have learned how to do it. What is new is not conditioning as an aspect of experience—which has been with us ever since we became us—but our new power to translate policy into a conditioning process imposed on a large and uniform scale.

Another addition to the impact of conditioning is that some of our former guides—living conditions, tradition, respect for institutional authority—compel us less, so that the way we have been bent directs us more. We used to revere tradition, not so much from the way we were conditioned as from a common belief—one that ignorance left unshaken—and from a rational reaction to existing conditions. A customary practice or outlook became a tradition, treated as a rule and given force by veneration for the hallowed past. We know more about the past than ever before and we still know that we are its servants because it has made us. But what Tocqueville called "the track of the generations" has been obscured. Less aware of continuity with the past, more aware of change, we have lost reverence for tradition. Although we still have customs, and by definition we still follow them, they bind us less. Custom no longer is supported by tradition and it has altered so many times that it has lost the force of permanence.

Our awareness of our leaders' fallibility and their lack of divine sanction has reduced respect for the institutions that they manage and thereby reduced their influence on our conduct.

Some retain belief in heavenly sponsorship for moral rules. But such faith guides the actions of but few among this few. At the same time, belief in personal moral responsibility has dropped. Most persons no longer think that one deserves either heaven or hell for his conduct because so much of it is ordained by the circumstances that shaped him. His character is his fate, his conduct deriving from his personality which in turn is produced by interaction of his inheritance and experience. Although our free will has not changed, the cessation of our belief in free will has freed us from servitude to moral principle.

The widened range of choice offered us by circumstance has come to cause the way we are conditioned to affect our conduct more. Simply as a species, we are offered many choices. Our biological makeup makes us less programmed machines than some of our fellow creatures.

The ratio of the number of our personal decisions to the number that the experience of the race has built into us is high, because so little is built in. The house fly makes some decisions of her own, but mostly uses the gradually acquired, the slowly trained mind of thousands of generations of flies.

HARLOW SHAPLEY

In times past, external pressures narrowly directed our conduct by making many choices so one-sided in their preferability that the details of an individual's personality bore less on his decisions. Survival without discomfort used to require most of a person's energetic hours. Everyone adjusted himself to surroundings over which he had almost no control. As savages we regarded nature as intractable and could alter only a small part of it. As a slave, the individual was likewise powerless and had to do all the adjusting. The choices offered by society and technology were few. They forced wide contradictions on us. The part of our self that lost out in the decision was more discomfited than it is now. The choice might be made between humiliating subservience to a master and going hungry; between grueling labor and a beating or between taking a husband who, to put it gently, was incompatible and spending your days keeping house for your parents and helping your sisters-in-law. In a certain season, regardless of your aptitude, inclination, capacity or taste, you picked up a scythe in the morning and swung it all day through the grain, since to do otherwise meant you first would be ostracized and then would starve.

Now that we have learned to subdue nature in drastic and elaborate ways, one has to make only minor adjustments of himself to his physical environment. (We are learning that society may not push nature too far, but the individual remains less in thrall to it.) We have broadened our choices further by an open and stable political system, by a social system that permits adoption and change of various roles, by accumulated wealth and knowledge and, above all, by expectation of a longer life.

It is as though we were ordering a meal and the number of items on the bill of fare over the years had grown. Yet someone embedded somewhere in us leans over our mental shoulder and tells us what to select. This diversity, plus our master's generosity, let us take a course more in harmony with our tastes and nature than the set of choices offered to our forefathers. Survival having ceased to be an urgent spur, the choice to undertake strenuous action depends less on our outer necessities' commands than on how a person responds to inner voices. The function of such voices, hitherto mere whispers, has expanded as the necessities' rule declined.

No longer so sharply limited by the narrow imperatives of a scarcity economy, confining roles, fixed beliefs and a short life, a person enabled to pursue his desires according to the particular configurations of his personality can be offered more chance to be himself. So the political issue of conditioning, whose powerful new methods are to some a threat of enslavement, is becoming enlivened by what to many is our liberating new conditions: our widened range of choice, loss of guiding beliefs, escape from a life of trudging down a tunnel of circumstance, and knowledge that how we will control each other by shaping each other constitutes a truly conscious choice.

The conditioning issue is not to be whether but what and how. Organized society might prevent any particular item of conditioning from taking place but it could not stop the overall process in any one. By their refusal to make concessions to the senses, the Protestant churches tried to escape this law of life but only altered its effects. In us all, this flow, which can be directed but not dammed, is certain, even without the presence or use of technical devices and without any direction by public policy. Everyone, no matter how free his personality, soon accumulates premises in his approach to the world, attitudes by definition nonrational though not necessarily irrational, but that cannot be escaped.

Even if we always could be reasonable, our reason remains the servant of our impulses and attitudes. Some may be more hospitable to reason than others, but reason always is directed, even if not impaired, by these attitudes. Like its cousin mathematics (or like money), reason never wants anything itself.

The conditioning process not only cannot be prevented, but the attitudes that it produces are essential to individuality. Without them, one would not be what we regard as a human being and would not have the capacity for personal freedom. We have not discovered how to eliminate them and we would not want to if we could. Since, in part, what we do is determined by nonrational attitudes, which are shaped by experience, which public policy can prescribe, the policy question involves in funda- mental conflict both our interests and our beliefs.

Although the political struggle may be ex- pected to take place over particular values and methods, a general principle is likely to underlie the common themes developed in dispute. Some of those who oppose any public policy on conditioning will argue, as follows, that a concerted affirmative policy to condition people according to a plan would not work.

People have shown an inherent resistance to the methods employed up to now, so most condi- tioning of adults has been only temporary. Sales resistance and sophistication have risen in response to manipulative power. As knowledge of how to influence minds has increased, so has the critical capacity to recognize the methods and avoid their effects. Our faculties for discerning assaults on our personalities are developed by experience of the danger just as persons living in the wilderness without elaborate tools develop keen eyes and ears for the presence of wild beasts. The experience of the Soviet Union shows that when a society with no tradition of independent thought enables its members to get an education, and not even a liberal education, some of them start getting independent ideas. The modern habit of thinking for oneself, especially in the physical sciences and other fields of self-disciplined, competitive and analytical thought, is hard to keep from people, especially if you want them trained to understand machines.

Then we are fenced in with what we have inherited, some within ourselves and some without. Anthropologists and biologists have discovered within us a body of inflexible material that limits our capacity to alter ourselves and our ways of living.

> The inexorable biological limitations of *homo sapiens* . . . the frontiers of social and technological limitations will be determined not by the extent to which man can manipulate the external world but by the limitations of his own biological and emotional nature.
>
> RENÉ DUBOS

This resistance, joined to inevitable mistakes in performance, would make a public policy for conditioning amount to no more than government meddling and muddling, giving us no benefit but burdening us with inconvenience and expense.

The rest of those who favor *laissez faire* would say a policy *will* work, and instead of what the proponents intend, the results will be enslavement from which it will be impossible to escape.

Without a unified policy, the present random

practices will stay varied, reflecting the diverse values among humankind. The risks that such a policy are supposed to protect against are exaggerated. And even if not, they are exceeded by the certain evils of a unified policy.

The biological limits will not be reached until the harm is done. Children have no sales resistance, and even for skeptical adults, the contest is unequal.

> There are more and more signs about us that our increasingly efficient and pervasive apparatus of mass suggestion is planing off individual differences, and making us more and more facile for mass manipulation.
>
> LEARNED HAND

Everyone, no matter how rational and resolute, or no matter how, because of a disturbed or distorted personality, unreachable by either reason or passion, can be manipulated. When sufficiently comprehensive and sustained, the devices and methods can alter attitudes and maintain the changes made. The methods of group offense are too powerful for an individual defense to resist or elude.

A concerted policy would cause us to be conditioned more intensively than is needed for maximum personal freedom. For example, extreme conditioning measures could make almost everyone unwilling to commit a crime. But the price of this would be narrowed and muted personalities. We now maximize freedom by conditioning people no more than just enough to make most of us unwilling to commit crimes. Those on whom the process does not succeed commit a crime once in a while. To keep us safe from them our conditioning is supplemented with reward and punishment to encourage and to deter, and with isolation to protect. A public policy of conditioning would go too far. We cannot maintain freedom of thought, freedom for citizens to choose the direction that society is to take, where leaders of a unified group can indoctrinate opinion.

Stalin called intellectual leaders "engineers of human souls." We may adopt this concept as a principle of government, substituting "positive thinking" for thought, determining not a proposition's truth but its appeal to the audience's psychic needs. People are gently guided as one blows a toy sailboat in a basin. The fatherly manipulators would become a self-perpetuating body like the board of a mutual insurance company. In this oligarch's paradise, impossible to overthrow, one would be denied even the modest privilege of martyrdom. Such a prospect would make one almost prefer to return to the brutal early days of social organization, when the *Arthasastra* declared, "Government is the science of punishment."

Some people reject the belief that to indoctrinate an enclosing framework of absolutes is to establish the necessary order within which one can be free, yet they believe that children can be protected from having any beliefs and attitudes implanted in them. But their mistake in thinking children can be kept as *tabulae rasae* does not show that public leaders—including those in the educational systems—are qualified to decide moral values for the schools to teach. In the days when the basis for morality (why be good) was agreed to be conscience or the church, such authoritative reason used to be fed to children as a proper absolute. Now we are not so sure. Even though it would not lead to despotism, we would be foolish to entrust to politicians that which we have withdrawn from clerics.

Mankind will not behave in a tolerably civilized way unless subjected to a strong authority, but (contrary to Hobbes' endearing trust in princes) since the governors themselves are little better than the rest of us, we cannot entrust them with powerful tools that can tempt them to make us content with them.

Those who favor an affirmative policy will argue as follows: The experiences that we are creating for each other, with our technology and through random combinations of social conditions and practice (in contrast to the past application of conditioning for better or worse by established institutions applying their values), have become so unpredictable, so unrelated to our overall desires, and so strong that they threaten our free thought more than do efforts to adopt the right kind of comprehensive, concerted program.

No longer confined to family, church and

class, the conditioning process now is shared by several groups and institutions, each of which implants a separate set of attitudes. The media operate without regard to their effects on the development of the young except for some limitations imposed by parents' pressures. Advertising and related entertainment have encouraged self-manipulation through chemicals by showing how eating, drinking and smoking certain substances are pleasing, comfortable, popular and safe.

The variety of resulting personalities that prevailed when parents held sway continues, but chance and irrelevant factors of strength have superseded reason and the consistency of tradition that often guided parental policies. The choice of values to be implanted depends in part on the resolution of forces, with the strongest groups prevailing, and in part on the random chemistry of the forces' interaction. This gives excessive strength to the mob with its numbers, to elite groups with their members' higher-than-average abilities, and worst of all, since no one is consulted, to chance.

We are approaching a state that combines the worst features of both haphazard and deliberate conditioning. Many of the voices that press upon us operate in a responsive, imitative way, rather than initiating. Instead of uttering what we have heard from an inner voice that speaks from a resolved harmony of prior conditioning, we often do little more than pass on what we have received from each other and what it seems to us that others want. A circular process unifies the voices, although without organizing direction. It is accentuated by the majority voices reinforcing each other and by their unity overshadowing, if not drowning out, the voices in dissent.

These new conditions may induce people to act capriciously. Before World War II, Arthur Koestler wrote, "We have thrown overboard all conventions, our sole guiding principle is that of consequent logic; we are sailing without ethical ballast." In many matters where people agree for a moment they no longer are impeded from acting forthwith, even though next morning they may feel regret. Lack of barriers to sudden and radical change except to the extent that people's impulses and tastes may cancel each other out may allow group whims to do things we abhor. If we tell ourselves that we are forbearing to presume to mold our fellow citizens' minds as we slide toward inadvertent unity, we abdicate our responsibility to preserve our own ideals of freedom because we allow each other to become slaves of the crowd.

Whether organized or anarchic, government by alteration of desire is uncontrolled. We have tried to limit the old forms of power and should do the same with the new. The weapons of mass destruction call for controls to enable survival of the human race, while the development of means to capture minds calls for controls to protect the freedom of our thought. The individual, powerless to resist these methods directly when they are used on him or his children, can join with others to restrict and guide these methods. However, since conditioning is inevitable in contrast to use of the weapons of mass destruction, prohibiting high pressure conditioning methods or bigoted values is not enough.

Our experience is sure to implant in us some nonrational premises, no matter how open-mindedly we were nurtured, no matter how rational, tolerant and liberating an education we were offered. Children cannot be counted on to cleave to the truth when they grow up merely so long as they have not been misled in childhood. They cannot be vacuum-packed until maturity. To try to do nothing but develop their powers of reason is to allow children to pick up their absolute beliefs from their experience of the world. In *Dennis v. U.S.*, when Chief Justice Vinson wrote, "Nothing is more certain in modern society than the principle that there are no absolutes," he declared an absolute. To teach children that there are none may be to make the same mistake.

Macaulay wrote that the Jesuits "discovered the precise point to which intellectual culture can be carried without risk of intellectual emancipation." But we have come to realize that good education is more than passing the point of emancipation just as it is more than "avoiding prejudice." In his will, Bertrand Russell's father appointed two atheists to be Bertrand's guardians, but the court set aside the will, and the boy was educated in the Christian faith. "I was afraid," wrote Russell, "that the result was disappointing but that was not the fault of the law. . . . A parent has the right to ordain that any imaginable superstition shall be instilled into his children after his death but has not the right to say that they shall be kept free of superstition." One may approve his objection to the law's inconsistency and consequent unfairness without thinking that to forbid teaching superstition is all we can do to let us make ourselves free.

Since it is impossible to keep people from acquiring premises of outlook, we should help them acquire what we think are the better ones. To instill a single set of attitudes (as among larger societies, only China has tried) would do more harm than our present nonsystem will do, but such a policy can be forestalled. A concerted program need not be a monolith of inculcated belief. It can be simply some bounds, requiring some values to be instilled by nongovernment agencies of differing points of view, forbidding other things, permitting the rest, and limiting scope and force. For long we have employed affirmative conditioning policies that liberate. For example, we try to require universal literacy by making children go to school.

Plato believed that the mass media equivalent of his day endangered children's proper development:

> And shall we just carelessly allow children to hear any casual tales which may be devised by casual persons, and to receive into their minds ideas for the most part the very opposite of those which we should wish them to have when they are grown up?

We cannot.

Then the first thing will be to establish a censorship of the writers of fiction, and let the censors receive any tale of fiction which is good, and reject the bad; and we will desire mothers and nurses to tell their children the authorized ones only. Let them fashion the mind with such tales, even more fondly than they mould the body with their hands; but most of those which are now in use must be discarded.

Without going so far as to establish public censors, as he recommended, we may enable parents to exercise greater selection over what their children consume. To restrict the more aggressive hucksters might restore to parents a portion of that control over their children's experience that has slipped away as the conditions of modern life have shifted it to other elements of society.

Public policy on conditioning should aim for personal freedom. Although *free will* may be a meaningless term, personal freedom is not; it is something we want even though we do not know how to define it precisely. (Ever since joining the profession dedicated to justice, my inability to define the term has grieved me, although like everyone else I feel qualified to express an opinion of its consequences. But this feeling comes from intellectual fastidiousness, not from any sense that one could not pursue an end that one could not clearly define.)

Let us examine this matter, using the less

ambitious and elusive term *free choice*, which depends on the opportunity for harmony between oneself and one's environment.

I am indeed rich, since my income is superior to my expense, and my expense is equal to my wishes.

GIBBON

Here are personality elements—aimed at increasing free choice—that public policy should direct, encourage or permit to be inculcated.

Minds should be taught to engage in independent, rational thought. John Stuart Mill wrote about how he was conditioned for an open mind. To do this we need not do to each child all the things that were done to him. For free thought are needed attitudes that minimize the force and scope of dogmatic beliefs and that let a belief be adopted or changed only on the basis of evidence and reason. Whatever first principles are implanted under this policy, their planting should be shallow on all points except the importance of rational and independent thought. To as great an extent as is psychologically possible, persons should be indoctrinated with attitudes that let their minds have another chance, attitudes that enable them in later years to reconsider their own premises and to do so only on reasonable grounds. (When Mill grew up he often contradicted his father, not from rebellion or perversity but because his father had taught him to think for himself, and his reason and experience led his thought on paths that sometimes departed from those of his father.) Such an approach may be criticized as an effort to make a god of free thought. However, since nonrational attitudes are going to be acquired, this is one that permits the person later to choose his own gods with greater freedom than if the conditioner had settled the matter.

Also, what should be pressed upon each person is some knowledge of mankind's accumulated and accepted works of thought and art. The best of the past lights our way into the darkness which surrounds us and it helps us to know what we most like and admire in art, conduct and style of life.

Confronting the great shapeless dream surging out of the unconscious of crowds, with its imperious demons, its childish angels and cheap heroes, stand the only forces as powerful as they, and which we acknowledge only by their victory over death. . . . Culture is the highest form of rivalry humanity knows. It orients [man's] fantasy-life, and orients it "up," by obliging it to compete with the greatest of human dreams. Thus [any great artist] tries to compete with [his predecessors] in the quality of the action they exert upon us. . . . However terrible an age, its art transmits only its music. The humanity of dead artists, when it transmits a scourge like the Assyrian horror, for all the torturer-kings of its bas-reliefs, fills our memory with the majesty of the *Wounded Lioness*. And one of the emotions this creature inspires in us is pity. If an art were to be born from the crematory ovens of our age, it would not express the executioners, it would express the martyrs.

In the battle for the human imagination, a civilization unwilling to impose dreams upon all its members must give each individual his opportunity. In other words, put the greatest number of great works in the service of the greatest number of men. Culture is the free world's most powerful guardian against the demons of its dreams, its most powerful ally in leading humanity to a dream worthy of man—because it is the heritage of the world's nobility.

ANDRÉ MALRAUX

A person must be cultivated in order to know more of what is beautiful and he must be educated to know more of what is true. Although this knowledge is not itself nonrational or instilled by nonrational means, it still shapes personality and basic outlook.

Also needed to be instilled is self-discipline. A wholly open mind can give its owner little freedom unless it can direct itself to some subject long enough to make discriminating choices. The mental discipline on which availability of choices depends is the capacity to discern what one wants, consider the array of choices and fit them to one's own desires. This requires knowledge, rationality and certain moral qualities. The moral discipline enables one to act in accord with his thought.

Conrad's point of view was far from modern. In the modern world there are two philosophies: the one, which stems from Rousseau, and sweeps aside discipline as unnecessary; the other, which finds its fullest expression in totalitarianism, which thinks of discipline as essentially imposed from without. Conrad adhered to the older tradition, that discipline should come from within. . . . His point of view, one might perhaps say, was the antithesis of Rousseau's: "Man is born in chains but he can become free." He becomes free, so I believe Conrad would have said, not by letting loose his impulses, not by being casual and uncontrolled, but by subduing wayward impulse to a dominant purpose.

BERTRAND RUSSELL

What must be instilled, of course, are not certain attitudes and values alone but the capacity to act upon them. Without self-discipline, values are no more than passive tastes. In some circles, some people believe in the so-called "cool" philosophy: the attempted substitution of indifference for self-discipline as a means to prevent anti-social conduct provoked by the passions. Whether or not this device achieves its intended purpose, it would not take one far on some demanding quest.

If we can be taught the fact of causality in human behavior, we may increase our freedom of choice by enabling us better to see things as they are, just as every substitution of knowledge for illusion gives us choices that are more free because more informed.

Accepting the idea of causality does not mean renouncing free choice, does not mean a resigned belief that life is so mechanistic and preordained that we might as well have a robot society. Freud, while demonstrating psychological causality (determinism if you will), sought to liberate people by enabling them to see reality.

Compelling evidence tells us that in the natural world—that is, all but the supernatural—each event is caused by a prior event. All events appear to belong to causal chains that operate like rows of dominoes where each that topples knocks over the next. In distance, these chains extend across the universe, and in time they reach back to the "beginning". Our inability to observe or explain more than a few links in any chain does not show causality to be other than a universal process. Causality appears to operate in living processes as well as inanimate ones, and in complex forms of life no less than in simple forms.

When we fly we feel assured that, whatever else may happen, the laws of aerodynamics will not betray us by changing. Yet causality seems to be even more universal a feature of the universe than the uniformity of physical laws. We have been discovering that some physical processes are not uniform except by a tendency. Our new knowledge is shifting part of our physical world from one of measurable causation to one of probability. But even chance events are caused. The results of flipped coins are attributed to chance, but they are also the result of existing but unobservable irregularities in the process as repeated. If the coin were evenly shaped and balanced, flipped the same way and landed on an even surface, the same side would come up every time. Where a deck of cards has been reshuffled and redealt in the same way, people have found—to their profit or their loss—that the same hands are dealt again. When Einstein said he could not see God playing dice with the universe he presumably meant he could not see an omniscient figure wondering what faces the dice would turn up. Even with the indeterminate, dancing particles of matter, we see no evidence that causation does not apply to them. When we attribute something to chance we do not deny causality but merely ascribe the event to a cause that we cannot discern or (except, in some cases of large numbers, by probability) predict.

Inexorable causality makes impossible such a thing as free will in any sense that a choice is free from the causes behind it. An audience does not give forth with "spontaneous applause" unless a stage performance has evoked it. If you sunbathe on the beach, when the tide comes in you can seek higher ground or lie still. Your choice—whether to be wet or dry—depends on how you have been made up to the moment that the tide touched your feet. When we come to a fork in the road, we are given a choice, which then is made by the compass needle in our mind. It turns to the alternative that we take, impelled by the response that the present situation provokes from what the past has made us. The point on the dial where it stops represents the resolution of those forces that we confront and those that fan out behind us, pressing on us the consequences of our background. The only alternative interpretation is that we make a choice by some sort of metaphysical spontaneity as our own uncaused first cause.

Sometimes a decision, especially one of those made between the ages of fifteen and twenty-five, has a profound effect on one's life, but the impact on oneself does not make the decision one's own in the sense of detaching it from causation. Nor does the unpredictability of a human act prove it should be ascribed to free will. Man's perverse unwillingness to follow rational codes and systems, his insistence on making his own decisions even when they do not accord with a sound view of what he may be expected to want—this proves only his complicated makeup, not his free will.

We always do that for which we have the strongest motive, supplied by causes outside us— our ancestors, our experiences and our expectations—bent and shaped by filtering through the prism of our personality. Doing something because you "want to do it" means doing it because part of your personality wants to do it, although other parts may prefer to do something else, and the first part wins control within you. An act of self-sacrifice means an act by which one part of the self directs an act that injures another part of the self and perhaps, as in a "voluntary" death, destroys the whole self. To say that one's strongest desire may be overcome by one's sense of duty is to say that one's sense of duty is itself a desire, and in this case is truly the strongest. What was said to be the "strongest desire" was actually the second strongest.

Reason performs a function in the resolution of these conflicts. "Reason is but choosing." It shows us how to get what we want, as the slave of our passions. When one makes a hard choice—a big price later versus cash now, more freedom versus more security, conscience versus pleasure, loyalty to A versus loyalty to B—feeling the burden of choosing rests heavily on the chooser alone, she performs as a combination of alert referee and tormented battleground for the contest between two or more dynamic elements of personality.

Henry Jekyll declared that the high level of his aspirations to grave dignity tended to clash with his "impatient gaiety of disposition." So to pursue the aim he felt required to conceal—and suppress—the impulse more than would have been necessary for a man whose inclinations were less contradictory.

Though so profound a double-dealer, I was in no sense a hypocrite; both sides of me were in dead earnest; I was no more myself when I laid aside restraint and plunged in shame, than when I labored, in the light of day, at the furtherance of knowledge or the relief of sorrow and suffering. . . . I thus drew steadily nearer to that truth . . . that man is not truly one, but truly two.

ROBERT LOUIS STEVENSON

Effort in pursuit of an ideal, in obedience to a duty, or in observance of a loyalty may be a natural exercise of a desire that wins out over other desires. Acceptance of causality gives no reason to quit so long as such effort fulfills a need within us. Because our actions that take moral effort matter to us, they may have worth.

To induce most people to behave tolerably toward each other—essential for any free choice in human relations—laws and rationality are not enough. Moral sanctions will not work as a social policy unless we instill in people four aspects of moral responsibility: conscience, habit, suscepti-bility to others' moral judgments (when others are right), and willingness to pass moral judgments on others. Margaret Mead has written:

> Now we have forgotten conscience. We worry only about what "other people" will say or think. But other people are so ever-present, and their knowledge of us is so thorough, that the guiding force is much more effective and reliable than it might have been in a more loosely organized society.

Since many people's commanding voice has shifted from conscience to the prospective opinion of others, and since that opinion often expresses taste rather than morality and in either case is often wrong, it seems useful to instill a sense of right and wrong and an inclination to do right.

The attitudes directed toward our own conduct, through habit and conscience, should apply to whatever those instilling the attitudes think has a moral element. But the attitudes to be instilled for passing moral judgment on others' behavior should cover the narrower range of where it is likely to work. As to another given person, the only decisions to be judged should be those of a kind that might be influenced by his awareness of potential approval or disapproval, measuring the person as a member of a class according to what is known about him. Where the prospect of praise or blame by others may influence one's conduct, there is where others should be taught to pass moral judgment.

Blaming others imposes a penalty. The judgment is imposed where, looking backward, the person judged might reasonably have been expected to have been influenced in his decision (for which he is now being held morally or legally responsible) by the threatened penalty. Where one is found legally responsible for having committed a crime, or is judged morally responsible for some act, it appears that the influence on him of the risk of judgment had been insufficient to guide his path where the rulemaker wished. However, the fact that it did not work on him does not invalidate the classification. The prisons are filled with those on whom the threat of penalties did not work, but those same threats keep most of the rest of us from doing what might send us to jail.

When the range of accountability was broader than the range set by people's capacity to be influenced by legal or moral sanctions, people sometimes were punished or praised without useful effect. Now moral responsibility has been withdrawn from those actions that we have come to realize moral pressures may not have been expected to influence. But it should be narrowed no further. Some people refuse to judge any act where they find an upstream cause. This attitude suggests that one is morally accountable only where either he is miraculously exempt from causation or where others are ignorant of his background. No one could be regarded as accountable for anything if all that was considered was whether his actions had been determined by all that had shaped his personality. The answer always would be yes, and the one who gave it might be a spectator or a historian but not a judge.

We should not let humility or sophistication inhibit us from passing judgments. Like judges in court, most of whom remember they are not God, we can with honesty and realism pass moral judgment on others and on ourselves. One does so in exercise of civic duty, helping to improve civilization, as music criticism improves musicians' performance. Mill remarked that "It would be a blessing if the doctrine of necessity could be believed by all *quoad* the character of others, and disbelieved in regard to their own." But without pining for such a blessing, we may make ourselves umpires or critics, bearing responsibility but not a burden of conclusive doom.

For a long time people have resisted the

notion of universal causality. Samuel Johnson said, "All theory is against freedom of the will, all experience for it." Not only is it hard for us to overcome our experience and reconcile causation with personal responsibility, but acknowledgment of causality has seemed irreverent toward Higher Powers. Plutarch observed:

> People would not then tolerate natural philosophers, and theorists, as they then called them, about things above; as lessening the divine power, by explaining away its agency into the operation of irrational causes and senseless forces acting by necessity, without anything of Providence or a free agent.

Even after we ceased to believe in the divine purpose that once was thought to help things along when free will took a rest, we continued to assume some purpose guiding events. When we discovered nature's regularities, we nonetheless applied to them not the term *practice*, indicating the way things are done, but the term *law*, indicating that Someone not only sees the sparrow fall but also commands the apple to fall.

Now that the universe shows us scant evidence of any underlying purpose, and belief in free will is not so confident, many people's effort flags. Some interpret causation as excusing retreat into lassitude, thinking, "Since we are bound in chains of causality, destiny rules. Why should I not sit back, coast and observe, letting destiny operate the machine?"

This fails to recognize that destiny lets us belong to it. You may have the choice of continuing to watch television from a warm chair or of shoveling snow from the front walk. A sense of duty toward your mother who is coming to call, pride toward a neighbor who is shoveling his walk, and satisfaction in performing a patriarchal role all press against inertia, a wish for comfort, and the pleasure of watching the show. By accepting determinism, you may be tilted to stay put. This supposes that the energy of the universe does not include one's own, that the failure to use one's own would have no significance to your surroundings or to you or that your life would be the same, determined by destiny, whether you got out of the chair or not. Our energies and will power are no less aspects of personality than are a bad temper or a strong back.

Of course, we reduce our freedom of choice when we butt our heads against the walls, failing to defer to necessity. But we make a like mistake if we decline effort and choice on the ground that everything is sure to happen as destiny decrees, regardless of what we do. Fatalism is unrealistic wherever it is applied to matters that our efforts can affect.

Existential thinkers seem to have been struggling with the problem for human action created by the combination of self-awareness and the compelling knowledge of causation. Concerned with refuting—or at least rebuking—the superficial interpretation of causality that leads people to narrow their horizons of possible choice, these thinkers argue, or point out, not that our will is free but that we broaden our range of choice by remembering that our decisions need not be confined by reference to our awareness of what has made us. Your past binds you but not in the particular pattern that you happen to know. Your background may have made you someone likely to do cowardly things, but in a given instance your awareness of your background need not dictate what you do. It may be determined by other factors, such as your wish to rise above yourself or to deny the expectations of others. Just as not every doctrine of government or history proclaimed as expressing necessity ("the tyrant's plea") is necessarily true, so to keep your decisions within limits that appear to be set for you by your own incomplete knowledge of how you have been made until today may deny you some alternatives that are truly yours.

Last, what needs to be instilled in each of us is a sense of desired direction, which is needed not only for personal identity but for free choice as well. Without purpose, the only way that a person could be regarded as free would be in the sense of the sole occupant of a spaceship that he can fly in any direction at the speed of light, in empty and infinite space.

All freedom is no more than the privilege to choose new goals of commitment and choose new paths of fulfillment. Who live in life-enhancing freedom live a certain way for particular purposes, not haphazardly and aimlessly.

JERRY BERLIN

We need personal independence, even to the point of perversity, for us to exercise freedom.

> It is man's inherent willfulness that I would preserve, and in which I wish to set the stronghold of that Liberty I prize.
>
> LEARNED HAND

But willfulness falls into triviality unless employed with a capacity for some sustained purpose.

Utopian thinking used to consider two variables: our outer selves and what surrounded us. The latter was how to subdue the physical world and to organize our practices with each other. We now must add a third variable: Whether and how to change our own natures. In time this conditioning question may perplex and divide politicians more than any other.

For long we have worked at harmonizing circumstances with ourselves. This is complicated enough, especially considering the related problem of harmonizing the separate, incorrigible selves that compose each of us. "And indeed what are we but sedition and discrepancy," wrote Montaigne.

We are told that we change a bit over the generations by adapting according to natural selection. Now natural selection further adapts to the culture that our species has made for itself, often with effects that multiply rather than neutralize.

The evolution of this species acquired and preserved a singular character. The genotypes which evolved and became established by natural selection facilitated the acquisition and transmission of culture. The establishment of these genotypes made possible rapid growth and development of culture. The sequence closed and became circular; the evolution of culture, of the human society, of technology and science, modifies the adoptive values, the Darwinian fitness of human genotypes. The process of natural selection is, therefore, channeled more and more toward adaptation to man-made environments.

THEODOSIUS DOBZHANSKY

When he told the House of Commons how important it was to choose the right design for the chamber it was to occupy, replacing the old one destroyed by German bombs, Churchill said, "We shape our buildings and afterwards our buildings shape us." Although we are changing our culture more these days, it still operates slowly on us through the breeding process. (Such alteration always is slow by the standards of the species doing the breeding.) But now, our power over each other and ourselves has grown from a chance to stimulate or give momentary solace to the capacity to change personality in basic ways. By such an alteration one does not merely adjust one's self to the surroundings (as in eating what is set before one or bending over to go through a low doorway). We are learning how to modify and determine our species. Such changes, interacting with the drastic changes that we make in our surroundings, can accelerate and extend the process. This power poses an issue that is not immediate but may soon beset us.

How far shall we remake ourselves, even going over the brink of discarding our present selves? Are we willing to commit a form of posteritycide? As Erasmus put it, "As if there were any difference between perishing and being another thing!" If we are willing to make such changes, then toward what end? With our increased power, if we could discern the answer we should be able to make ourselves happier and better.

> I think it not improbable that man, like the grub that prepares a chamber for the winged thing it has never seen but is to be—that man may have cosmic destinies that he does not understand.
>
> HOLMES

But how can we know what "better" is? If we develop new types, they in turn may have new wants about what their species should be.

How can we know how to make people free— by giving a sense of direction—until we know what to make of ourselves? Our earlier notion of freedom as possessing available choices to permit attainment of harmony is incomplete. Our new knowledge gives us power yet takes from us our knowledge of how to approach freedom. With two variables to adjust—our outer selves and our environment—an aimed-for harmony was visible though often not attainable. Always we had a constant for reference, our basic selves. But with our core changeable as well as our skin, with three variables and no constant, what and where are the measuring sticks? With which of our potential natures should we try to live in harmony?

> We have learned that we do not see directly, but mediately, and that we have no means of correcting these colored and distorting lenses which we are, or of computing the amount of their errors. Perhaps these subject-lenses have a creative power; perhaps there are no objects. Once we lived in what we saw; now, the rapaciousness of this new power, which threatens to absorb all things, engages us.
>
> EMERSON

Since we are what we are, the only way we can consider what we ought to be is by considering our possibilities. What standard of value should we use to measure and compare them? Unless we have a self-image for which to aim, we cannot know what to do with either ourselves or our environment.

Can man be used as "the measure of all things" if he himself is variable? What we are never has been something precisely identifiable, like our social security number, and now with self-alteration capacity, is it even loosely identifiable? To learn what we should make of ourselves, should we try to plumb our unconscious minds, there to discover our "true" selves, or, even in truth, would we desire them?

That even through desire, man does not
know how to find what he needs; that not by
enjoyment, not even by imagination and wish, can
we agree about what we need for our contentment.
Let our thought cut out and sew at its pleasure, it
will not even be able to desire what is fit for it, and
satisfy itself.

MONTAIGNE

Left with only bootstrap reasoning available
to us, lacking points of reference on which to guide
ourselves, we resemble a composer who is told he
can use any combination of pitches to constitute the
scale within which he will construct music. We frail
mortals, dismayed at our newfound power over
ourselves, wonder how we can choose a course to
steer when our only guide is the light on the ship's
prow. We no longer can turn to the Westminster
Catechism to tell us (first question) what is man's
chief end. We have reason to think that our
knowledge of what has happened before us is becoming more comprehensive and more accurate.
Nor is it as useless as Coleridge suggested with his
analogy of the lantern at the stern. But like retaining
a lawyer who can better point out pitfalls than
discover loopholes, knowing and heeding history
help us less to choose where to go than to make
fewer mistakes.

Until we know better what we want, we might
postpone experimental alteration of our species.
Although no such delay can keep our culture from
changing, and us with it, we might attend to the

ideal of what a person should do and be within the limits of our species as it is. This lighthouse manufactured for our use requires values other than free choice. Merely to say the ideal type is a free human begs the question. For our purposes out at this limit, free choice is only a means, not an end. In relation to our present horizons, the goals that we select should be distant, should constitute ends.

As a child, read to by my mother, I was thrilled by Horatius's words as he stepped out on the Tiber bridge against the Tuscan ranks:

> To every man upon this earth, death cometh
>   soon or late.
> And how can man die better than by facing
>   fearful odds,
> For the ashes of his fathers and the temples
>   of his gods.

But now the chance for heroism in death is small, for better and for worse. We hardly die at all; we disintegrate and peter out. The chance to help others to a better life by dying for one's country has dwindled. Submission to a living death of some sort may be a useful sacrifice in its place, but heroic action for nationalism, despite its popularity some places on the earth, seems to offer doubtful value and narrow scope. Leopold Bloom's drunken companion complained: "Let my country die for me."

Our life expectancy's extension changes the kind of disaster that always lurks beneath our feet but it does not thicken the floor.

> I felt . . . that he [Joseph Conrad] thought of civilized and morally tolerable human life as a dangerous walk on a thin crust of barely cooled lava which at any moment might break and let the unwary sink into fiery depths.
>
> BERTRAND RUSSELL

Although we now can better justify future plans, our lives' duration, quality and worth remain uncertain, making paramount our conduct and enjoyment of the present moment. On a crystal summer morning after breakfast, hearing distant music of silver bells and a resonant horn, one may think to himself, "How can one live better than sustained and soothed, protected and corrected, animated and amused and encouraged, by a good family and friends, work and play, belonging to a community on this ancient planet hanging in the stars?" Yet facing oneself, gemütlich reverie turned stale, this insubstantial pageant faded, no aimless existential heroism will suffice, and to remove the insecurity would leave life as dull as Paradise.

Long ago, with short and brutish lives, few men and fewer women lived on a high plane. But now, although we cannot longer give our death as payment for an ideal, many of us can live in an elevated way. We can commit ourselves to some high purpose, make sacrifices and take risks like

Cortez, who dismantled his ships on the Mexican beach, and Spartacus, who drew his sword and killed his horse before the final battle in the Servile War, showing his men he would not have a chance to flee.

Life now resembles the central chamber that once was built in a pagan temple. Its only opening to the outdoors was a hole drilled through the thick, domed roof. Astronomical calculations fixed the angle of the hole so that once a year the sun crossed the axis. The room stayed dark except on the day when the sun filled it with light. We have no hope that patient waiting will bring us such a day. The only way we can light our room is by action to set our course toward elevated goals.

INDEX

About the author

All his life Stimson Bullitt has belonged to
Seattle, with excursions elsewhere that included under-
graduate years at Yale and another four in the Navy
(where he was wounded by shrapnel as a member of a
volunteer landing party at Leyte). A ninth-generation
American lawyer, his first political activity was a solo
letter-writing campaign in 1942-43 in defense of
Japanese-Americans. He has taken part in civic affairs,
locally and nationally, in the fields of government
reorganization, political process reforms, race relations,
foreign affairs and conservation. Among honors he has
received, perhaps the best known was Nixon's "Enemies List".

MORE TITLES
FROM WILLOWS PRESS

By Stimson Bullitt

To Be A Politician	Hard Cover	$22.95
	Soft Bound	$15.95
River Dark and Bright	Hard Cover	$22.95
(available fall 1994)	Soft Bound	$15.95
Ancestral Histories of Scott Bullitt and Dorothy Stimson	Hard Cover	$29.95
(available summer 1994)		

By Lawrence Kreisman

The Stimson Legacy: Architecture in the Urban West	Hard Cover	$55.00
	Soft Bound	$35.00

You may order these books directly from the publisher. Please include $3.00 for postage and handling (and 8.2% state sales tax if you are a Washington State resident). Allow two weeks for delivery.

Willows Press
1204 Minor Avenue
Seattle, Washington 98101

Please send me _____copies of _____

@ $ _____ per copy, for a total price of_____, including tax.

Name: _____

Address: _____

City/State/Zip: _____